CHRISTMAS
IN AMERICA

CHRISTMAS IN AMERICA

A HISTORY

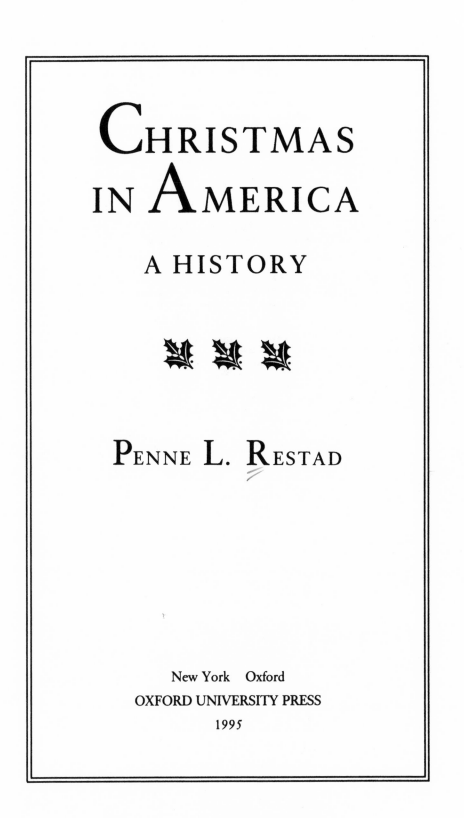

PENNE L. RESTAD

New York   Oxford
OXFORD UNIVERSITY PRESS
1995

JUL 9 6

achi
'okyo

Melbourne   Auckland   Madrid

and associated companies in

Berlin   Ibadan

Copyright © 1995 by Penne L. Restad

Published by Oxford University Press, Inc.,
198 Madison Avenue, New York, New York 10016

Oxford is a registered trademark of Oxford University Press

Library of Congress Cataloging-in-Publication Data
Restad, Penne L.
Christmas in America : a history / Penne L. Restad.
p. cm.
Includes bibliographical references and index.
ISBN 0-19-509300-3
1. Christmas—United States—History.
2. United States—Socal life and customs.
I. Title.
GT4986.A1R47   1995   394.2'663'09—dc20   94-42357

2   4   6   8   9   7   5   3   1

Printed in the United States of America
on acid-free paper

For Robert,
Benjamin, and Johanna

Foreword

There exists a commonplace history of America's Christmas: Dour Puritan forefathers banned its observance and the effects of their prohibition lingered into the nineteenth century, when the Christmas stories of Washington Irving and Charles Dickens, the customs of new immigrants, and the expansion of commerce invigorated and widened our notion of the holiday. By the 1870s, Americans eagerly decorated trees, sang carols, shopped for gifts, and spent hot hours in kitchens preparing festive dishes. They dashed over snow-laden fields and impatiently awaited the arrival of Santa Claus. By the end of the century, they had forged a new, splendid, and popular Christmas. Since then, the familiar wisdom concludes, materialism, aided by media, modern advertising, and mass marketing, has overtaken and profaned this most glorious of holidays.

This account has guided much of the popular as well as academic writing on the holiday. Many have approached Christmas with an antiquarian's passion, searching out the origins and details of the festival's customs and habits in order to acquaint us with its former grandeur. Their efforts have rewarded us with rich descriptions of ornaments, toys, trees, rituals, stories, and menus. More recently, scholarly forays into the universe of Yuletide have yielded important perspectives on Christmas and the roles of commerce and class conflict. Yet, whether etched as nostalgic fact- and object-finding or incorporated into the latest demystified view of the American past, each elaboration mainly reaffirms clichés. [1]

Christmas in America places these understandings within a broad and often paradoxical chronicle, one that considers the holiday's rich and changing spiritual, social, material, and personal meanings. It addresses those mythic qualities of Christmas that make it more than a simple winter festival, and shows it to be, at least for our own era, a time of considerable private and social consequence. Within communities and even for the nation, the celebration briefly unites a disparate people in rites and impulses that hold almost universal appeal. For individuals, it cradles myriad sentiments concerning friends, family, age, place, heritage, and values.

The chapters that follow provide an explanation for how such a Christmas came to be. In part, they comprise a narrative running from seventeenth-century Jamestown, and before, to the present. They tell how Christmas has been celebrated or ignored at various times and in various places in America. This history also explores what Terence Ranger and Eric Hobsbawm called the "invention of tradition." At certain critical times, they argued, a particular culture invents new symbols and ceremonies that help define and reflect its character. These actions or icons soon become so closely associated with a people as to seem or feel as if they had been in place for ages past. For instance, Scotsmen did not always wear kilts, nor did the Queen of England always address her realm on Christmas Day. Yet these traditions have about them a timelessness that orders the history and meaning of Scottish nationalism in one case and English society in another.[2]

Given that, historically, not all Americans kept Christmas and that those who did had celebrated it in ways that varied by region and religion, Hobsbawm and Ranger's theory suggests that the American Christmas as it evolved in the nineteenth century was just such an "invented" tradition. Its rise corresponded with America's struggle to find its own identity and its need to bind together the peoples of many nationalities who made this country home.

The concept of "invention" provides a useful starting point, but leaves much to be considered and explained. We know, for example, that Americans began to celebrate Christmas widely only in the last half of the nineteenth century. Even as Americans framed the holiday, they revealed a self-conscious awareness that it was significantly different from earlier celebrations of Jesus' birth. We also know that the holiday matured in an era marked by the Civil War and titanic social change. The creation of the Christmas we celebrate cannot be considered apart from these tumultuous events. Indeed, any explanation of our Christmas must draw upon many themes, ones as pervasive as a remolding of religious expressions, the rise and dominance of science and a new rationality, the efforts of accommodate an unprecedented heterogeneity in the nation, and the changing social and economic roles of both individuals and groups within an ever-expanding industrial economy.

In the twentieth century, Christmas has continued to reveal the nature of American life. Of the innumerable conversations about the holiday that I have enjoyed, many began with a person's memories of his or her own Christmas and often focused on traditions brought from other nations or from different areas within the United States. American Finns, Germans, Mexicans, African-Americans, and Balinese all have unique stories. Californians, Pennsylvanians, Texans, and Montanans have others. These accounts, fascinating in their detail and variety, are all the more arresting for their similarities. How is it that from so many types and sorts of people, we can genuinely speak of Christmas as a common experience? "Invention" is a helpful but too singular and static a word to encompass and explain the American Christmas.

Looking at the full sweep of this holiday's history in our culture, we can begin to see its relationship to ethnic pluralism, its meaning for non-Christians, and its unchallenged position as the most important of national holidays within a culture that also values religious freedom and separation of church and state. Only then can we approach an answer to perennial concerns about the holiday, ones that range from the nagging feeling that Christmas is in decline to the more specific charge that materialism has destroyed its spiritual message.

Given this breadth of inquiry, *Christmas in America* attempts to chart the evolution of our Christmas from its colonial days, when the marks of religion and region were most distinct, to its incarnation by media and money in the twentieth century. For the most part, though, this book concentrates on events and conditions of the nineteenth century that have indelibly shaped the Christmas we keep and the attitudes we hold about it. It emphasizes the elastic and ever-changing nature of the American calendar and its holidays, as well as the interaction of political, social, economic, and religious realms. It seeks to analyze rather than moralize the issues of materialism and gift-giving, and to bring new insights to such familiar elements of the festival as trees, cards, and Santa. Ultimately, it wills the reader to understand Christmas through the lens of history and, through Christmas, the ambiguities and paradoxes of our culture.

I owe a debt of gratitude to those people who have helped me in thinking and writing about Christmas. First of all, my parents, Mary and Lee

Restad, who teach me, every year, the meaning of the holiday. For this, and many more things, I am always thankful.

I note with great appreciation the help of Galen Wilson, who went far beyond the call of an archivist's duty in locating material for this work. To Dave Bowman, William Goetzmann, Jeffrey Meikle, Mark Smith, Bill Stott, and Clarence Walker, I give credit and thanks for thoughtful critiques of the dissertation on which I have based this book. Another thank you goes to the University of Texas for granting me a welcome year of financial support in the form of a Graduate Continuing Fellowship. I am even more grateful to my friend and advisor, Howard Miller, whose support, confidence, advice, and careful reading of these pages has been of inestimable help and importance to me.

I cannot begin to acknowledge the contribution of my husband, Robert Abzug, whose patience, example, and wisdom I rely upon daily. To this list, I must add Benjamin, who inspires me with his questions, and Johanna, who heartens me with her cheer.

Contents

CHRISTMAS
IN AMERICA

CHAPTER 1

European Inheritances: Christmas in the Colonies

"Shall we have Christmas?" was the way one Pennsylvanian asked the question in 1810. Throughout their colonial history and well into nationhood, not only the matter of "shall" but of "how shall" Christmas be celebrated challenged Americans. Their search for answers to these two difficult and sometimes divisive issues can be found in a chronicle of evolving customs, cultural discord, and striking invention. It begins with the first European émigrés, who brought to America an ambiguous legacy concerning the holiday that was almost as old as the Christian Church itself.[1]

Christians had wrestled for centuries with questions of if, when, and how to celebrate Jesus' birth. As a commemoration of the miracle that established the Godly paternity of Jesus, Christmas was a celebration of the event upon which the existence of Christianity depended. At the same time, the festival functioned from its inception as an end-of-year substitute for pagan rites and quickly absorbed many profane elements, ones that remain among its most attractive features. As the observance of Christmas spread, the details of its celebration became as varied as the cultures that kept it and as changeable as the history of those cultures. But the radically paradoxical mix of both the sacred and the profane remained.

The earliest Christians gave little attention to Jesus' birth. They expected the Second Coming any day, and in any case viewed birthday celebrations as heathen. As the possibility of his imminent return faded, the faithful took a more historical perspective and began to search for evidence of the day or even season of Jesus' birth. They found no clues in the Gospels. Nor could they locate any other reliable sources to pinpoint his nativity. Undeterred, some placed his birth on May 20 and others on April 19 or 20. Clement, Bishop of Alexandria (died c. 215), nominated November 18. Hippolytus (died c. 236) calculated that Christ must have been born on Wednesday, the same day God created the sun. The *De Pascha Compu-tus*, written anonymously in North Africa about 243, posited that the first day of creation coincided with the first day of spring, on March 25, and contended that Jesus' birthday fell four days later, on March 28.[2]

Sometime in the fourth century of the Common Era, the Roman Church began to celebrate a Feast of the Nativity and to do so on December 25. A variety of issues influenced the decision. Internally, heresies plagued Church authority. Arianism, one of the most threatening, regarded Jesus as a solely human agent of God. The Church insisted on his divinity. By assigning him one human quality—a birthday—it appropriated some of Arianism's appeal, but sustained Jesus' place in the Holy Trinity.[3]

The Church had also grown concerned about the increasing popularity of pagan religions and mystery cults in Rome. Each year beginning on December 17, the first day of Saturnalia, and continuing through Kalends, the first day of January, most Romans feasted, gamed, reveled, paraded, and joined in other festivities as they paid homage to their deities. The Church's alarm deepened when Emperor Aurelian, noticing that the pagan rituals had begun to converge around Mithras, the solar god, decreed in 274 C.E. that December 25, the winter solstice on the Julian Calendar, be kept as a public festival in honor of the Invincible Sun. Rome's Christians challenged paganism directly by specifying December 25, rather than some other date, as the day for their Nativity Feast.[4]

Exactly when the Church of Rome began to keep Christmas, however, is not known. The first extant reference to the Feast of the Nativity may be as old as 336, in the earliest list of martyrs of the Roman Church. Perhaps Christmas was celebrated even earlier. Some scholars believe that Emperor Constantine (ruled 312–337 C.E.), who had converted to Christianity and built the Vatican atop the hill where the Mithras cult worshipped the sun, may have instituted the festival.[5]

In any case, by the middle of the fourth century, the Church had boldly declared its Nativity holy day to be observed on the same day as the winter solstice. The concurrence of the two celebrations gave the Church an opportunity to turn elements of the Saturnalia itself to Christian ends. For example, it used the creation of the sun, the center of the Saturnalia, to reinforce and symbolize frequent scriptural and doctrinal imagery of God as the sun, and of Jesus' role as Son of God. The creation of Christmas was thus a measure of Christianity's growing power, challenging the crowds enjoying Saturnalian revelry to join the once secretive Christians in a celebration not of the birth of the sun, but rather the birth of Jesus, the Son of God.[6]

The overlapping of Saturnalia and the Feast of the Nativity set the terms of all future debate over the Christmas festival. Its Christian aspects, at least in their most intense form, emphasized heavenly afterlife. The heathen elements absorbed into the festival affirmed life and exalted its annual renewal. The Church made no clear separations between the two perspectives. Instead, it layered profane activities with sacred ends to answer the needs, spiritual and physical, of the total person. This combination of sacred and profane made some religious leaders uncomfortable. For example, Gregory of Nazianzen (died 389) urged that "the celebration of the [Christmas] festival [be conducted] after an heavenly and not after an earthly manner" and cautioned against "feasting to excess, dancing and crowning the doors." Indeed, the paradox of purpose forged an enduring Christmas reality. As one historian succinctly characterized it: "The pagan Romans became Christians—but the Saturnalia remained."[7]

The custom of honoring Jesus' birth on December 25 quickly spread to the Eastern Church. By 380, Christians in Constantinople honored it as "Theophany or the Birthday." These Christians had once observed Epiphany, January 6, as a joint Feast of the Nativity and Baptism. This was the same date that popular legends held pagan gods made themselves known to humans. "Deep in the tradition of the Church's spirituality," writes John Gunstone, "was the idea that Christ's appearance in flesh was the consummation of all epiphanies." During the Christological controversies of the fourth and fifth centuries, the celebration of Epiphany spread westward, but the Roman Church, with its celebration of the Nativity set in late December and its emphasis on Jesus' incarnation and divinity, recast it to commemorate the adoration of the Magi. In Constantinople, Epiphany continued to consecrate Jesus' baptism, but the Eastern Church began to mark December 25 as the day of his birth. The dual celebration, that of birth and baptism, that had defined the old holy day ceased to exist.[8]

Over the next thousand years, the observance of Christmas followed the expanding community of Christianity. By 432, Egyptians kept it. By the end of the sixth century, Christianity had taken the holiday far northward and into England. During the next two hundred years in Scandinavia it became fused with the pagan Norse feast season known as Yule, the time of year also known as the Teutonic "Midwinter." Sometime around the Norman incursion in 1050, the Old English word Christes maesse (festival of Christ) entered the English language, and as early as the twelfth century "Xmas" had come into use. From the thirteenth century on, nearly all Europe kept Jesus' birth.[9]

The tension between the folk and ecclesiastical qualities of the holy day did not ease with the advance of Christmas-keeping. Documents of the Middle Ages, Tristram Coffin has noted, were "fat with decrees against the abuses of Christmas merriment," an indication "that people at large [were] doing just what they ha[d] always done and paying little attention to the debates of the moralists." Some clergy stressed that fallen humankind needed a season of abandon and excess, as long as it was carried on under the umbrella of Christian supervision. Others argued that all vestiges of paganism must be removed from the holiday. Less fervent Christians complained about the unreasonableness of Church law and its attempts to change custom. Yet the Church sustained the hope that sacred would eventually overtake profane as pagans gave up their revels and turned to Christianity.[10]

These conflicts continued during the Protestant Reformation, but with little promise of resolution. In England, the Anglican Church repeatedly, but with little success, tried to gain control over the day. Its custom had been to begin Christmas on December 16 (known as "O Sapientia") and celebrate for nine days. But during King Alfred's reign (871–899 C.E.), a law passed extending the celebration to twelve days, ending on Epiphany.[11]

Celebrants devoted much of the season to pagan pleasures that were discouraged during the remainder of the year. The annual indulgence in eating, dancing, singing, sporting, card playing, and gambling escalated to magnificent proportions. By the seventeenth century, under the reigns of the Tudors and Stuarts, the Christmas season featured elaborate masques, mummeries, and pageants. In 1607, King James I insisted that a play be acted on Christmas night and that the court indulge in games. One account of an evening's "moderate dinner" noted a first course of sixteen dishes. In 1626, the Duke of Buckingham found that the captains, masters, boatswains, gunners, and carpenters of three ships had abandoned their service in favor of Christmas revels, leaving their vessels prey to any enemy. In

1633, the four Inns of Court presented a masque, "The Triumph of Peace," at a cost of £20,000.

It fell to Puritan reformers to put a stop to the unholy merriment and to bend arguments over the proper keeping of Christmas into an older and more basic one—whether there should even be an observance of the day. Defying the decision of the Anglican Convocation of 1562 to maintain the church calendar, the Puritans struck Christmas, along with all saints' days, from their own list of holy days. The Bible, they held, expressly commanded keeping only the Sabbath. That would be their practice as well.[12]

In taking the offensive against Christmas-keeping, Puritans distributed colorful diatribes against the excesses of the holiday. Philip Stubbes's *Anatomy of Abuses* (1583) condemned revelous celebrants as "hel hounds" in a "Deville's daunce" of merriment. William Prynne's *Histriomastix* (1633) inveighed against plays, masques, balls, and the decking of houses with greens. "Into what a stupendous *height* of more than pagan impiety . . . have we not now *degenerated*!" he lamented. Christmas, he thought, ought to be "rather a day of mourning than rejoicing," not a time spent in "amorous mixt, voluptuous, unchristian, that I say not pagan, dancing, to God's, to Christ's dishonour, religion's scandal, chastities' shipwracke and sinne's advantage."[13]

Even as Puritan condemnation of Christmas intensified, the economic and social upheaval of the late sixteenth and early seventeenth century had begun to alter English life. The standing social order, along with the paternalism of its manor system, was crumbling. Christmas, in its role as a part of the old structure, could not escape unscathed. In some years, the lavish celebrations lapsed. In many cases, the emphases of the holiday changed. It transformed, in the words of J. M. Golby and A. W. Purdue, into "a symbol for hospitality towards the poor, an understanding between the different levels of society, and happier and more prosperous times in now neglected villages." King Charles I (1625–1649) went so far as to direct his noblemen and gentry to return to their landed estates in midwinter in order to keep up their old style of Christmas generosity.[14]

The rise of Oliver Cromwell's Puritan Commonwealth dealt another staggering blow to England's Christmas celebrations. Parliament outlawed seasonal plays in 1642. It ordered that the monthly fast, which coincidentally fell on Christmas in 1644, be kept. Parliament purposely met on every Christmas from 1644 to 1652. In 1647, it declared Christmas a day of penance, not feasting, and in 1652 "strongly prohibited" its observance.

Ministers who preached on the Nativity risked imprisonment. Churchwardens faced fines for decorating their churches. By law, shops stayed open on Christmas as if it were any regular business day.[15]

Yet resistance was not uncommon. One year, protesting Londoners decorated churches and shops with swags of bay, rosemary, box, holly, privit, and ivy, only to watch the Lord Mayor and City Marshal ride about setting fire to their handiwork. The populace "so roughly used" the merchants who ventured to open shop in 1646 that the shopkeepers petitioned Parliament for protection. In Canterbury, when the Lord Mayor ordered that the markets be kept open that Christmas, a "serious disturbance ensued . . . wherein many were severly hurt."[16]

It was within this particularly turbulent era that English Christmas customs entered early Virginia and New England. Most settlers and adventurers arriving in the New World welcomed Christmas as a day of respite from the routines of work and hardship. Some observed it, at least in part, as a holy day. Others attempted to feast. On Christmas, 1608, Captain John Smith and his men, having endured for "six or seven dayes the extreame winde, rayne, frost and snow" as they traveled among the Indians of Virginia colony, "were never more merry, nor fed on more plentie of good Oysters, Fish, Flesh, Wild-foule, and good bread; nor never had better fires in *England*." Maryland-bound passengers aboard the *Ark* in 1633 "so immoderately" drank wine on Christmas that "the next day 30 sickened of feve[r]s and whereof about a dozen died afterward."[17]

Only Dissenters tried to ignore the holiday. The *Mayflower* Pilgrims, who arrived at Plymouth in December 1620, spent Christmas building "the first house for commone use to receive them and their goods." Within a year, however, the Pilgrims themselves had to face dissent. On the morning of December 25, 1621, less reform-minded newcomers to the colony "excused them selves and said it wente against their consciences to work on that day." Governor William Bradford allowed the "lusty yonge" Englishmen to rest, saying he "would spare them till they were better informed." But at noon he found them playing games in the street. Angered, Bradford told the frolickers that it ran against *his* conscience that they should play while others worked. If they desired to keep Christmas as a matter of devotion they should stay in their houses, he said, "but ther should be no gameing or revelling in the streets." Nor did the Puritans of Massachusetts Bay Colony observe Christmas. Governor John Winthrop entered nothing in his diary on his first Christmas in America in 1630, and in succeeding years he attempted to suppress the holiday.[18]

In the early non-English settlements, sparse evidence points to a more traditional attitude toward the holiday. In 1604, for instance, French settlers of St. Croix Island, off the coast of Maine, held religious services and spent the remainder of Christmas Day playing games. In 1686 LaSalle's French colony on Garcita Creek celebrated what was probably the first Christmas in Texas. "[W]e first kept the Christmas *Holy-Days*. The Midnight Mass was sung, and on *Twelve-Day*, we cry'd *The king drinks* . . . tho' we had only Water. . . ."[19]

As the first settlements grew into more established communities, patterns of Christmas celebration peculiar to the colonies began to appear. Geographic separation from European homelands, the proximity of disparate religious and ethnic groups to each other, and the hardship of new beginnings disrupted old habits and holidays. In Dutch New Amsterdam, early in the seventeenth century, eighteen languages could be heard among the 500 or so inhabitants. Numerous Christmases abounded, persisting as an expression of individual heritages. In large towns, where various groups lived close together, the common ground for celebration could often be found in public and secular rather than in potentially divisive religious areas. Thus, Christmas, although widely celebrated, retained little importance in society as a whole precisely because of religious and cultural diversity.[20]

Particularly in the middle colonies, a wide range of ethnicities and religions prevented a shared ecclesiastic and religious holiday. Pennsylvania Quakers scorned Christmas as adamantly as Puritans did. Huguenots, Moravians, Dutch Reformed, and Anglicans, who also lived in the colony, all kept Christmas in their own way. Shortly after Americans had won their independence, Elizabeth Drinker, a Quaker herself, divided Philadelphians into three categories. There were Quakers, who "make no more account of it [Christmas] than another day," those who were religious, and the rest who "spend it in riot and dissipation."[21]

"Frolicking," the name many gave to this sort of boisterous Christmas and New Year's fun, could be found throughout the colonies. In the New England countryside, revelous intruders entered houses with a speech and swords at Christmas time. Far into the eighteenth century, masked merrymakers roved Pennsylvania's Delaware Valley "making sport for everyone." Southerners shot guns, a custom similar to one practiced in northern England.[22]

The antecedents to this seasonal phenomenon have been traced to Roman times, when early Christians, seeking to ridicule pagan superstition and the Roman custom of masquerading, masked themselves on New Year's Day. Many, however, flagged in their intent and joined in the heathens' frolics. Church officials attempted to persuade members to desist, but failed. In time, even clergy could be found in full disguise, taking part in miracle and mystery plays performed during the Christmas season.[23]

The convention of disguising, or mumming, and performing plays and skits dispersed throughout nearly all European countries. In England, beginning under the reign of Edward III (1327–1377), it became a form of royal entertainment. It peaked in the fifteenth and sixteenth centuries, when elaborate dress and formal presentations, such as Ben Johnson's *Masque of Christmas* and that in Shakespeare's *Henry VIII*, were the order of the season. Enthusiasm for court masques diminished thereafter, dampened by the Puritan Directory. But the tradition of masquerading and mumming continued to thrive in more rustic forms. In parts of England, householders, family, guests, and servants donned masks and painted their faces or darkened them with soot to become "guisers," "geese-dancers," or "morris dancers." Often they dressed as animals. Sometimes men and women exchanged clothes with each other. Disguised, they played crude tricks on one another, or went from house to house and entered without permission. There they might dance, sing, feast, and act "a rude drama," mocking propriety and challenging the social order.[24]

American colonists engaged in similar antics, though usually without the performance of even a rudimentary play. They concentrated instead on disguises, noisy good humor, and chaotic peregrinations through neighborhoods. Across the land, revelers, almost always males, gathered to shoot off firecrackers and guns, paraded with musical instruments, call from house to house in garish disguise, and beg for food and drink on December 25 and, in some places, on New Year's.[25]

Such frolics, drawn from the custom of English Anglicans, as well as those of Swedish, German, and other settlers, were especially prominent in New York and Pennsylvania. Samuel Breck remembered maskers from his Pennsylvania childhood in the late eighteenth century. "They were a set of the lowest blackguards," he wrote, "who, disguised in filthy clothes and ofttimes with masked faces, went from house to house in large companies, . . . obtruding themselves everywhere, particularly into the rooms that were occupied by parties of ladies and gentlemen, [and] would demean themselves with great insolence." As the elder Breck and his friends played cards, Samuel had watched the mummers "take possession of a table, seat themselves on rich furniture and proceed to handle the cards, to the great annoyance of the company." He could only get rid of them by "giv[ing] them money, and listen[ing] patiently to a foolish dialogue between two or more of them . . . "[26]

Usually an informal code regulated the mummers' reception. According to one set of rules, "the proper custom" had been to ask the uninvited guests "into the house and regale them with mulled cider, or small beer, and home-made cakes," or "give the leading mummers a few pence as a dole, which . . . they would 'pool,' and buy cakes and beer." One never "address[ed] or otherwise recognize[d] the mummer by any other name than the name of the character he was assuming."[27]

In New York, the calling ritual varied slightly. Men had gone from house to house, firing their guns, on New Year's Day since "time immemorial." At each place, after being invited in for food and drink, the men of the household joined them. "[T]hus they went on increasing their numbers until the whole neighborhood had been saluted and visited. . . . " The remainder of the day the shooters engaged in contests of marksmanship and other sports. At least one, the "very barbarous amusement" of "Shooting Turkeys," required a keen eye and sharp betting skills.[28]

The southern colonies, largely rural and unhampered by Quaker and Puritan dissenters and whose white population was comparatively less diverse, cultivated Christmases of a very different sort. Decentralized living, a dearth of women, and a high death rate kept the holiday at bay during the first decades of settlement. As social and political conditions stabilized, southerners began to look to England for models of dress, manner, and social behavior. Their Christmas, like that of the English manor, evolved as an interval of leisure rather than a set of rituals assigned to one particular day. During the season, Virginians, Carolinians, and Marylanders especially enjoyed dancing, but also engaged in card playing, cock fighting, nine-pins, and horse racing. Anglicanism, the established religion in most of the planting colonies, did not pressure its members into sacred observance.[29]

While southerners may have aspired to recreate a sense of the English Christmas, its authentic reproduction eluded them. No pre-Revolutionary account mentions boars' heads or wassail bowls, mummers or waits. In England those traditions had been on the wane when John Smith first ventured through Virginia, and by the 1650s had been mortally threatened by Cromwell's Parliament. A French traveler, who along with his entourage of nearly twenty stopped unannounced at the Virginia home of Colonel William Fitzhugh in 1680, left one of the few accounts from the seventeenth century. "[T]here was good wine and all kinds of beverages, so there was a great deal of carousing," the visitor wrote. For entertainment, Fitzhugh provided "three fiddlers, a jester, a tight-rope walker, and an acrobat who tumbled around." When the travelers left the next day, Fitzhugh sent wine and punch to the river's edge for them and then lent them his boat.[30]

By the middle of the eighteenth century, tales of Virginia Christmases had spread back to England and began to create an aura of romance around the South. "All over the Colony, a universal Hospitality reigns," *London Magazine* reported in 1746; "full Tables and open Doors, the kind salute, the generous Detention, speak somewhat like the old Roast-beef Ages of our Fore-fathers. . . . Strangers are fought after with Greediness, as they pass the Country, to be invited."[31]

Evidence of eighteenth-century Christmas celebrations is nearly as scarce as for the seventeenth. Best known is the Christmas chronicled by Philip Vickers Fithian, a Presbyterian tutor from New Jersey. Fithian spent a single Christmas season, in 1773, at Nomini Hall, a plantation owned by Robert Carter, one of the wealthiest Tidewater planters. The first sign of the season he recorded occurred on Monday, December 18; students barred one of Fithian's colleagues from teaching school until "twelfth-day" (January 6), a custom known throughout the British Commonwealth. However, Fithian continued to teach, noting proudly that his "scholars are a more quiet nature, and have consented to have four or five Days now, and to have their full Holiday in May next. . . ."[32]

Excitement built as the holiday approached. "Nothing is now to be heard of in conversation, but the *Balls*, the *Fox-hunts*, the fine *entertainments*, and the good fellowship . . . ," Fithian wrote on the 18th. His entry for Christmas Day began, "Guns fired all round the House," after which the various "Servants" who regularly attended him greeted him with "Joyful Christmas." He rewarded them with the expected small change and a donation to a "Christmas *Box*." As for Christmas dinner, Fithian noted that it "was no otherwise than common yet as elegant" as any he had ever attended. Not until the following Sunday, December 26, did he and the Carters go to church. The minister "preach'd from Isaiah 9.6 For unto us a child is Born &c. his sermon was fifteen Minutes long! very fashionable—," but few attended. Fithian reopened his school the following Wednesday, December 29. The holidays at Nomini Hall had ended.[33]

Not all southerners partook of the sumptuous Christmases reported in London or witnessed by Fithian. Neither ritually exacting nor regularly held, the holiday on each plantation seemed to have its own style of celebration. In 1709, William Byrd began Christmas by attending church, where he "received the sacrament with great devoutness." Afterward, he dined on roast beef with friends and "in the evening we were merry with nonsense and so were my servants. . . . " The following year he spent Christmas quite differently, reading a sermon and dining alone. Thomas Jefferson rarely mentioned Christmas. George Washington frequently spent his holiday hunting and settling such year-end financial matters as renewing the terms of indenture for his servants, and attending church.[34]

Perhaps, as Julian Boyd has suggested, the Enlightenment, which uprooted superstitions and redefined social classes, prevented a precise duplication of an English Christmas. Indeed, there may even have been some attempt to rationalize the Christmas festival. In December 1739, the *Virginia Gazette* briefly recounted a history of the holiday, noting that some Christians "celebrate this Season in a Mixture of *Piety* and *Licentiousness*," others "in a *pious Way* only," others "behave themselves *profusely* and *extravagantly alone*." The last category was comprised of the many who "pass over the *Holy Time*, without paying any Regard to it at all." The writer concluded that "On the whole, they who will be over-religious at this Time, must be pardoned and pitied; they who are falsely religious, censured; they who are downright criminal, condemned; and the Little Liberties of the old *Roman December*, which are taken by the Multitude, ought to be overlooked and excused, for an Hundred Reasons. . . . "[35]

This broadly permissive approach to Christmas contrasted sharply with prevailing attitudes in New England. Like their forebears in England, the Puritan leaders of New England sought to expunge the holiday altogether. Their struggle betokened a broader battle against growing numbers of non-Puritans in the region and periodic intervention in religious affairs on the part of the Crown.

The entry of non-Puritans began at the founding of Plymouth and Massachusetts Bay colonies, and increasingly presented a problem as displaced English workers, many of them Anglican, bolstered the labor-short economies. At first, Puritans relied on what one historian called the "infor-

mal pressure of like minded co-religionists" to quell the observance of Jesus'
birth. But this strategy proved inadequate. In 1659, in an atmosphere of
tension over Anglicanism, other heresies, new trade, and general disarray,
the Massachusetts Bay General Court banned the keeping of Christmas by
"forebearing of labour, feasting, or any other way." The law aimed to
prevent the recurrence of further, unspecified "disorders" which had apparently arisen in "seuerall places . . . by reason of some still observing such
Festiualls," and provided that "whosoeuer shall be found observing any
such day as Xmas or the like . . . " would be fined. [36]

Pressure from England contributed to the troubled atmosphere. All of
the once forbidden holiday rites had begun to be practiced once again
during the Restoration in Britain, in forms more extreme than before.
As early as 1665, Charles II demanded that Massachusetts rescind its
anti-Christmas law to reflect these changes. Finally in 1681, Massachusetts
issued a repeal, citing as a reason that a ban on Christmas would be a
derogation of the King's honor. Still, in 1686, Puritan militants barred
newly appointed English Governor Andros from holding his Christmas
services in their meeting house and forced him to move to the Boston
Town Hall. [37]

The renewed English fervor for the raucous excesses of Christmas began
to wane almost as rapidly as it had revived, while New England's Puritan
leadership gave little indication that it had gained much tolerance for the
holiday. "[M]en dishonour Christ more in the 12 days of Christmas than
in all the 12 months besides," wrote Increase Mather in his diary. He
reiterated the case against Christmas in *A Testimony Against Several Profane
and Superstitious Customs Now Practiced by Some in New England*, a tract
published in England in 1687. "In the Apostolical times," Mather wrote,
"the Feast of the Nativity was not observed. . . . It can never be proved
that Christ was born on December 25. . . . The New Testament allows of
no stated Holy-Day but the Lords-day. . . . It was in compliance with the
Pagan saturnalia that Christmas Holy-dayes were first invented. The manner of Christmas-keeping, as generally observed, is highly dishonourable to
the Name of Christ." [38]

Increase's son Cotton escalated the rhetoric against the holiday by making more explicit the fearful connection between Christmas and sin. He
even linked it to Salem's witchcraft. "On the twenty-fifth of December it
was," he wrote, "that Mercy [Short] said, They were going to have a
Dance; and immediately those that were attending her, most plainly Heard
and Felt a Dance, as of Barefooted People, upon the Floor. . . . " Mather

later denounced the holiday in more general terms. "I hear a Number of people of both Sexes, belonging, many of them to my Flock, who have had on Christmas-night, this last Week, a Frolick, a revelling Feast, and Ball, which discovers their Corruption, and has a Tendency to corrupt them yett more, and provoke the Holy One to give them up into eternal Hardness of Heart."[39]

Despite his strong tone, Cotton Mather did not forthrightly condemn Christmas itself. Like Bradford, who in 1621 had stopped the newcomers' street revelry, he expressed more concern for the liberties taken during the celebration of Christmas than for the fact of celebration. Calling the merrymaking an "affront unto the grace of God," he tacitly turned the question of "should" to one of "how" to hallow Jesus' birth. "Can you in your consciences think that our holy saviour is honored by mirth, by long eating, by hard drinking, by lewd gaming, by rude revelling, by a mass fit for none but a Saturn or a Bacchus, or the light of Mahametan Romandon?" he asked. "Shall it be said that at the birth of our Saviour . . . we take the time to please the hellish legions and to do actions that have much more of hell than of heaven in them?"[40]

In all, Christmas became a point at which Puritan piety and autonomy grated against English custom, British authority, and Anglican influence. Bostonians, for example, openly repudiated Anglicanism by refusing to close their businesses on Christmas. "Carts come to Town and Shops open as is usual," Judge Samuel Sewall noted on December 24, 1685 (and nearly every year after). That same year Sewall smugly noted that he thought the British colonial officials were "vexed . . . that the Body of the People profane it [Christmas]," and thanked God that there was "no Authority yet to compell them [i.e. Puritans] to keep it." The Crown-appointed governor twice took Sewall aside in 1722 to discuss recessing the General Court on Christmas. Sewall opposed adjournment, but suggested (after a discussion with Cotton Mather) that the matter be voted on by the Council and Representatives. The governor took the opposite side, arguing that "All kept Christmas" except the Puritans. Provoked, Sewall responded: "the Dissenters came a great way for their Liberties and now the [Anglican] Church had theirs, yet they could not be contented, except they might Tread all others down." Ultimately, the governor ignored Sewall's entreaty and closed the court on Saturday until the following Wednesday, December 26.[41]

Others besides the British government challenged the Puritans on Christmas. Holiday rituals in observing churches attracted a fair number of putative Calvinists at Christmastide. Ebenezer Miller, graduate of Harvard but recently ordained an Anglican, Sewall noted in 1727, "keeps the day in his New church at Braintrey: people flock thither." On another occasion he spoke to a Mr. Newman "about his partaking with the French church on the 25th of December, on account of its being Christmas, as they abusively call it." Congregational ministers countered by ordering fasts on Christmas Day and tried in other ways to show their disregard for the festival. One spent the Sunday preceding Christmas outlining his proof that the celebration of Jesus' birth was "Popery and prelatic tyranny, a destroyer of consciences."[42]

In the end, whether slowly in New England or more rapidly in the middle colonies and the South, the forces of pluralism and the need for social harmony shaped and encouraged Christmas celebration. Yet its status as a holiday remained haphazard and varied widely. Like the colonies in general on the eve of the Revolution, regions and communities were as notable for their different approaches to the holiday as for their commonalities. It would take the project of nation-building in the wake of the Revolution to begin to define an American conception of Christmas.

CHAPTER 2

Red-Letter Days:
Christmas and
the New American Calendar

The shaping of an American Christmas in the hundred years after the Revolution must be understood within a stark and salient reality. Americans celebrated few holidays before independence and even fewer after. The English actress Fanny Kemble noted this fact on Christmas Day, 1832. "Comparatively no observances of tides and times" punctuated the American year, she observed. "Christmas day is no religious day and hardly a holiday with them: New-year's day is perhaps a little, but only a little more so. For Twelfth-day, it is unknown; and the household private festivals of birthdays are almost universally passed by unsevered from the rest of the toilsome days devoted to the curse of labour." Elizabeth Cady Stanton and Samuel Goodrich, both New Englanders, recalled the Fourth of July, Thanksgiving, and "training day" as the only "great festivals" of their early-nineteenth-century youths. An 80-year-old New Yorker wrote that in 1818 his boarding school allowed but two week-long vacations, plus the Fourth of July and Thanksgiving, during the entire year. Christmas and New Year's were ignored. [1]

By contrast, Fanny Kemble's England kept numerous festival days. The Bank of England closed annually for no fewer than eighteen holidays, including Good Friday, Christmas Day, and the firsts of May and November (Whitsun and All Saints'). In addition, the British observed a wide variety of local holidays, festivities, fairs, and wakes, many of which people enjoyed in spite of employers' objections. [2]

England's web of holidays was thin compared with that of Catholic Europe. The Roman Church had gradually established Easter, Pentecost, Epiphany, Nativity, Ascension, and Rogation Days. It added commemorative days for Saints Peter, Paul, and Stephen; four feasts for Mary; and one each for the archangel Michael and the martyrs and confessors. In 1232, Pope Gregory IX declared 95 such days of universal observance, but each diocese proclaimed additional local holidays. By the time of the Reformation, so much had pageantry and spectacle come to characterize the wealth of holy days that protesting theologians maneuvered to excise many of them from the calendars of their native lands. Martin Luther, for example, proposed eliminating all but the Sabbath, which he thought should be kept in order that workers might rest and worship. Still, European calendars modified by the Reformation remained rich in comparison with those of America.[3]

The spare American calendar seems even more unusual when one considers the almost universal appearance and function of holidays in cultures throughout the world. Interspersed among ordinary days, special religious and civic days temporarily release celebrants from the everydayness of life to renew social, religious, and civic commitments. Holidays, as Emile Durkheim argued, fulfill a fundamental need to differentiate and to alternate among various existential domains. Placed amid ordinary days, they punctuate the rhythm of the calendrical year, helping to describe and characterize units of time and to give them significance. In short, holidays define and reflect the nature and needs of the societies in which they exist. Such days, and their pattern on the yearly calendar, are essential to the formation of a cultural identity.[4]

The condition of American calendars of the early nineteenth century can be traced back to the cultural variety and displacement endemic to pre-Revolutionary days. No single calendar served all of the colonists. Dutch settlers, and presumably Germans, Swedes, and other Continental Europeans, used the Gregorian calendar. Until the British government switched to the Gregorian in 1752/3, English settlers used the Julian calendar. Dissenters in New England and Quakers in the Delaware Valley of Pennsylvania used the same calendar, but renamed the months and days to avoid referring to their pagan origins. January became First Month, and Sunday became First Day.[5]

Nor did colonists celebrate the same holidays. Sectarian religious differences and church decrees hindered the observance of some festivals in the New World, while the passage of time and distance from native villages eroded the symbolic importance of others. In New Amsterdam, the Dutch celebrated May Day, New Year's, and an assortment of religious days, including Voorbereyding (Preparation for the Lord's Supper, observed quarterly), Christmas, Palm Sunday, Paasche (Passover or Easter), Ascension Day, and Pinxxter (Whitsuntide). Washington Irving tells us (although the accuracy of his history might be questioned) that Governor Peter Stuyvesant "was a great promoter of holydays. Under his reign there was a great cracking of eggs at Paas or Easter . . . and never were stockings better filled on the eve of the blessed St. Nicholas."[6]

In New England the staunchest Calvinists kept only the Sabbath, but farmers often noted other holidays in their private almanacs and journals. Many interrupted their work routines on Election Day and Harvard's Commencement Day, as well as on sporadic feast and other special days. According to one historian, the Connecticut clergy "generally found their people woefully ignorant of the Church year, and tried to persuade them to lie [*sic*] according to the Christian calendar."[7]

Southern colonists commemorated most English folk and Anglican religious holidays. As in southern England, accounts and rents in Virginia usually fell due on Lady Day (March 25), Midsummer's Day (June 24), Michaelmas (September 29), and Christmas Day. Other days, such as Shrovetide, Lent, Easter, Easter Monday, and Hock Tuesday, were also kept. In 1662, a Virginia law set aside May 29 to celebrate the birthday and restoration of King Charles II.[8]

Southerners, as well as other colonists, occasionally celebrated Epiphany, or Twelfth Night, alternately bidding a solemn farewell to the winter's religious season and inaugurating pre-Lenten revelry. William Byrd, although he rarely mentioned the occasion, wrote that on Twelfth Day, 1740, he read Hebrew and Greek, then played billiards. After dinner he "talked to my people, drew twelfth cake, gave the people cake and cider, and prayed." In the 1770s, Landon Carter and his family "ventured through the rain" to share twelfth cake on the invitation of old Captain Beale. George Washington married Martha on "Twelfth night or 'Old Christmas' Eve" in 1759. In 1774, an English traveler attended a Scots-Irish Twelfth Night Ball in Alexandria, Virginia. There he saw "about 37 ladies dressed and powdered to the life." He thought "it look[ed] more like a Bacchanalian dance than one in a polite assembly," and "went home about two o'clock, but part of the company stayed, got drunk and had a fight."[9]

Throughout the colonies, drinking, fighting, revelry, and squandering money had become a fairly routine way to spend almost any holiday. Such indulgence particularly irritated New England's leaders, as high spirits on muster and election days and at other civil events increasingly threatened public decorum and piety. On Shrove Tuesday (Mardi Gras), antics in Boston sometimes rivaled those in England, where the church holiday had a history of raucous behavior. On that occasion in 1686/7, Samuel Sewall noted in his diary that "Jos. Maylem carries a Cock at his back, with a Bell in 's hand, in the Main Street; several follow him blindfold, and under pretence of striking him or 's cock, with great cart-whips strike passengers, and make great disturbance."[10]

Sermonizing preachers dominated Election Day, but some activities gave it an "unreligious tone." One minister complained that rather than praying, men met "to smoke, carouse, and swagger, and dishonor God with great bravery." Misbehavior on Guy Fawkes' Day became such a problem that New England authorities tried to end it. Each July, Harvard Commencement Day brought together a host of reputable participants. However, it also summoned "a great gathering of hucksters and vast crowds of country people." By the 1730s, officials fixed ceremonies on Fridays, so there would be "less remaining time in the week to be spent in frolicking." Rowdiness even imperiled Thanksgiving. Or so said one minister, who "express'd his dislike of the Guns fired by the Ships and Castle, as not sutable [*sic*]" for the day.[11]

Geography and community diversity made the dates of holiday observance a crazy quilt of timing. No single set of traditions dominated colonial life. Beginning with fall harvest and stretching as far as Candlemas in February, winter holidays such as Thanksgiving, New Year's, St. Stephen's, and Twelfth Night graced some calendars, but not all. Shrove Tuesday, St. Valentine's Day, Guy Fawkes' Day, and Good Friday scattered across others. The traditional English harvest festival came at the right time for a New England Thanksgiving but too early for the Chesapeake. Whitsuntide, the seventh Sunday after Easter, synchronized well with the completion of tobacco planting and made a fine southern holiday. It often went unacknowledged elsewhere. Perhaps only the British closing of colonial ports and other government offices on Sundays and 23 official red letter days each year gave a semblance of calendrical unity in the colonies.[12]

That Americans neither celebrated as many holidays as Europeans nor held many in common among themselves caused little if any stir in the pre-Revolutionary era. However, the Revolution altered American calendars. Revolutionary patriots revoked all official British holidays on the thirteen colonial calendars, but did nothing to replace them. They neither rejected the Gregorian calendar, which had been imposed by British rule, nor consolidated its many colonial versions into a single, national calendar that encoded republican and democratic values. Consistent with the principles of federalism, they forfeited authority over such matters to states, communities, and individuals. National holidays simply did not exist. Moreover, disestablishment eliminated many religious holidays and insured that none would receive state sanction. Thus, the American calendar at the beginning of nationhood actually looked more barren than it had early in the seventeenth century.[13]

In America—young, dynamic, criss-crossed with linguistic, ethnic, and regional differences—the "nature and needs" of its society as a whole were as yet incompletely formed. Nature and the nature of work did provide basic rhythms. Dawn, dusk, and the weather shaped work days. Plantings and harvests defined years. Leisure and work intertwined. Blacksmiths breakfasted as their forges heated. Tradesmen and laborers met at the local tavern before finishing the day. Only a few holidays, however, transcended everyday life.

As the nation became more enmeshed in commerce and as some regions even began to industrialize, Americans became more conscious of regulated time. Cycles of traditional life yielded to linear time. New imperatives discouraged irregular work patterns and time-consuming traditional holidays. Modern merchants and factory owners, looking to future profits, emphasized efficiency, speed, and productivity. Their more rigorous attention to labor routines and goals altered old relationships between work and play, splitting life and livelihood into regular intervals of work and leisure. Leisure became something to be pursued away from the workplace, and the number of leisure days dwindled even further.[14]

By the 1830s, a handful of holidays—New Year's, Thanksgiving, Independence Day, and Christmas—had emerged as nascent national celebrations on otherwise eclectic and diminished calendars. Even these now familiar days Americans of the post-Revolutionary era observed irregularly and with little ceremonial consistency. Indeed, observance in a single community might shift between enthusiasm and passivity over a stretch of years.

The early history of America's Independence Day celebrations illustrated the widely varied holiday habits of the nation. Massachusetts, in 1781, had been the first among the states to give official recognition to the Fourth of July. Other northern states soon followed. By the early nineteenth century, organized civic ceremonies commemorating independence had settled into a routine of noise, parades, speeches, food, and fireworks. Typical of these was the celebration of the fiftieth anniversary of American independence in Thomaston, Maine. It opened with "The roar of cannon . . . , a salute of 24 guns from a brass six pounder . . . , [and] the ringing of bells." Nearly 300 townspeople gathered to hear a reading of the Declaration of Independence, toast nation and community, and drink and dine together. After being entertained by "some fine patriotic songs and towards the last of it some comic songs in fine style," they enjoyed "a fine display of fireworks." Accounts survive of similar festivities in Fredericksburg, Virginia, Gambier, Ohio, Quincy, Massachusetts, and presumably many other towns noted the day with equal verve. [15]

Yet much depended on geography and circumstance. Fourth of July celebrations were more common in the North than the South. Especially in the countryside, dominated by local custom, the holiday claimed relatively little attention. William Sewall, teaching in Maryland in 1821, for example, remarked that the day did not "seem any different than other days for all is still and tranquil around here." [16]

As for Thanksgiving, most considered it a New England feast. Pilgrims reputedly held the first one in 1621, where, as recounted by one nineteenth-century writer, they abandoned themselves to "every kind of merrymaking, and almost every species of sport" to feast with Chief Massasoit and "his ninety swarthy retainers" for three days. During the next several decades, they repeated the community holiday only sporadically. Gradually, though, other New England towns adopted the practice. The Journal of Captain Francis Goelet sheds some light on the regard in which Thanksgiving was held. Writing on November 1, 1750, he noted, "This Being a General Thanksgiving day, was Strictly Observed heere and more so by the Presbyterians, its Call[e]d their Christmas, and is the Greatest Holyday they have in the Year and is Observed more Strict than Sunday." [17]

By the middle of the seventeenth century, civil governments throughout the region, rather than churches, were declaring a Thursday in late fall to give thanks. The feast soon gained a fairly secure place on the calendar, but often it merited no more mention than a comment such as "Very Comfortable Thanksgiving Day" in diaries. In the nineteenth century, the popularity of the Pilgrim holiday continued to grow. Thanksgiving "dont [*sic*] take quite so strong hold of 'Friends' as of others," John Greenleaf Whittier explained in 1842, "but even *they* feel its contagious influence more or less." Indeed, by many accounts, Thanksgiving provided for an "outpouring of the heart" that Charles Francis Adams thought so necessary to human happiness.[18]

New Year's, for most Americans, was simply a social festival. Dutch and English settlers had long welcomed it with great ceremony. In the week preceding New Year's in New York City, the rich dined with each other at elaborate dinner parties. On January 1, etiquette required men to call on every family member, friend, and acquaintance, while women held open house. The custom charmed visitors and temporary residents, and they often carried it home with them. George Washington, after living in New York City, received New Year's visitors throughout his presidency in Philadelphia. Thomas Jefferson and other Presidents continued the practice of keeping their doors open to visitors on January 1.[19]

Outside New York City, the pleasures of New Year's were as agreeable if perhaps less genteel. Calvin Fletcher of Indianapolis "had a Stein in company of [various men] then returned home and spent the fore part of the day rather sluggishly" on New Year's Day, 1822. Later he and his wife met "about 20 couple" for a party. In 1835, Mary Austin Holley celebrated New Year's Eve in Brazoria, Texas, "with a supper—present some young ladies & gentlemen, Drank champagne—sung & danced in the New Year."[20]

In addition to Thanksgiving, Independence Day, and New Year's, Christmas also gained prominence on the calendar as the new nation matured. Yet Americans continued to celebrate it in diverse ways. In some places, the radical Protestant rejection of the festival as non-scriptural remained. Few of Pennsylvania's citizens observed Christmas, reported the Philadelphia *Democratic Press* in 1810. During the War of 1812, the state legislature adjourned at Christmas, but soldiers continued to fight, prompting one newspaper in the Quaker region of West Chester to editorialize: "The poor solider gets only 30 cents a day, in the field, for having . . . 'bayonets poked through his ribs and his sides bored with bullets,' while his brother legislators draw *three dollars* a day for eating Christmas pies." By contrast, southerners tended to keep the festival. "The Christmas holiday, from Christmas to newyears are regarded with much attention here," Nathaniel Wright had written from Virginia in 1816. "It is always a great holiday in [E]piscopal places."[21]

Individual behavior also varied widely. Couples often chose December 25 to marry. Funerals were not uncommon. German immigrants traditionally kept two days of Christmas, one devoted to religious sentiment and the second to more temporal pleasures. If Christmas fell on a Sunday, the holiday would last three days. The Rev. Francis Asbury professed Christmas Day to be "the worst in the whole year on which to preach Christ." However, the Rev. Heman Bangs, an itinerant Methodist preacher, had a "glorious Christmas" in 1826. It began at six in the morning with "a blessed prayer-meeting." At eleven he "attended service at the Episcopal Church; at two in the afternoon, preached to the children, and catechised them; at night, a delightful Love feast; some shouted for joy, some wept for mercy."[22]

On the frontier, Christmas evoked a memory of civilization and occasionally gave an excuse to enjoy extra rations for merriment's sake. William Clark and Meriwether Lewis spent the winter of 1805 at Fort Clatsop at the mouth of the Columbia. Clark wrote that "we would have Spent this day the nativity of Christ in feasting, had we any thing either to raise our Sperits or even gratify our appetites, our Diner, concisted of pore Elk, so much Spoiled that we eate it thro' mear necessity, some Spoiled pounded fish and a fiew roots." Ross Cox only dreamed of Christmas when he spent the winter of 1821 among the Flathead Indians. Nonetheless, its importance to him was clear. Asleep that holiday he imagined he was at his "father's table, surrounded by the smiling domestic group, all anxious to partake of a smoking sirloin, and a richly dotted plumb-pudding, while the juvenile members recounted to each other with triumphant joy the amount of their Christmas boxes; but alas!" Francis A. Chardon, a fur trader based at Fort Clark on the upper Missouri River, recorded that his men fired several salutes on Christmas 1836. He "gave them a feast, of eatables but [had] no drinkables to give them."[23]

However, in the nation's rising trade centers, where the bustle of trade brought people together in new and sustaining combinations, December 25 often differed little from any other day. Newspapers seldom took note of Christmas, indicating either that their readers paid little heed to its importance or that the matter lay primarily in the church rather than the public sphere. The *Richmond Enquirer*, printed on Christmas Day in 1804, said nothing of the holiday. It remained silent on the matter as late as 1833. The *Salisbury* (North Carolina) *Western Carolinian* did not mention Christmas in its regular "Religious" column for December 25, 1821. The *Providence* (Rhode Island) *Gazette* allowed only a few lines about Christmas in 1823, noting on December 24 that Christians could not agree on an exact date of Christ's birth.[24]

Work time mixed with holiday time as businessmen pursued their business-as-usual routines. Courts convened, offices hummed with industry, and legislatures debated and voted. Samuel Rodman, a Quaker, could usually be found at the "counting house" on Christmas. In 1823, Hezekiah Prince, Jr., attended court on Christmas Day. Edwin Martin Stone reported an official bridge opening on Christmas Day, 1828. Isaiah Thomas, on Christmas 1819, settled a financial dispute, allowing G. A. Trumbull "60 dollars for which he had no honourable claim." William Sewall, great-grandson of Puritan Judge Samuel Sewall, often wrote of other holidays in his diary, but never described any special event on December 25th except to note "CHRISTMAS," which in 1817 he spent "rambling around town."[25]

Brief social notes on the holiday, however, many underscoring business associations, became more common in private diaries. Calvin Fletcher, who had just arrived in Indianapolis, headed down to the river on Christmas Eve in 1821 to join "a larg[e] collection of men Principly the candidate[s] for the New county." There they unheaded a barrel of cider and "all permiscussously drank. . . ." Meanwhile, his wife Sarah and two women friends read the Bible together. Another Christmas, they "had a party of a ball" attended by "about 30 couple[s]." In 1829, after attending court, Christopher Columbus Baldwin went to a party at Sheriff Willard's with other members of the bar. Isaiah Thomas spent his Christmas in 1829 with the county sheriff and "about 20 others" at Sike's Coffee House. Another made it "a rule to have several of our friends and our connexions here to take Christmas dinner with us every year."[26]

The paucity of holidays almost inevitably made Christmas, New Year's, Thanksgiving, and Independence Day important. Yet just as these were not universally kept, neither was the manner of their observance uniform. Regional practices associated with a holiday in one place seemed out of place in another. New Englanders, Charles Francis Adams noted, transferred the customs that "ought to come at Christmas and New Year" to "Thanksgiving, an Institution of their own." Southerners tipped faithful servants and shot off guns at Christmas, behavior similar to what a rural Pennsylvanian or New Yorker might do on New Year's. Harvard student Jacob Rhett Motte, when awakened "by the ringing of bells and firing of guns" on the Fourth of July, compared it to Christmas in the South. On Independence Day in his hometown of Charleston, he wrote, "nothing is heard, thought or dreamt of, but pleasure and enjoyment; from the proudest aristocrat to the humblest negro." Thanksgiving feasts in New York paralleled those of the Puritans but were held far less frequently. Virginia had no annual feast day, probably owing to the work requirements of raising tobacco.[27]

James Iredell, Jr., a southerner who had been sent off to Princeton for his schooling, quickly learned that not everyone celebrated Christmas. "You will naturally suppose we had a good deal of diversion on Christmas," he wrote home to his friend Ebenezer Pettigrew in 1805. "But this day, which in Carolina is welcomed with so many demonstrations of joy, is here [at Princeton] regarded almost with perfect indifference & passed over as but little more than an ordinary day." Pettigrew responded that he found the inattention "a little surprising." Until his friend had encountered the Calvinists of Princeton, Pettigrew had "thought it was a day of mirth with a great majority of the people in all countries of the Christian wourld [sic]."[28]

"E.F." expressed similar wonderment. Two days after Christmas, in 1819, he wrote home to his sister in New York that in New Orleans, in addition to the common gentlemen's amusements of billiards and gambling, they "were *pitching dollars* in the streets, and getting drunk, the latter particularly is very much in vogue at this season." The "great doings at the Chapel" especially caught his attention. There "a guard of gens d'armes, with fixed bayonets were employed all Christmas eve in watching a *waxen baby*, which they call the infant Jesus!!! — ."[29]

Early in the nineteenth century, a few thoughtful Americans voiced concern over the nation's sparse and ragtag calendar. Same faulted religion for its condition. "Our Protestant Faith affords no religious holidays & processions like the Catholics," John Pintard remarked in 1823. "From the period of the Jews and Heathens down thro the Greeks & Romans, the Celts, Druids, even our Indians all had & have their religious Festivals." England, he noted, retained numerous "red letter days as they are called" which, in addition to Christmas, Easter, and Whitsun, "afford intervals of rest . . . , but with us, we have only Independence Christmas & New Year, 3 solitary days. . . ."[30]

Pintard's friend Washington Irving blamed not only America's lack of traditions, but also the "degeneracy and refinement" of new conditions that destroyed the geniality and generosity of the imagined past. "The good old Dutch festivals," which had been so "faithfully observed in the mansion of Governor Stuyvesant," Irving noted in *A History of New York* (1809), had "fall[en] into sad disuse among my fellow-citizens." New Year's, the governor's favorite festival, had once been "truly a day of open-handed liberality, of jocund revelry and warm-hearted congratulation, . . . genial good fellowship, . . . unceremonious freedom, and honest broad-mouthed merriment." A character in one of Irving's stories spoke for the author: "One of the least pleasing effects of modern refinement is the havoc it has made among the hearty old holiday customs." Modernity had "completely taken off the sharp touchings and spirited reliefs of these embellishments of life."[31]

Significantly, Irving turned to Christmas for his richest evocation of a golden age. At one point, perhaps in search of a proper format for his own stories, he transcribed into his journal the text of a 1652 English tract titled "Vindication of Christmas." In it, the character "Christmas," upon leaving the country house where he had spent the holiday in exile during the reign of Cromwell, gives "this christian exhortation to all people in general. Love one another, as my master loved you: relieve the oppressed: call home exiles: help the fatherless: cherish the widow, and restore to every man his due. . . ."[32]

Yet Irving knew the importance of Christmas was more complex than simple Christian moralizing. He saw in it a potential to bind society together and to provide an antidote for the ills of modern life.

Irving explored the social implications and usefulness of a traditional English Christmas in five essays published in *The Sketchbook of Geoffrey Crayon, Gent.* (1819–1820). He told the story of himself, young "Geoffrey Crayon," who happened to meet a former traveling companion, Frank Bracebridge, while touring England. It being the holiday season, Frank promptly invited him to his father's country home, Bracebridge Mansion. When they arrived on Christmas Eve, Crayon found gentry and servants gathered around a roaring fire in the great hall to enjoy the heartiness, hospitality, and communal good feeling associated with a "traditional" old English Christmas. They feasted from a table "literally loaded with good cheer," including, to Crayon's delight, his "old friend minced-pie." Afterward, the servants engaged in "a great deal of revelry."[33]

Geoffrey Crayon soon discovered the entire celebration had been invented by the Squire as part of an effort to recreate the hierarchical social order over which he had once presided. On the condition that "every thing was done conformably to ancient usage," Bracebridge encouraged servants and guests to enjoy the holiday's full twelve days. He believed the old customs and games fundamental to the restoration of the imagined harmonies of earlier times. They made the peasant fond of his home and his lord, and in all "make the times merrier, and kinder, and better."[34]

For all his purpose, though, the Squire could not revive an idyllic past. The country people did not know how to act and so had to be taught the old games. The parson, "[s]hut up among [his] worm-eaten tomes," still believed Christmas needed only be reclaimed from the condemnation of Cromwell's Puritans to achieve its old glories. He gave "a most erudite sermon on the rites and ceremonies" of the holiday but had forgotten that "nearly two centuries had elapsed since the fiery persecution of poor Mince pie throughout the land." Worse, even the Squire could not bring himself into full conformity with tradition. Rather than kill a peacock in order to use its magnificent tail to decorate the traditional pie, he made the pie of pheasant.

The irony of the Bracebridge Christmas did not elude Irving. Although the Squire had attempted to ignore the changed circumstances of the modern world, both he and Irving understood the futility of his undertaking. "The nation . . . is altered," Squire Bracebridge mourned. "[W]e have almost lost our simple true hearted peasantry." They "talk[ed] of reform," thought their interests unrelated to the upper classes, and had become "too knowing" from reading newspapers and listening to "alehouse politicians." Yet the struggle with such yearnings for Christmas, even when admittedly irrelevant to the world around them, hinted that some new form of celebration was in the offing.

CHAPTER 3

![holly leaf ornament]

The Beginnings
of a Modern Christmas

Despite whatever fears Irving had about the fate of holidays, "modernity" did not doom Christmas. Changed times simply meant changed holidays. The Christmas that the Squire of Bracebridge tried to recreate may have, at a time long past, affirmed unity and hierarchy among landholders and laborers in the English countryside. Similarly, the varied and sometimes quite minor significance that colonial Americans placed upon Christmas suited their society, one physically truncated from traditional life in England and continental Europe and subject to the usual pace of change. The holiday that came to be celebrated in the nineteenth century reflected yet another setting. It emerged as a response to new circumstances shaped by the American Revolution and America's participation in a worldwide revolution in commerce and industry. Irving's yearning for some festival to bind members of the community, in fact, expressed the changed needs of a new nation more than it marked the passing of some real or imagined golden age.

The most striking and visible transformations began to materialize in the 1820s, in the realms of commerce, communications, and industry. A growing network of roads and railroads and, beginning in the 1840s, an increasingly effective national mail system connected Americans as never before. Cities expanded to fit growing numbers of European immigrants, rural transplants, and a burgeoning middle class. Cheap newspapers, books, and magazines reached new audiences. Inventions and scientific discoveries

29

pushed aside tradition and exacerbated the contrast between the present and romantic memories of a more leisurely and harmonious pre-industrial life. Everywhere, signs of progress tested old bonds of religion and community.

Even before such palpable transformations of American life began to sweep the nation, signs that Americans had started to experiment, mostly unwittingly, with the essence of a new Christmas tradition appeared. One began to see individuals using the holiday as a means of coming face to face with other communities in the pluralistic worlds of town and city. The experience of the Reverend Ezra Stiles is one example. Schooled in Calvinism at Yale and minister of Newport, Rhode Island's Second Congregational Church, he should have had no interest in Christmas. His diary suggests otherwise. First in 1769, then again in 1770, he attended pietistic German Lutheran Christmas services at the local Moravian church.[1]

To some extent, such behavior reflected Stiles's penchant for religious experimentation. He had come near to being a Deist in his first years of training. Furthermore, Rhode Island was the most religiously tolerant of the New England colonies. Yet something more was going on, something that impelled Stiles to partake of the Moravians' sacred Christmas despite Congregationalism's official rejection of the holiday.[2]

Stiles did not limit his interest to Moravians. He was particularly struck by the Baptists' interest in Christmas. They, like the Congregationalists, found no scriptural grounds for celebrating Christ's birth. However, on December 25, 1772, the Baptist Church of Newport observed Christmas for the first time in its history. Its minister, a Mr. Kelly, had begun holding lectures on alternate Wednesdays in 1771. Since Christmas coincidentally fell on Wednesday that year, Kelly had adapted his sermon to "celebrate the Birth and Incarnation of the blessed Savior." The following year, Kelly more openly challenged Baptist doctrine by giving his talk "not on Wednesday but Friday expressly because it was Christmas." To Stiles, who attended Kelly's Christmas service, "this looked more like keeping Christmas than any Thing that ever before appeared among the Baptists or Congregationalists in New England. . . . [I]t is probable," he prophesied, "this will begin the Introduction of Christmas among the Baptist Churches, about one hundred and fifty years from the first planting of New England and *near one hundred and thirty years* from the foundation of the first *Baptist Church* in New England."[3]

Stiles accepted such momentous change with some apprehension. "Had it been the will of Christ that the Anniversary of his Nativity should have been celebrated," he reasoned, "he would have at least let us have known the day." By 1782, however, Stiles felt comfortable enough with Christmas to "cordially joyn with the greatest part of christendom this day in celebrating the nativity of a divine Savior; altho' I well know from Ecclesiastical History that this is not the true day of his Nativity. . . . "[4]

When Mr. Kelly and Stiles broke with Calvinist tradition on the matter of Christmas, they defined a new community within Newport, one highlighted by a broader, more generic Christian experience that relied less singularly on the doctrine of individual churches. The yearning for such a common identity more and more surfaced as a counterpoint to sectarianism, despite or perhaps because of the rise of so many new faiths in the early nineteenth century. And Stiles's penchant for visiting the churches of others continued as a means toward preparing a broad Christian identity.

Christmas endured as the occasion for such explorations. Among the members of those churches that traditionally rejected Christmas or found it of only minor importance, celebrations at Episcopal and Catholic churches often proved magnetic. William Bentley noted in 1808 that "The English Church tho' usually very thin was full this day & chiefly from the most rigid sects. We see the attraction of the decorations of a Church still in New England." In 1812, the Universalists met on Christmas Day, which, wrote Bentley, "is somewhat extraordinary, as they profess to be no observers of times & seasons which beguile men." Thomas Robbins, although apparently still a Congregational minister, habitually slipped into an Episcopal church at Christmas. While Samuel Rodman attended a meeting of fellow Quakers, his children went to the Episcopal church, "it being Christmas and the house decorated with evergreens." On Christmas, 1851, Rev. Dr. James Waddel Alexander, a Presbyterian minister in New York City, attended "nine churches: St. Francis Xavier's, St. Patrick's Cathedral, St. Joseph's, St. Vincent de Paul, St. Somebody's (German), Bellows', Grace, Calvary, and Muhlenberg's Little Gothic Free Seat Chapel."[5]

Even those from the most powerfully Calvinistic background felt drawn by the luster of the holiday. Born in 1813 and raised in the orthodox household of his father Lyman, Henry Ward Beecher knew virtually nothing of Christmas until he was thirty years old. However, as a child he exhibited much fascination with the Christmas music and lights at Litchfield, Connecticut's Episcopal church. "To me Christmas was a foreign day," wrote Beecher in 1874. "When I was a boy I wondered what Christmas was. I knew there was such a time, because we had an Episcopal church in our town, and I saw them dressing it with evergreens, and wondered what they were taking the woods in church for; but I got no satisfactory explanation. A little later I understood it was a Romish institution, kept up by the Romish Church."[6]

Many masked their "sin" of Christmas visitation by using it as a pretext for an aesthetic critique on Roman Catholicism. In 1801, Manasseh Cutler reported on attending the Catholic church in Georgetown as if he had gone to the theatre: "Much insignificant ceremony; poor sermon, but excellent singing." One woman found the music in the Catholic church on Christmas "almost equal on this occasion to an *Opera*." George Templeton Strong, who had forsaken his Congregational upbringing in college to become, as he declared, a "violent High Churchman," took the occasion of Christmas, 1841, to attend St. Paul's in New York City. "Then went to St. Peters—Church jammed—squeeze terrific—," he observed. "[S]uch church music I never heard before—they had a choir of 50 or so—Well drilled—& the effect with which the choir & the full organ . . . with the Hallelujah Chorus at the end of the services was great. . . . It's a shame that the Church cant or dont have such music as is thrown away on those rowdies at St. Peter's."[7]

Rather than condemning these divergences, some Calvinist denominations began to acknowledge the nativity feast. Early in the century, Tocqueville had made the broad observation that "all the clergy of America freely adopt the general views of their time and country and let themselves go unresistingly with the tide of feeling and opinion which carries everything around them along with it." One can track an instance of this behavior in the journal of Congregationalist Thomas Robbins. Robbins began his diary in 1796, but made no entry concerning Christmas until 1804, when he "[w]as invited to an entertainment with a number of people, it being Christmas." The people who invited him, he noted, were "not Episcopalians," a comment suggesting that the hosts belonged to a denomination that did not traditionally celebrate Christmas. In his Christmas entry for 1807, Robbins recorded that he had kept the day solemnly "fasting, reading the Bible, and [in] prayer." However, in 1808 he ventured to preach "a little in reference to Christmas Day" during his sermon on the 25th and to enjoy a Christmas dinner on the 26th.[8]

Robbins's diary remained silent on Christmas for several years. Then, in 1821, for the first time he took note of what was still something of a rarity: "Many people went to Hartford to Christmas," he wrote, probably at an Episcopal church. Two years later he noted the turning of yet another Calvinist congregation to Christmas. The Congregationalists of Hartford had a Christmas meeting, he recorded, "I presume for the first time."

In their observances of Christmas, Americans had begun to create a symbol of non-denominational Protestantism that fit well into the pluralist culture in which they lived. The festive air of churches, draped with nature's greenery, shining with candles, and filled with music, invited wary strangers to enter. Inside, they could imagine a haven in which old and cherished values survived, a world removed from an ever more complex and confusing temporal one. Church visitors and members alike could bypass the theological questions that divided them along sectarian lines and participate together in the pomp and ritual of the services. Synthetic, short-lived, and to some degree superficial, this association of believers at Christmas helped satisfy a vague but growing need to identify and solidify a sense of community that went beyond the confines of church walls.

As the festive, communal appeal of Christmas evoked curiosity and began to erode opposition to its celebration, other forces began to mold the holiday in new and more public ways. This was especially so in the cities, those centers of new forms of commerce and industry destined to transform society from top to bottom. Growing cities created societies of strangers and fostered a new middle class bent upon defining an appropriate familial and public life for America. For them, sobriety, gentility, moral living, prosperity, and a well-ordered civic existence became ideals for the entire nation.

The public conviviality of Christmas and New Year's brought this highly diverse urban population together. Only a decade after the publication of *Bracebridge Hall* (1819), in which Washington Irving mourned the passing of Christmas, New York City was reinventing the holiday season. "The week between Christmas and New Year is, and always was," Gabriel Furman wrote, "emphatically a week of Holidays. . . . [New Yorkers] greet everyone with 'Merry Christmas.'" Although Furman cast an aura of timelessness over Christmas, December 25 had only recently and quite abruptly gained such prominence as a holiday in that city. Fifteen years earlier, in 1815, the local newspaper had printed but one reminder of Christmas's appearance, a nativity poem by Sir Walter Scott.[9]

Now, New York's stores in the city stayed open until midnight during the Christmas season. Bright gas lights illuminated "[w]hole rows of confectionery stores and toy shops, fancifully, and often splendidly, decorated with festoons of bright silk drapery, interspersed with flowers and evergreens." In the evenings and into the late night, "visitors of both sexes and all ages" filled the streets, "some selecting toys and fruit for holiday presents; others merely lounging from shop to shop to enjoy the varied scene." [10]

Even the major strongholds of Calvinism and Quakerism shared in the new focus on Christmas and New Year's. In Boston, the last day of 1834, a sunny day "warm enough to melt much of the snow," found Charles Francis Adams among the crowds who had turned "out at the shops in the busy occupation of purchasing for New Year's day." On Monday, the day after Christmas, 1842, Isaac Mickle "crossed over to Philadelphia and walked up and down Chestnut Street with some friends. I never saw so many people turned out to celebrate Christmas," he wrote. "The main streets were literally jammed." [11]

Holiday street scenes rich in the imagery of commerce and fellowship and churches overflowing with holiday greens provided for Americans an affirmation of human community in the midst of their thriving cities. This was especially important for members of the urban middle class. As forceful engineers of change, they experienced perhaps most keenly the absence of stabilizing religious and folk traditions. In particular, they felt a need to preserve those old ideals that best promoted the moral values they espoused for society as a whole, and to create new ways and manners to help knit society into modern fabric. These insurgent middle classes, especially those of Calvinist background, showed little tolerance for customs and ideas that ran counter to their vision. In the case of Christmas, they sought to transcend the legacy of Puritan rejection and at the same time control the holiday rowdiness that seemed endemic to the lower classes. [12]

Privately and publicly, the gulf between the tenacious influence of Puritan thought and the attractiveness of Christmas brought forth increasingly sharp condemnation of Puritan asceticism. In Boston, once a bastion of Puritan resistance to the holiday, local newspapers had as early as 1833 called for a "more marked observance of Christmas day." In 1840, George Templeton Strong assailed Puritans and other non-observers as "papaphobic dissenters" for their opposition to the holiday. "I really wish—for the aggravation of Schismatics in general that *churches* could be Christmas-greened outside & in—that triple bobmajors could be sung from Every Church steeple in the City from Christmas morn'g till Christmas night:—a salute of 100 guns fired in Trinity Church yard, and every churchman's house in the City illuminated from garret to cellar," he wrote. "—It would make them so gloriously indignant." [13]

A short story published by *Godey's Lady's Magazine* in 1849, just as forthright if not as acerbic, also condemned Puritan fustiness. One winter the Rev. Mr. Jason Archer, a "good man, but with his mind sadly warped through early prejudices, long confirmed," that is, a Puritan of the old school and strongly against "fashionable follie," journeyed from his New England village to visit a niece in the city. He arrived to find her family preparing for its annual "merry old Christmas" party. At first reluctant, the Reverend could not resist joining in. The innocent enjoyments of the holiday convinced him he had been too cautious. Christmas, while not as solemn and austere as he might have wished, was not as rowdy as he had feared.[14]

Endorsements of a moderate Christmas celebration embodying broad Protestant values came from many quarters. Horace Bushnell, Congregational theologian and author of *Christian Nurture*, was quite willing to subvert the theology of Calvinism for the sake of community values. Echoing the qualifying arguments voiced by William Bradford and later by Cotton Mather, he objected not to the actual keeping of Christmas, but to the manner in which it was sometimes celebrated. Christmas, he asserted, "may be greatly abused by what is really unchristian; what is sensual and low, and very close to vice itself. . . . " He regretted that its celebration, "otherwise so beautiful and appropriate, taken as a Christian commemoration of the greatest fact of the world's history, has been so commonly associated with traditional loseness and excess." Bushnell hoped that Christmas would "clear it entirely of the excess and profane jollity by which it was made to commemorate any thing and every thing but Christ," and charged them to make it "a genuine religious festivity" that "all friends of Christ" could observe universally.[15]

That Bushnell, in the middle of the nineteenth century, could complain of "excess and profane jollity" emphasized the persistence of some of the noisier holiday customs: revelry, mumming, and shooting off guns and fireworks. In Europe and England, myriad customs of outlawry, role reversal, and colorful mockery of the existing order punctuated the year. Similar outbreaks of raucous play had been a common part of American life in the countryside and frontier throughout the colonial period. By the early nineteenth century, Americans had developed strong, albeit informal, regional traditions of Christmas revelry. The concussion of guns filled the void of silence on the open frontier on Christmas morning and in sparsely settled areas it signaled a holiday greeting to distant neighbors. Ritual processions from house to house created comparable feelings of community. These amusements also punctuated the dreary routine of rural life.[16]

Frontier celebrations were of the broadest and most boisterous variety. In 1791, the crew of the *Colombia* kept Christmas "in mirth and festivity" in the wilds of Puget Sound. Sergeant John Ordway, wintering with William Clark's expedition near present day Bismarck, North Dakota, saluted Christmas, 1804, by shooting "Swivels at day break." Untroubled by "Savages," who had been warned to stay away on that "Great Medician day," the men drank "Taffee" (rum), ate as well as possible, and "continued firing danceing & frolicking" until nine that evening. Hosea Stout dotted his diary with references to seasonal high spirits. "San Bernardino, California," he wrote on Christmas in 1852, "sounded like a battle field[.] The boys are celebrating Christmas." In Mormon Utah, according to John Lee, "The reports of guns were heard in every direction, which is nothing uncommon about chrismas times." The boys, he said, were "waisting their Powder as usual on such ocasions. . . ."[17]

Sometimes Christmas revelers engineered spectacular blasts. In 1844, Thomas A. Hord's children, on their isolated homestead on the Trinity River in Texas, dug a deep hole and exploded a major cache of gunpowder stolen from their father's supplies. Just as satisfying were the impromptu fetes. A government exploration party, finding itself in northern Arizona in sub-zero weather on Christmas Eve in 1853, razed a grove of pines surrounding the camp. "The fireworks were decidedly magnificent," wrote Lieut. Amiel A. W. Whipple. "The flames leaped to the treetops, and then, dying away, sent up innumerable brilliant sparks."[18]

Such revelries knew no end of variety. One man remembered that in his Missouri boyhood he and his brother had divided the bladders of freshly butchered hogs between them. Working with great care, they "blew them up as tight as they could bear, then laid them away for our Christmas guns!" On Christmas Day they planned to "lay the bladders down on the ice and with a big paddle strike them sharply," making "a noise louder than a pop-gun. Oh, but it was fun!" James Lamar remembered that each Christmas Eve during his youth in Georgia, he and eight or ten of his friends armed themselves with "anything that would shoot." Later in the night, they set out "for miles and miles visiting every house far and near in the whole neighborhood." At each house, they sneaked as close to the bedroom as possible. With cocked guns in hand, they "became as still as death," waiting for the "whispered command *fire*! . . . And by the time the man [of the house] had fallen over a few chairs, and the women screamed and the babies squalled a little, they found out that it was Christmas Eve." Sometimes the householders invited the boys in for "Christmas pies and things, including, perhaps, a little extemporized egg-nogg." Lamar called his youthful holiday activities "anything but creditable," but nevertheless defended them. "[I]t should not be forgotten that we were country boys; that life in general was dull and monotonous."[19]

These rowdy and sometimes dangerous customs were not solely rural phenomena. Cities and towns, north and south, were scenes of year-end revelry. From Jeffersonville, Indiana, to Alexandria, Virginia, and many places between and beyond, boys and men claimed the streets for themselves at Christmas and New Year's. In 1819, James Flint, while traveling through Indiana, noted that beginning at dusk the night before Christmas, boys made "a great noise by firing guns and pistols." Adults created their own noise, swearing and fighting among themselves. J. C. A. Hamilton wrote that in his southern town, "all the big and little Boys" had been out all Christmas night, "Band serenading and the rest ringing the Fire bell[,] placing boxes across the streets[,] running out the fire apparatus Horse fiddles. Tin Horns + etc." Another wrote that although Christmas was over in Alexandria, Virginia, "the effects of it are still seen in the streets. It was like a Fourth of July."[20]

During the "Christmas Serenade," in St. Augustine, Texas, a band of "pleasant spirits . . . blowing tin horns and beating tin pans" blazed their own trail of havoc. They visited every house in town, "kicking in doors and pulling down fences until every male member of the family had appeared with appropriate instruments and joined the merry party." Their ceremony ended in the square "with a centupled tin row." "As strangers," Frederick Law Olmsted wrote, "we were not urged to participate."[21]

Alcohol often fueled, and frequently defined, holiday amusements. On Christmas, 1806, a Manchester, Ohio, "grog shop" invited patrons to partake of a concoction of "about a dozen eggs," slightly stirred, "about a pound of sugar and a little milk," amply laced with whiskey. After they had "suped . . . with spoons!," the crowd "began to cut up, and especially a professor of religion." In Houston, one young German businessman feared that he, like his Texas hosts, would spend New Year's of 1839 "wallow[ing] on the buffalo skin, sunk in melancholic reveries." Taking action, he gathered the whiskey, guns, and powder necessary for the enjoyment he planned for "these backwoods people" and declared the "watchword for the evening" to be "whisky!" Mormon Hosea Stout described his town on Christmas in 1858 as being "in a universal good natured drunk hollowing and yelling." In Harmony, Utah, John Lee, after being "ser[e]naded with the martial Band & nearly all the young men in town" at two in the morning, responded in a time-honored manner by treating "them to about 6 gallons Beer & all the Pies & cakes that they would Eat."[22]

Scholars of mumming, masking, and similar forms of ritualized revelry have seen the antics as, in the words of one folklorist, a "temporary plunge into chaos." The sharp contrast between mumming and everyday civil behavior, she argued, tended to reaffirm and strengthen the prevailing social order and values of the community. Revelry thus provided a release for pent-up anger and hostility, clarified the border of work and play, and, paradoxically, reinforced social connection. Another scholar stressed the importance of reversing civil order, but asserted that a deeper conviction, that freedom and innocence is achieved only by turning society upside down, underlay revelers' anarchy. Roger D. Abrahams and Richard Bauman arrived at a less romantic view of the process, finding that those who so aggressively disrupted the holiday caused similar problems throughout the rest of the year. Mumming, they suggested, accented the "general interrelationship between order and disorder in the moral and social universe of the communities. . . . "[23]

Each of these interpretations explains at least some aspects of the revelry that Americans across the nation witnessed and participated in during the early nineteenth century. But the free-form holiday mayhem was of a different order than the ritualized mumming and masquerading of European tradition. In Europe, such ceremonies thrived in small communities, where familiarity and the firmness of the social order buffered the holiday anarchy. In America, church and social hierarchy did not have such power.

The riotous behavior did not oppose, promote, or provide an alternative to the social order. Furthermore, eyewitnesses sometimes could make no specific connection between American revelry and Christmas or any other holiday. James Flint, awakened in Cincinnati at 5 a.m. by the firing of pistols and guns on Christmas Day, 1818, expressly noted that he "heard no one speak of the nature of the event that they were commemorating." A German settler in Missouri concluded that "a religious observance [of Christmas] was out of the question. . . . There was just shooting." Nor was the rowdiness many engaged in at Christmas and New Year's confined to that season alone. Fireworks and alcohol were often as conspicuous a part of Fourth of July celebrations."[24]

While the revelers and their mischief, gun play, and drinking may have been tolerated, accepted, ignored, or even encouraged in the countryside and in small towns, they met serious opposition in urban settings, even during the colonial era. Philadelphians, in an effort to curb public disorder, banned mumming by law. In 1702, they cited one John Smith for dressing in women's clothing and walking "openly through the streets of this citty from house to house on or about the 26th of the 10th month [i.e. the day after Christmas on the Quaker calendar]." Dorothy Canterill and Sarah Stoner were also charged "for masking in men's clothes." In 1675, officials in colonial New York City banned shooting on New Year's. Soon after, however, New Yorkers began to celebrate Christmas Eve noisily as well. So, in 1785, the state legislature reinstated the colonial law, extending it to prevent firing any arms, rockets, squibs, and other fireworks on Christmas Eve or New Year's. In 1808, Philadelphia declared "Masquerades and Masqued Balls to be Common Nuisances. . . ."[25]

However, legal prohibitions did little to alter custom. In New York City, the practice of shooting in the New Year continued into the 1830s. Philadelphia's mumming law proved more effective in ending masked balls than in stopping masquerades. Across the river in Camden, New Jersey, Isaac Mickle noted in 1842 that "the boys" were "very busy" firing guns to welcome the New Year. Thomas Cope, who had earlier thought there was "some diminution of this absurd fervour," observed in 1844 that "[t]he long accustomed practice among us of firing away the old & saluting the new year was not forgotten today. . . ."[26]

In fact, the noise, intimidation, and destructiveness of holiday antics seemed to intensify in the face of middle-class displeasure. Mocking the genteel manners of the upper classes, revelers made social visits to the homes of the city elite, paraded to cacophony down the main streets, and demanded attention in their outrageous costumes. During the 1820s, '30s, and '40s, urban rowdies—young, male, and usually poor—built on the general license of the season and began to cross the line from ritualized mayhem to anarchic mêlée. Mobs known as Callithumpian bands roamed New York City, banging and blowing on homemade instruments, intent on creating mischief to match their noise.

Gabriel Furman specifically remembered the New Year's Eve of 1828 as one of New York City's worst ever. In Philadelphia, on Christmas Eve, 1833, young men, rebelling against the constraints of urban routine, wandered in packs, drinking in taverns and fighting on street corners. Philadelphia's *Daily Chronicle* reported that "riot, noise, and uproar prevailed, uncontrolled and uninterrupted in many of our central and most orderly streets. Gangs of boys and young men howled and shouted as if possessed by the demon of disorder." In Pittsburgh, "[t]he screams of alarmed ladies, as some young rogue discharges his fire crackers at their feet," augmented the din created by "juvenile artillerists" who invaded that city at Christmas time. "Wretched is now the youngest who cannot raise powder; and proud, indeed, is the warlike owner of a pistol. . . ," concluded that city's newspaper after Christmas 1848.[27]

The prevalence of such fearful reports from the late 1820s through the early 1850s coincided not only with a probable increase of activity, but also with several phenomena deeply threatening to an aspiring middle class of devout Christians. First, for many of the middle class, Jackson's election in 1828 foretold doom at the hands of mobs, and the increasing occurrence of riots throughout the year fanned concern for the potential for violence among mummers. Quite as important, the rise of the temperance movement electrified a great many Americans with the notion that a sober society might lead America to the millennium. Moreover, the merrymaking flouted the demands of market and industry within a commercial culture that had come to see family, sobriety, and privacy as signal social virtues. In short, ritualized revelry posed political, social, and moral challenges to the hegemony of the middle and ruling classes.[28]

Some historians have labeled these boisterous displays emblematic of a class consciousness and elements of a working-class culture of antebellum America. Certainly there is truth to this interpretation. Not only did revelers taunt social superiors, but they also assailed ethnic groups in the lower strata of the economy whose competition they feared and against whom they measured their own status. In Philadelphia, men who had worn only partial or semi-human disguises began to impersonate national and racial types, dramatizing a sometimes hidden world of ethnic tension. In 1834, for instance, the *Easton* (Pennsylvania) *Sentinel* reported a "parade of fantasticals" which included a Callithumpian band uniformed as "Indians, negroes, hunters, Falstaffs, Jim Crows and nondescripts" on New Year's Day. As the frolics took on new forms, they were seen to embody new kinds of dangers to the community. Issues of rich versus poor, ethnicity versus nativism, public versus private, work productivity, and gender shaded the culture's response to the antics.[29]

Mummers and revelers, then, alarmed "respectable" city dwellers because of the disorder they caused, the saturnalian cast of their rituals, and most of all because they were almost inevitably strangers who did not conform to middle-class ideals of urban life that shunned unregulated behavior. Pressures against reveling began to mount. In many cities, the increasing influence of temperance doctrine promoted by the middle classes began, to some degree, to check the use of drink. One Indianian credited

"Temperance & Sabbath School societies" in his town for having "produced almost a calm" on the day before Christmas, 1829. Noting that "formerly New Years was a riotous day," John Pintard commented in 1828 that "it is right to lay the dram aside."[30]

Other opposition incorporated traditional distrust of Catholic and Anglican propensities toward "pagan" ceremony, and especially the belief that the Catholic Church promoted ignorance and immoral abandon. The presence of Catholic newcomers from Germany and other European countries strengthened prejudices against masking by posing a double threat of religion and ethnicity. One Quaker newspaper testified to the jumble of cultural tensions enveloped in the Christmas season when it editorialized that Christmas had "tended more to open licentiousness of manners, than to the increase and encouragement of sound morality and religion. The mummery . . . and the childish and superficial ideas which are propagated" through the "corrupt and interested medium" of some of the churches, it believed, were "wonderfully calculated to enlarge the sphere of stupidity, and to increase the shades of moral darkness over the minds of mankind."[31]

By the 1860s, dissatisfaction with the excesses of mumming could be found nearly everywhere. John Lee, the Mormon who had a number of previous Christmas and New Year's days generously and cheerfully supplied food and alcohol to his rowdy callers, lost patience with them in 1867. "The Party as usual was inturupted by those worthless Jolly Boys," he wrote. "The House was densly crowded & no comforte to be had in the midst of confusion & disorder. . . . " Lee's remarks echoed issues that had been raised in the larger cities for decades. The general disorder caused by "worthless" guests, not just to individual households but to entire communities, had made the old traditions of mumming, even as they had been declining over the decades, no longer tolerable.[32]

Thus a new kind of public notice of Christmas took hold in the cities, and the more raucous celebrations lost favor. Americans, especially the rising middle class, fostered at least a fictive sense of harmony and common focus with neighbors of different religions, nationalities, and classes. If in a small and more familiar community one reaffirmed the social order by occasionally and harmlessly overturning it, in a society of strangers one cemented order and reduced fear by partaking of "other" culture and life in the safe setting of the churches and, as would become increasingly apparent, at home.

CHAPTER 4

Home for Christmas:
Family, Religion, and Santa Claus

"At present time," wrote Lydia Maria Child in 1842, "indications are numerous that the human mind is tired out in the gymnasium of controversy, and asks earnestly for repose, protection, mystery, and undoubting faith." Middle-class antebellum Americans, even as they tried to shape the public world about them into a more perfect and orderly place, looked to home and family for respite from its trials and challenges. Through their idealization of the private virtues of domesticity, they hoped not only to escape physically from the strains and stresses of the profane world outside their door but to satisfy their need for a place of comfort, piety, security, and spiritual unity. In simplest terms, Americans molded the idea of home into a spiritual and metaphorical sanctuary from the awesome changes that modern life had brought them.[1]

Within this sphere of domesticity, woman played a unique and central role as wife, mother, and keeper of hearth and faith. Corseted by the demands of society and church and shut out of the world of commerce, she worked to make house and household, as one advice book directed, an "elysium" where her husband could "find rest from the stormy strife of a selfish world" in which he had to make a living. Mother especially, Horace Bushnell advised, must "find methods of making the house no mere prison, but a place of attraction, and of always cheerful and pleasant society." She took charge of the spiritual welfare of her home as well. She and her sisters, drawing on their repertoire of Christian experience and belief, relocated the emphases of Protestant faith within its walls. There they guarded and embellished traditional Christian values and reinstituted the order, cohesion, and moral authority that churches had once theoretically exercised over the larger community.[2]

This theology of home Protestantism focused on Christ's birth. Early in the century, German historians found new literary evidence that Christ had a human form and an earthly existence. Their discoveries influenced Christian theology, shifting its historical emphasis on God the Father to his son, Jesus the Savior and the Son of Man. In matters of faith, Jesus' birth figured more importantly than it had ever before.[3]

At the hearth, removed from the tangles of church history, Jesus' life story resonated with special meaning. Neither Catholic nor Protestant faiths considered birth a holy sacrament, and so traditionally neither emphasized it. However, as birth rates began to decline among middle-class women, childbirth became a more momentous occasion, and families came to appreciate childhood as a distinctive stage of life. These sociological changes in turn influenced the way in which Protestants understood and acted upon their faith. Jesus' birth, unlike his Easter resurrection, was rationally comprehensible as human experience, radiating the aura of the miraculous that attended all births. For his followers, who found themselves on the brink of a new social and political economy, his thirty years of mortal life exemplified the human hope and innocence of new beginnings.

For women, the image of Jesus as "a human dominated by love, sacrificing himself for others, asking nothing but giving everything and forgiving" had unique import. "The new Christ," according to Barbara Welter, "was the exemplar of meekness and humility, the sacrificial victim," a model for women in their domestic calling. The advice Bronson Alcott gave his daughters one Christmas made this role clear. "This is the Birth Night of one of the best men ever born into this world," he wrote. "He was a good and wise Child, and grew into a good and wise man, living for the good of those who lived with him, and going about to make men wise and happy as himself. He was a friend of children and like them was innocent and pure in his thought and feelings. . . . " Alcott believed his daughters should "be ready like him to bear unkindness, and to suffer for doing right. To feel and do so will be keeping his Birth day in the truest way, and continuing to do so will make you a Christian, this is, a person like Jesus, and all your days will be Christmas days—your life holy and good like his."[4]

Even as women came to identify with the suffering Christ, his blameless goodness informed the way in which pious middle-class parents were learning to treat their children. Gradually forsaking the belief that all youngsters were born sinners who had to be broken of their innate ungodliness, mothers, fathers, and ministers began to perceive in children an innocence that had to be cultivated. Advice books and tracts, written mostly by women and clergy, now encouraged women to raise children with a gentle voice and tolerant hand in the hope that Christian love would make them productive and faithful adults. Beriah Green, pastor of the Whitestown, New York, Congregational church, asserted that the circumstances and relationships of a young child at home gave "parents high advantages for instructing and impressing him respecting his relations, duties, and prospects, as a creature of God. Now is the time," he declared, "to conduct him to the bosom of the saviour." In *Christian Nurture*, Horace Bushnell advocated play as a way to encourage children's religious bent. "[R]*eligion loves too much the plays and pleasures of childhood, to limit or suppress them by any kind of needless austerity*," he counseled.[5]

The private calendar of family life, structured on a cyclical pattern of pre-industrial time, encoded the evolving attitudes of home life, child-rearing, woman's role, and religion and set the household rhythm. In nearly every American community, Protestant influence had discouraged to varying degrees the reinstitution of the decorative and ceremonial lushness of pre-Reformation Christianity. However, antebellum wives and mothers began to recreate for certain days a texture of ritual detail within their domestic sphere. In this way, they established a sense of sacred time and sacred space that set home apart from the profane outer world. They made funeral ceremonies into new and more elaborate events and found that the seasonal and symbolic attributes of devotional holidays such as Thanksgiving rekindled spiritual and humane sensibilities, which increased in importance as the secular world seemed to become more inhospitable.[6]

Of all holidays, Christmas was a perfect agency for transporting religion and religious feeling into the home and for righting the excesses and failures of the public world. Through a selective reworking of older practices, nineteenth-century Americans recast the holiday to fit American culture. The festival focused on the very essence of Christian home sentiment that venerated Jesus and honored children. At the same time, it held the potential to reflect the complicated interrelationships between faith, market, community, and family that attended the dawning age. Gift-giving, gestures of charity, even the friendly exchange of a holiday greeting and the decoration and enjoyment of an evergreen tree set in a parlor or, later, a Sunday school hall, linked members of each nuclear family to one another, to church, and to society. At Christmas time, these acts and icons symbolically bridged the widening gap between rich and poor, rejuvenated the weakening bonds between church and family, and channeled the immoderation of the marketplace into charitable goodwill.

At the center of this new domestic holiday stood Santa Claus, who, laden with small toys and treats, called on more and more American children each year. This stealthy saint traced his lineage back through many centuries to St. Nicholas. A very old and useful saint, St. Nick was born in Patara, near Myra in present-day Turkey, possibly in 280 C.E. He died sometime in the middle of the fourth century, reputedly on December 6. Known first for his piety (when a newborn, he had refused to suckle his mother on a religious fast day), he was best remembered for bestowing gifts upon the three young daughters of a destitute and widowed nobleman, who had intended to sell each daughter into slavery or prostitution. Nicholas rescued them by throwing bags of gold through the window so that each had a proper dowry. The father caught him, but Nicholas swore him to secrecy. [7]

Stories about Nicholas's good deeds multiplied. He became known as a protector and rescuer of children and, later, of parents, schoolboys, sailors, and numerous others. Many came to regard December 6 as a lucky day, one for making important purchases, conducting business transactions, or getting married. By the time of the Renaissance, St. Nicholas had become, according to Martin Ebon, the "Favorite Saint" of nearly everyone: "yearning virgins, barren wives, helpless infants, thieves and financiers, traveling students and pirating Vandals." When during the Protestant Reformation veneration of saints was generally discouraged, St. Nicholas's reputation remained strong in Holland and in many other Protestant strongholds. [8]

Notwithstanding, St. Nicholas had no real history in colonial America. Not until the Revolution, when a New York paper, *Rivington's Gazeteer*, noted on December 23, 1773, that the anniversary of St. Nicholas, "otherwise called St. a Claus," had been celebrated the previous Monday by "a great number of Sons of that ancient Saint," was any reference made to him. The following year, the same newspaper announced a second gathering of the "descendants of the ancient Dutch families," to be held Monday, December 8, it "being the anniversary of St. Nicholas." [9]

In fact, the *Gazeteer* most likely reported the meeting of a saint society, not a celebration of the saint himself. Such associations were fairly common in the colonies. Scots, Irish, and Welsh immigrants created them to promote fellowship and to perpetuate their countries' traditions. The English, for example, invoked the protection of St. George and designated April 23, his feast day, as a legal holiday throughout the colonies. In 1772 Philadelphia patriots, deciding they needed their own saint, chose Tammany, a seventeenth-century Delaware Indian chief as their protector and renamed him "Saint Tammany." In all likelihood, the revival of St. Nicholas started as a New Yorker's bit of such patriotic, perhaps derisive, fun. [10]

After the Revolution, New York City's boosters, in their efforts to promote the rising commercial and political importance of their city, renewed more strongly an investment in their history as Dutch colonists. For men with such diverse interests as John Pintard, Washington Irving, and other prominent citizens, especially those of Dutch ancestry, the old Dutch St. Nicholas afforded a serviceable icon. Pintard fostered a particular fascination with the old saint. When in 1810 the New-York Historical Society, which he had helped found in 1804, set its annual meeting on December 6, the Festival of St. Nicholas, Pintard distributed a woodcut to each member. It pictured St. Nick holding a money purse in one hand and a "Birchen Rod" in the other. In the background, a pair of "Blue Yarn Stockings" hung over the fireplace. One was filled with "toys, Oranges, Sugar plumbs, and Oley cooks." The other, apparently belonging to a hopeful but bad child, held only a stick. As for St. Nicholas himself, the *New York Advertiser* reported that his wooden image bore a striking likeness "*no doubt*" to the original. [11]

Not surprisingly, Pintard also promoted the Dutch saint within his own family. "In the old times," he reminisced to his daughter in 1819, "St Claas used to cross the Atlantic & brought immense supplies of cookies &c. from Amsterdam," visiting every house and family, "not only in this city, but in Albany & all the immediate towns. . . . " In 1832, Pintard went as far as to stage a personal visit. On Christmas Eve, he had made a figure of "this children's friend" and fitted it with "a small white mask." While the family waited silently at one end of the nursery, Pintard contrived to have the masked head gradually rise over the door at the other end of the room. As Pintard told the story, "Poor [younger] Pintard immed[iately] skriemd out, that it was his dear departed little brother." Another child joined in. A third child, though he "behaved with fortitude," admitted that he was afraid. [12]

As Pintard's enthusiasm helped promote St. Nicholas locally, Washington Irving's *History of New York* (1809) introduced him to a growing national readership. Full of references to St. Nicholas as the patron of New York and, with sly humor, dedicated to the New-York Historical Society, this quasi-history provided the first descriptive outlines of what was to become an American counterpart to the European saint. In it, Irving claimed that the masthead of the first Dutch ship to enter New York Harbor had been carved in the saint's image. It was, he wrote, a figure with "a low, broad-brimmed hat, a huge pair of Flemish trunk hose and a pipe that reached to the end of the bowsprit." [13]

Irving's literary circle of *Salmagundi* friends reworked and embellished the basic Nicholas fiction, adapting it bit by bit to the American environment. James K. Paulding, Irving's brother-in-law, made the first significant change. He kept to the Dutch imagery, portraying Nick as "a little rascal with a three-cornered cocked hat, decked with old gold lace, a blue Dutch sort of short pea jacket, red waistcoat, breeks of the same colour, yellow stockings, and honest thick-soled shoes, ornamented with a pair of skates." However, his Santa arrived on New Year's Eve, not on the traditional December 6. Paulding accounted for the change as a confusion over the shift to the New Style calendar, although it was more likely a reasonable accommodation to the prevalence of English Christmas custom. [14]

Clement Clarke Moore, an acquaintance of Irving, made more radical alterations. Born in 1779 of Dutch Walloon ancestry and raised in the Protestant Episcopal Church, Moore had helped found the General Theological Seminary, where he taught Oriental and Greek literature. In 1822, he briefly stepped out of character to write a long and clever poem for his three children, Margaret, Charity, and Mary. The piece, "An Account of a Visit from St. Nicholas," created for St. Nick a new physical appearance and bright personality and, at least in some versions, set his visit on Christmas Eve. It tells of a "right jolly old elf," who arrives amid much noise in a sleigh pulled by flying reindeer. He stuffs toys in children's stockings, then lays his finger along the side of his nose, nods his head, and ascends up the chimney. As he flies off in a sleigh, he is heard shouting a benediction to all below: "Merry Christmas to all and to all a good night." [15]

This Santa had no precedent in history. Moore said he modeled Nick on "a portly rubicund Dutchman," who lived near his father's home in New York. He bore little resemblance to the centuries-old St. Nicholas of Europe, and but faintly recalled the depictions by Irving and Paulding. Yet

Moore clearly drew inspiration for his yarn from Irving's *History* and a number of other sources. [16]

To be sure, Moore's St. Nick reprised Wouter Van Twiller, the first governor of New Netherlands. Van Twiller, by Irving's account, looked a little like "a beer-barrel on skids." He measured "exactly five feet six inches in height, and six feet five inches in circumference, . . . [being] particularly capacious at bottom." As to visage, he had "[t]wo small gray eyes" which "twinkled feebly . . . like two stars of lesser magnitude in a hazy firmament, and his full-fed cheeks, which seemed to have taken toll of everything that went into his mouth, were curiously mottled and streaked with dusky red, like a spitzenberg apple." Upon reaching a decision, Van Twiller, like the St. Nicholas in Moore's poem, laid his finger beside his nose. [17]

Olaffe Van Kortlandt, another of Irving's characters, suggested additional details. He dreamed that "the good St. Nicholas came riding over the tops of the trees, in that self-same wagon wherein he brings his yearly presents to children. . . . " The figure landed and "sat himself down and smoked; and as he smoked, the smoke from his pipe ascended into the air and spread like a cloud over head. . . . " At the end of the dream, St. Nicholas twisted his pipe "in his hat-band, and laying his finger beside his nose, gave the astonished Van Kortlandt a very significant look, then mounting his wagon, he returned over the tree-tops and disappeared." [18]

The "eight tiny reindeer" who pulled the "miniature sleigh" through the skies were not entirely original either. Reindeer had never been part of St. Nicholas's European background, but in 1821, William Gilley, an American bookseller, published a poem that began:

> Old santeclause with much delight
> His reindeer drives this frosty night

Whether a single or several deer, Moore made their number eight, and named them Dasher, Dancer, Prancer, Vixen, Comet, Cupid, Donder, and Blitzen. [19]

Even the poem's imagery had antecedents. Robert H. Woodward suggested that Moore, in describing the children snug in their beds and other scenes, borrowed, consciously or not, the opening images of Michael Wigglesworth's "The Day of Doom." Written in 1662, this didactic Puritan poem had a similar sing-song rhythm, and, certainly, textual comparisons can be drawn. Moore's lines

'Twas the night before Christmas, when all through the house,
Not a creature was stirring, not even a mouse,

echo Wigglesworth's

Still was the night, Serene and bright, when all Men sleeping lay.

A similar comparison can be made between

I sprang from the bed to see what was the matter
Away to the window I flew like a flash,
. . . The moon on the breast of the new-fallen snow
Gave the luster of mid-day to objects below,

and lines from "The Day of Doom" that run:

They rush from Beds with giddy heads, and to their windows run,
Viewing this light, which shines more bright then doth the Noon-
    day Sun.

It is entirely possible that Moore had found inspiration in Wigglesworth, but "A Visit" bears no hint of irony or lesson. The two poems can hardly be more different in intent and import, for Moore created an effect infinitely cheerier than Wigglesworth's dire warning of sin and apocalypse.[20]

Whatever his influences, Moore wove a subtle reinterpretation of the gift-bringer into a memorable vignette that balanced magic with reality. His "little old driver so lively and quick" was a genial and generous American saint, more good-natured, even self-consciously so, than any before. His physical solidity conferred credibility:

trimmed up with fur from his head to his foot,
. . . His eyes—how they twinkled! his dimples—how merry!
His cheeks were like roses, his nose like a cherry;
His droll little mouth was drawn up like a bow,
And the beard on his chin was as white as the snow,
The stump of a pipe he held tight in his teeth,
. . . He had a broad face, and a little round belly
That shook, when he laughed, like a bowl full of jelly,
He was chubby and plump, a right jolly old elf. . . .

The domestic setting in which Santa revealed himself lent an additional touch of realism to the story. Moore authenticated it all by having the father of the household, the male authority, bear witness to the fabulous event. Through these stratagems, Moore made readers privy to a delightful secret and the impossible became plausible.[21]

Moore apparently meant only to entertain his family, but a year later, on December 23, 1823, the *Troy* (New York) *Sentinel* reprinted his poem. No one knows if the *Sentinel's* copy was contributed anonymously or whether the editor deliberately falsified the source. The story goes that Harriet Butler, who was visiting the Moore home, copied it into her album, and from there its public life began. After that, "A Visit from St. Nicholas" appeared sporadically but seasonally in newspapers throughout the nation (but especially in New York) and as a news carrier's holiday gift to customers. Eventually Moore himself published "A Visit," along with other of his verses, in 1844, in a volume titled *Poems by Clement C. Moore, LL.D.*[22]

As the widening circulation of Moore's poem helped establish a common imagery for Santa Claus and his deeds, Santa began to take over the largely rural routes of two other folk figures. During the first part of the century, Belsnickel and Christkindel, Old World relatives of St. Nicholas, maintained active seasonal lives in the German communities of Pennsylvania and elsewhere. Belsnickel usually traveled alone when he delivered gifts and not infrequently used the stick he carried to discipline youngsters. Occasionally, he called in the Dutch communities of Michigan and Iowa on the evening of December 5, bringing with him oranges and switches. In Buffalo, New York, where many Germans congregated in the 1840s, he also arrived on December 5 "to take orders for presents to be delivered for Christmas."[23]

Christkindel ("Christ Child") usually traveled the back roads too, but bore more resemblance to Belsnickel than to Jesus, the Christ Child. He visited every home in the community where one visitor spent Christmas Eve in 1821. Dressed "in ludicrous masquerade," and carrying "a rod [in] one hand & nuts & cakes in his pockets," this "Christkinkle," awarded the rod to the "idle & ignorant" and gave favors to the deserving only after they had repeated "a tremendous round of [D]utch prayers."[24]

However, by the beginning of the Civil War, Christkindel and Belsnickel had faded. The most significant transition took place in the urban setting of Philadelphia. There publishers distilled the rich Old World saint lore of its German settlers and reformed it into a virtual likeness of Santa. They did so with the publication of *Kriss Kringle's Book*, in 1842, and *Kriss*

Kringle's Christmas Tree. a holliday present for boys and girls, in 1845. Designed to counter Washington Irving's Saint Nicholas, this Kriss Kringle resembled Moore's Santa, except that he put his gifts on the branches of the Christmas tree and not in stockings. [25]

Few claimed to have actually beheld the American Santa Claus. St. Aclaus, St. Iclaus, Sancte Klaas, St Claas, Santeclaw, and St. a claus, in addition to Santa Claus and St. Nicholas, were just some of the ways to call him forth. By any name, this elusive and all-knowing folk figure, who, in silent league with parents, visited sleeping children, was becoming a familiar necessity to many a family Christmas. But he served a larger purpose than mere delivery man. Put to work in the domestic sphere, Santa combined characteristics of God, Jesus, and human parents into a presence embodying love, generosity, good humor, and transcendence. Through him, children learned about the rewards of good and bad behavior, and also about the miraculous realities of the invisible world. [26]

Preparation for Santa's arrival occupied considerable amounts of time in many households. The night before Christmas, children chose their largest stockings to hang for him to find. The stockings, claimed Mrs. Schuyler Van Rensselaer in her history of New York, represented the shoes that children of New Amsterdam had once set in the chimney corners on St. Nicholas Eve. Usually, children placed them near the fireplace, perhaps because of an old belief that Hertha, the Norse goddess of happiness, appeared in fireplaces at the winter solstice bringing happiness and good luck. But other places—a bedpost or a bannister—seemed to serve as well. Knowing that "St. Nicholas was supposed to come down the chimney," Elizabeth Cady Stanton pinned her stocking "on a broomstick, laid across two chairs in front of the fireplace." On the plantation where Susan Dabney Smedes grew up, everyone hung up a "sock or stocking" along the hall staircase. One time she counted "twenty-two of them," including "the dainty pink sock of the three-weeks-old baby." "It would have stimulated a manyfactureer [*sic*] to see the rows of stockings, of all sizes and hues, that were hung in the capacious corners at the Elms, to receive the tribute of St. Nicholas," remembered Charlotte Gilman of her plantation Christmases. [27]

The next step usually proved more difficult, as childhood memories attested. It was when, in one writer's words, "hopeful little heads went to bed early in order to be up at the first peep of dawn." However, most were "scarce able to keep in their pallets for excitement. . . . " Many "listened for the jingling of his sleigh bells" all through the long night. At daybreak, the waiting ended. "All the stockings came down quicker than they had gone up."[28]

If lucky enough, children found oranges, candies, candles, nuts, toys, gloves, or other such trifles tucked in their stockings. Elizabeth Cady Stanton recalled that one of hers contained "a little paper of candy, one of raisins, another of nuts, a red apple, an *olie-koek* [cookie], and a bright silver quarter of a dollar in the toe." At the Smedes', children scrambled to find prose and poetry notes. For many children, discovering evidence of Santa's visit as well as the ritual of preparing for his arrival had an enduring appeal. As one young girl testified in 1876: "We have hung up our stockings, ever since I can remember; and we all think that as each of us, one after another, settle[s] down in homes of our own, we shall still cling to, and cherish this custom of our childhood, and youth, that our children may be happy even as we have been."[29]

Critical to understanding the place of Santa in the household was his strong, though generally unarticulated, association with Jesus. Nineteenth-century American families invested in Santa Claus qualities they had come to associate with Jesus and thereby introduced children to the possibility of the miraculous. The Santa myth made available a personage that could further the child's understanding of religion and fortify symbolically the parents' own sense of the same. As John Shlien, writing on the role of Santa in twentieth-century America, suggests, "The ceremony of Santa Claus may explain in a very literal way the nature of primary religious experience." Children are "simply *taught* to believe in a supernatural being with magical powers and omniscience—a belief supported by the whole society, demanding moral behavior, involving prayer, public ritual, and every element of religious faith."[30]

Anthropologically and sociologically, the essential characteristics of Santa match those associated with Jesus. Jesus fulfills the criteria for a mythic hero, and so does St. Nicholas. St. Nicholas's birth and the ongoing embroidery and ritualization of tales of his magical appearances, generosity, and immortality parallel Jesus' story. In fact, Shlien calls Santa Claus "a full-fledged hero," which, he argues, makes him "a genuinely sacred figure by virtue of his classical heroic traits and his intimate historical and verbal linkage to Christ. . . ."[31]

In the sphere of antebellum domesticity, the womanly ideal of meekness and compassion, patterned on the example of Jesus, triangulated the interconnection between Santa and Jesus. Their various qualities of moral authority, presence—heavenly, physical, or ethereal—and even voice compelled children, through reward or punishment, to follow a moral path.

The relationship has intrigued scholars, but none has explored its implications. Folklorist Alan Dundes has suggested that in Christmas "one has the celebration of the 'mother-son' complex," that is, the relationship of Mary and Jesus. Since Protestants venerate Jesus far more than Mary, they place more importance on the male role in the drama. Dundes thinks that this same "complex" may explain why Santa Claus is male. Implicitly, he considers Santa to be the secular equivalent of Jesus. Dundes also argues that Santa Claus reflects Mary. He correlates the saint's bulging, "unnaturally pregnant" sack with the supernaturally pregnant Mary. Some years earlier, in 1941, Richard Sterba offered a more radically inventive version of Santa's relationship to woman. Writing in *Psychoanalytic Quarterly*, he asserted that "Santa Claus with his fat belly is a pregnant woman. . . . The presents come down the chimney since the fireplace and chimney signify vulva and vagina of the unconscious and the child-present thus comes out of the birth canal."[32]

Nineteenth-century magazines, of course, used a different interpretive vocabulary. While they did not speculate on woman's role, a connection between Jesus and Santa did not elude them. German lore, as printed in such magazines as *Godey's*, provided a model for the merging of these two kind spirits—Jesus and Santa—into one. One article written in the late 1840s informed readers that after dinner on Christmas Eve, German children were shown into a dark room and left to think about the gifts they would get. When the mother and father came for them, they would announce "that the little infant Jesus had paid them a visit, and left them tokens of His love." Another piece reported that Germans taught their children "to believe that our Saviour, on the anniversary of his birth, travels all over the world to visit children that love him and their parents, to bestow on them some token of his affection." American children seldom questioned the link. James S. Hogg, governor of Texas, remembered that as a child in the late 1850s he had created a theory about Santa Claus. "I thought that in a great battle with the devil, God had won and sent Santa around to celebrate the victory by making presents to the children on His side." Another man wrote that in his youth he believed in Santa "as implicitly" as he believed "the Ten Commandments, or the story of David and Goliath."[33]

By any account, Santa symbolized a miracle, getting and giving forth his gifts in as mysterious a manner as Mary did hers. As believers struggled to retain a sense of spiritual wonder amid the rationalism of the modern world, they necessarily devised new codes and symbols to transfer the experience of faith to the next generation. Santa embodied the demands of faith itself. Children did not see him; they merely had to believe, in the words of William James, in the "reality of the unseen."

Coming of age in an era of growing material prosperity in which some questioned harsh child-rearing, Santa Claus also functioned as a conduit of parental authority, parental love, and, not incidentally, consumerism. Through this American saint, parents schooled their children in the subtle inflections of the dawning Victorian era, coaching them on the fundamentals of pluralistic Protestantism, demonstrating their affection, and domesticating the new forces of the marketplace by buying toys and other gifts.

The relationship between God, parents, and Santa Claus could be found in a number of places. A poem written in Santa's voice and published in *The Children's Friend* in 1821 advised young readers on the importance of good behavior and endorsed parental punishment by Santa as a decree by God: When, "Old Santeclaus,"

> . . . The steady friend of virtuous youth,
> The friend of duty, and of truth, . . .
> . . . found good girls or boys,
> That hated quarrels, strife and noise, [he]
> left an apple, or a tart,
> Or wooden gun or painted cart.

However, should the saint find

> . . . the children naughty,
> In manners rude, in tempers haughty,
> Thankless to parents, liars, swearers,
> Boxers, or cheats, or base tale-bearers, [he]
>
> left a long, black, birchen rod,
> Such as the dread command of God
> Directs a parent's hand to use. . . . [34]

Fanny Longfellow (Mrs. Henry Wadsworth Longfellow) admonished her children more gently than did the poetic Santa Claus. Each Christmas she wrote Charley and Erney Santa letters. In them Santa remarked on the boys' behavior, how to improve, and what gifts he was leaving. "I wish I could say you had been as good boys this year as last," he wrote them from "Chimney Corner" in 1853. "You have not been so obedient and gentle and kind and loving to your parents and little sister as I like to have you." Theodore Ledyard Cuyler once received "an autograph letter from Santa Claus, full of good counsels." Their black cook, he said, "actually saw the veritable old visitor light a candle and sit down at the table and write it!"[35]

Children understood fully that Santa expected and exacted good behavior. "About the first of December," one writer recalled, "I was duly told that if I was not a good boy my stockings in the big fireplace would get little or no recognition." He added that staying out of "boyish pranks and mischief for three weeks took some of the charm out of Christmas enjoyment for us young lads." Elizabeth Cady Stanton, who described her parents as "kind, indulgent, and considerate as the Puritan ideas of those days permitted," believed that "fear, rather than love, of God and parents alike, predominated." If a child showed especially good behavior, Santa might leave "an illustrated catechism or the New Testament." However, if a child were "guilty of any erratic performances during the year," which, she confessed, was often her case, "a long stick would protrude from the stocking." The evidence proved to her "that the St. Nicholas of that time held decided views on discipline and ethics."[36]

Sometimes Santa's judgment seemed especially cruel. Marion Harland kept a sour memory of one Christmas in which some "visitor in the family" put a "lithe, keen, wicked-looking rod" in her Christmas stocking as a joke. Another person reminisced that one Christmas Eve he and his brothers had carefully hung their stockings on the chimney and gone to bed to dream "of the great Santa Claus, plum-cakes, sugar plums, comfits, toys, etc." They rose early the next morning, "eager to get our rewards." The first stocking "was loaded with luxuries." The second "contained an orange and beautiful edition of *Jack the giant killer*." Trembling, the author put his hand out for his own stocking. "[I]t was light—and my heart sunk within me—my elder brother seized it, and laughing while I wept, drew out a rod!" The boy could not guess how Santa Claus knew that he had been truant from school the previous day, but from then on, he wrote, "I slept with my stockings on."[37]

Had disappointed children read *Kriss Kringle's Book for All Good Boys and Girls* (1852), they might have guessed their fates each Christmas before they hung their stockings. "If there should chance to be any idle, disobedient, bad-tempered boy or girl in the house, who neglects lessons, beats brothers and sisters, scratches faces, tells lies, breaks things, &c. &c.," it warned, "Saint Nicholas, instead of giving him toys," would leave "a rattan rod, brought for that special purpose all the way from the East

Indies." A child receiving this token would "feel very much chagrined, and look very silly the next morning when all the other children are laughing and clapping their hands at Kriss Kringle's presents." [38]

Santa could also be, and increasingly proved to be, an open-handed and forgiving soul. As the range of his Christmas Eve deliveries expanded, so too did his tendency to reward rather than discipline children. He overlooked with heartening frequency the recalcitrance of more than a few children. In this Santa received encouragement. In 1848, one writer declared in Philadelphia's *Saturday Courier* that no stockings should "hang empty in the chimney corner; and even if Harry and Natty haven't been quite as good children as they ought to have been, don't disappoint them with a whip or an old rusty jewsharp by way of punishment." [39]

By mid-century, Santa had nearly universally become a very good old saint, who rewarded children with toys and candies, and (almost) never chastised them. He allowed parents to indulge their children's material wishes without compromising other family virtues such as frugality and the value of earning what one received. At the same time, the fantastic appearance of Santa's gifts in the night removed them from the profane context of money and work that charted consumer cravings. Indeed, Wendell H. Oswalt has suggested that as an American myth, Santa "may have been created to counteract the harsh materialism of the newly emerging country." [40]

Santa Claus's legend particularly suited the age and country. Irving had removed the taint of old world saints and Roman Catholicism by making him a cheerful Dutch immigrant. Paulding, Moore, and others had shown him to be quite adaptable to his new home. His reputation for beneficence and growing familiarity made this new American Santa increasingly congenial. Associated with dollars, good fortune, and children, as well as generosity and good nature, he seemed a natural for Americans.

Santa had, in fact, become part of a nascent national folklore, a full-fledged product of American humor and naive optimism. John Henry or Davy Crockett may have inspired more stories, but no American folk character was more widely embraced and accepted as real. No others even raised the question of belief. Santa differed from other mythic Americans in another way. He seemed to prefer the city. For it was in cities that Santa Claus mediated the often disparate aspirations of the emerging middle-class as each year he skated along the uncertain line between reality and miracle, between market and hearth. [41]

CHAPTER 5

Home for Christmas: Christmas Trees and Christmas Giving

The arrival of Santa Claus was but one part of the transformation of Christmas into a home festival. Nineteenth-century Americans embraced and adapted many traditions from the many old Christmases around them to create the modern domestic holiday. Of these, the decorated evergreen tree and exchange of gifts among family and friends proved to be the most broadly significant and seductive.

The tree that graced the parlors of many American homes at Christmas had a long history. In pre-Christian times, Romans used evergreens, symbols of fertility and regeneration, to trim their houses at the Kalends of January. Eventually, Christians appropriated the use of evergreens for their Christmas celebration. To remove the taint of paganism, they associated it with new beginnings and man's second chance with God. The tree became for pious folk a representation of Jesus as the Light of the World, Tree of Life, and second Adam born to right the sins of the first.[1]

Christians also invented a number of stories to explain the custom's origin. One legend credited St. Winfred, reputed to have felled a giant oak that had been used for Druidic worship, with dedicating the evergreen tree to Christmas. "This little tree," he is said to have told the crowd of converts who looked on, "shall be your holy tree to-night. . . . Let this be called the tree of the Christ-child; gather about it . . . in your own homes; there it will shelter no deeds of blood, but loving gifts and rites of kindness." One of the most enduring tales attributes the invention of the tree custom to

Martin Luther. Walking in the German woods one Christmas Eve, Luther had felt particularly inspired by God's work. He hoped to convey this experience to his children, so he returned home with an evergreen which he decked with candles representative of the stars of heaven.[2]

At least some Christians had been bringing trees into their homes since the Reformation. However, not until the seventeenth century is there any record of trimming the Christmas evergreens. A diarist in Strasbourg wrote about Christmas in 1605: "they set up fir-trees in the parlours . . . and hang thereon roses cut out of many-coloured paper, apples, wafers, gold foil, sweets, &c." By the first decades of the nineteenth century, German Protestants had taken the tree as an emblem of their faith. German Catholics, inspired by St. Francis of Assisi, had already adopted the *Krippe*, or holy manger, as an icon distinctly theirs. But slowly the tree custom gained acceptance among them as well.[3]

Meanwhile, the practice had begun to spread throughout Europe. By 1830, Danes and Norwegians knew of Christmas trees; by 1840, the French. (However, the French middle class tended to consider it "an intruder of Alsatian origin" until around 1870, when it became readily available in Paris markets.) Swedes added trimmed evergreens to their Christmas celebration in the 1860s. The festive trees may have been in England as early as 1789. An English memoir mentions one complete with candles and gifts in 1829, noting, "Here [in England] it was only for the children; in Germany the custom extended to persons of all ages." The more widely told version, though, ascribes the introduction of the Christmas tree to the English to Prince Albert, who in 1840 gave one as a gift to Victoria.[4]

Americans were also making a niche for the tree. Pennsylvania Dutch had brought the custom of Christmas trees to the United States in the early part of the nineteenth century, probably as much a reminder of their German homeland as a religious symbol. One Matthew Zahm of Lancaster, Pennsylvania, in one of the earliest documented American references to a holiday tree, recorded on December 20, 1821, that "Sally & our Thos. & Wm. Hensel was out for Christmas trees, on the hill at Kendrick's saw mill."[5]

The Zahm and Hensel families would probably have decorated their trees, for it seems to have been the custom among German settlers. About 1820, John Lewis Krimmel, an artist from Germantown, Pennsylvania, sketched a small holly tree trimmed with cookies and surrounded by a miniature picket fence and toy animals. Another account, dating from the same time, describes a tree in Lancaster that stood about four feet tall. "[E]very available branch" on it held ginger bread cut into stars, hearts, the "bad man," and other "grotesque forms," each coated "with a mixture of starch and sugar." However, if all went as planned, the Society of Bachelors in York, Pennsylvania, enjoyed the grandest of these first American trees. The decorations on their "*Krischtkintle Bauhm*," they promised in 1823, would "be superb, superfine, superfrostical, shnockagastical, double re-fined, mill'twill'd made of Dog's Wool, Swingling Tow, and Posnum fur; which cannot fail to gratify taste."[6]

In fact, the German immigrants' custom of a Christmas tree became a point of fascination for other Americans. Charles Haswell remembered that, as a teen in the 1830s, he braved "a very stormy and wet night" to go to Brooklyn, where the number of German families had increased significantly, to see their "custom of dressing a 'Christmas Tree.'" A story titled "New Year's Day," which appeared in *Token and Atlantic Souvenir* (1836), told of a German maid who decorated her mistress's tree in the custom of her homeland. She loaded the thickest branches with books and toys, and attached birds, animals, "cherries, plums, strawberries and fine peaches, as tempting and at least as sweet as the fruits of paradise" to the others. "Never did [a] Christmas tree bear more multifarious fruit."[7]

Often owing to the influence of German natives, evergreens began to appear in the homes of prominent Bostonians, Philadelphians, New York-ers, and residents of other cities during the 1830s and early 1840s. In 1842, Charles Minnegerode, who had recently arrived from Hesse, Ger-many, and taught classics at William and Mary College, introduced the custom into Virginia when he took a tree to the Williamsburg home of his friend Judge Nathaniel Beverly Tucker. Four years after Minnegerode's contribution, in 1846, citizens of Richmond saw their first Christmas trees. In 1832, Charles Follen, a Hessian and the first professor of German at Harvard College, put up a tree in his home in Cambridge and decorated it with "7 dozen wax tapers, gilded egg cups, paper cornucopiae filled with comfits, lozenges and barley sugar." Dr. Constantin Hering and a teacher named Frederick Knerr, attended closely by boys who laughed, shouted, at threw stones at them, apparently brought the first trees into Philadelphia in 1834.[8]

In St. Louis, Gustave Koerner, a German immigrant, jurist, and political advisor to Abraham Lincoln, and his host could not find a tree on the barren western frontier. They improvised, making "a kind of pedestal" of "the top of a young sassafras tree" on Christmas Day, which "the girls" decorated "with ribbons and bits of colored paper, wax candles, little red apples and nuts and all sorts of confectionary. . . . " Although the tree was not a traditional evergreen, Koerner claimed it to be "perhaps the first lighted tree on the banks of the Mississippi." The influence of German custom was also felt in the Ohio home of future President Rutherford Hayes. He wrote in 1858 that the family's "German girls" worked in the cellar until three in the morning to surprise the family with "a beautiful Christmas tree."[9]

While German Americans perpetuated in their own homes the custom of trimming Christmas trees, the middle and upper classes of the cities often mimicked colorful dramatic Christmas presentation ceremonies they had seen first hand in Germany or in their neighbors' homes. For example, Bostonians Anna and George Ticknor spent Christmas, 1835, in Dresden. Few families "passed this evening without a 'Christ Baum' in some form or another," Anna Ticknor wrote in her travel journal. Their landlord's tree, which they had asked to see, was in fact "three little pine trees, lighted with multitudes of tapers, hung with little cakes, and comfits" arranged on a "long table, which was perfectly covered with all manner of toys for four little children."[10]

Anna Ticknor declined Baron Ungern Sternberg's invitation to witness a German Christmas in his home, but her husband attended and described what he had seen. On that evening, George Ticknor wrote, a bell rang and everyone went into a room "where the presents which the children had secretly prepared for the elder members of the family were placed under the tree." Another bell summoned family and guests to a different room, "and we were led through a passage-way purposely kept dark, where two folding-doors were thrown open and we were all at once in a large and handsome saloon, where was brilliantly lighted up and where were the presents which the parents had provided for the children" placed on individual little tables surrounding the tree.[11]

The degree to which the Baron's entertainment had captured the imagination of the Ticknors became quite clear several years later. In 1843, they held a Christmas party at their home in Boston. In its essentials, the gala bore the distinct imprint of the Dresden Christmas they had participated in years earlier. Mrs. Henry Wadsworth Longfellow attended and later wrote in her diary that there was "a beautiful Christmas tree decorated with presents from one relation to another." It was the first she had seen and she "was as much excited as the children when the folding doors opened and the pyramid of lights sparkled from the dark boughs of a lofty pine. . . ."[12]

Other American visitors to Germany seemed as taken by the German Christmas ceremonies as the Ticknors had been. William Wetmore Story and his family spent Christmas, 1849, in Heidelberg. "[A]s soon as the lamps were light[ed]," the Storys decorated three branches with "all sorts of little presents" they "had purchased at the booths scattered every where about. & lighted little candles among them. It showed very splendid." On the tablecloth beneath the tree, they strewed additional "little presents and all was reflected in the mirror before which it was placed. Then the door was opened & the children came in—What joy! What rapture! What wonder!" The children "danced round the tree, examined all the curious fruits we'd hung upon it . . . & then they fell to wondering how Christkein- chen came in & whether he had wings and how he knew what would please each one. . . ."[13]

No matter the newfound awe and delight some Americans held for Christmas trees, others still objected. Often, their reasoning rested on their embrace of Calvinism. Although Robert Blair Risk lived in Lancaster, Pennsylvania, he nearly reached adulthood before seeing a Christmas tree. "Such a symbol of the christmas tide," he wrote, "was too Germanic for [his] Scotch-Irish appreciation." Lydia Maria Child had similar views. In 1845, she wrote to her friend that although she admired much about German literature and character, "the Puritan blood still flows too briskly in my veins to allow me to relish over much the Christmas tree. . . ."[14]

Harriet Beecher Stowe, daughter of Lyman Beecher, also retained much of her orthodox heritage. However, at Christmas she relaxed her Calvinism enough to allow her daughter Hattie a "fine spruce." They set it upon the table, its branches touching the walls, and decorated it with apples, nuts, and "four gilt stars." A winged fairy doll clothed in gauze and spangles, with "a star on her forehead & a long gilt wand with a star on the end," graced the top of the tree.[15]

Harriet Martineau had predicted the popularity of Christmas trees as early as 1832, when she noted that she had "little doubt" they would "become one of the most flourishing exotics of New England." The reasons for their success were not hard to discern. Candies, toys, and candles transformed a common tree into an exotic and fanciful vision of delight that lightened the gloom of winter. At the same time, it expressed perfectly the age's romanticism that made nature a metaphor for moral ideals. Its symmetry and perpetual green when all outside was barren reflected beauty, order, and life in God-created nature. Its presence in the parlor attested to the importance of the Christmas holiday and enhanced profane, domestic, and even sacred holiday rituals.[16]

More down-to-earth forces also insured the fulfillment of Martineau's prophecy. An increasingly affluent and mobile urban class had grown fond of traveling in Europe, where it sampled what to many seemed exotic customs. A flourishing print industry provided another source of information. Each year new books, magazines, and pamphlets of all sorts became more widely distributed and less expensive. A third element, an entrepreneurial spirit, helped make available the wonderful Christmas evergreens that print, gossip, and contact with German customs had made increasingly familiar.

Christmas trees soon started to appear in church and marketplace, in turn widening their use in homes. Sunday schools, persuaded by the hazy aura of religion and morals and the more direct delight and sociability elicited by Christmas trees, began to decorate their auditoriums with them. The *Youth's Friend*, an American Sunday School Union magazine for children, had never mentioned Christmas except as a date until 1846. Only a year later, William A. Muhlenberg, a native of Reading, Pennsylvania, had seen fit to put a tree in his Sunday school in New York City, making it the first to boast its own Christmas evergreen. Within a decade trees were common, although not universal, in New York's Sabbath schools and not uncommon in other regions. "We have had a Christmas tree and many other attractions in seminary chapel," one Caroline Richards noted matter-of-factly in 1859. Abraham Warner, an Episcopalian minister in Illinois, commented that on Christmas Day, 1864, "the children met at the Parsonage 2 P.M. to receive some presents & to see the Christmas tree which had been prepared for them."[17]

A Sunday school tree provided a number of advantages for teaching and recruiting young Christians. Children who memorized and recited Bible verses correctly might be invited to enjoy the bounty of trinkets and candies placed among the tree's branches. A tree provided just the right sort of incentive to persuade some children of the benefits of enrolling as regular students. And during the winter months when attendance diminished, a tree enticed both children and parents to brave the cold. However, despite the demonstrated effectiveness of Sunday school trees, congregations did not quickly allow them to be placed in the church proper. In Cleveland, Ohio, in 1851, the Reverend Henry Schwan, a German immigrant, put an evergreen in his church and nearly lost his pulpit because of it.[18]

As it gained acceptance the novelty of the tree gave rise to money-making plans. A farmer's wife from Monmouth County, New Jersey, made one of the earliest ventures into tree-selling in 1840. That December, along with the hogs and chickens, she packed a bundle of pine greens, planning to sell all in New York City. The *New York Tribune* had carried advertisements for "Christmas Trees" and decorations as early as 1843. And in 1851, one Mark Carr set up the first tree concession in the city, paying one dollar to rent sidewalk space in Washington Market. Soon markets in Philadelphia and other large cities sold trees. In fact, so popular had the Christmas tree become by 1852 that *Gleason's Pictorial* noted that "[a]lready is the annual Christmas Tree established as one of the household gods of New England and a large portion of the States." President Franklin Pierce confirmed the observation. He put the first tree in the White House in 1856, a tradition that had become established by the 1880s.[19]

Magazines provided another introduction to Christmas trees. In 1851, when her "children had such a number of gifts," Mahala Eggleston, who lived on Learmont Plantation near Vicksburg, "made a Christmas tree for them." She had learned about them "from some of the German stories" she had been reading. "Mother, Aunt and Liz came down to see it; all said it was something new to them," she wrote in her diary.[20]

Godey's, especially, helped define the tree's place in Christmas and in American life, grafting on to it a vaguely religious motif and planting it at the heart of the American home. In 1850, it published in its December issue the first widely circulated picture of a decorated evergreen, placed atop a table and surrounded by a family. The picture had appeared two years earlier, in the *Illustrated London News*, but with a twist. Originally titled "Christmas Tree at Windsor Castle," the English engraving showed Queen Victoria, Prince Albert, and their family standing next to a tree. *Godey's* copied it exactly, except that it removed the queen's crown and other royal symbols, remaking the engraving into a very American Christmas scene.[21]

Godey's, at least for a time, had even attempted to delineate a religious iconography for the tree. Christmas, it noted, followed Adam and Eve's Day (December 24). Therefore, "an orthodox Christmas-Tree will have the figures of our first parents at its foot, and the serpent twining himself round its stem." With its properly decorated branches and candles, the tree could then be "understood to typify the genealogy of our Lord," culminating as it did in "the most luminous apex the sun of light and life. . . . " In fact, the tree did greater service as an icon of family. The same issue of *Godey's* featured an engraving titled "The Christmas Tree" which displayed neither serpent nor images of Adam and Eve. Rather, adults and children gathered around a handsomely trimmed fir, giving testimony to the role it played in the new American Christmas, that of a visual magnet for a familial holiday season. [22]

Mothers and fathers, charged by influential advisors such as Beriah Green and Horace Bushnell to make the home environment particularly appealing to children, needed little instruction on the impact a tree would make on their youngsters. Women usually supervised the task of transforming this ancient fertility symbol into a moral talisman of domestic order. First, a place for it was found, usually the front parlor where it would dominate most if not all the ceremonies of the important holiday, from the pageants, dinners, and callers to the finale of gift-trading. Home trees had once been squat bushes, no more than two or three feet high, set on a table top, but in many households, this no longer sufficed. They became American-sized. In 1860, *Godey's* described one as an "evergreen, reaching almost to the ceiling," big enough "for *all* the family presents" beneath and resting upon a "large baize covering" in the middle of the parlor floor. [23]

Trimming came next. *Godey's* suggested "tiny tapers, . . . strings of beads, tiny flags of gay ribbons, stars and shields of gilt paper, lace bags filled with colored candies, knots of bright ribbons," all made by hand. Nuts, popcorn, seeds, cookies, bits of ribbon, cut paper, and other readily available items civilized the tree's wild beauty and attested to the workings of an inventive and home-minded decorator. A "bag of pecans," provided by Robert E. Lee, decorated Miss Nellie Whitely's tree. Abby Howland Woolsey festooned hers, "a very large one," with "the most hideous Chinese toys" (which she described in another letter as "a number of small colored lanterns and a great variety of beautiful and cunning toys"). When affixed to branches, such ornaments represented not the everyday world, but a whimsical one. [24]

Candles added the perfecting touch. Mrs. Woolsey estimated it would "take a whole box of one hundred colored candles" to illuminate her tree properly. The earliest Christians had shunned candles because they were used in pagan ceremonies and gift-giving. By the Middle Ages the attitude had apparently changed. Burning Yule logs and giving candles became common seasonal customs. By the mid-nineteenth century, neither concerns about paganism nor even the imminent threat of fire prevented

Americans from completing the dressing of their Christmas trees with tapers.[25]

While candles, ribbons, trinkets, and other ornaments commanded attention be paid to the evergreen, a good part of its charm, of course, lay in the gifts tied to its branches with colorful string or spread beneath it. Like Christmas trees, the idea of giving gifts at Christmas time, for most Americans, was a fairly recent one, but holiday giving was an old custom. Ancient Romans made gifts of twigs at midwinter. Later, they offered the emperor *strenae* (gifts) to assure him of their loyalty or exchanged them privately at Kalends. At first these were substantive items, but they gradually degenerated into what two historians described as "useless little terracotta lamps, clay tablets with pictures of fruits, garlands or cornucopiae with such inscriptions as 'Happiness in the New Year.'"[26]

Early Christians refrained from gift-giving because it reminded them of the Roman Saturnalia. But during the sixteenth and seventeenth centuries, the English revived the custom. Women often received expensive gloves or pins, sometimes accompanied by money, a custom that gave rise to the terms "pin money" and "glove money." By the middle of the seventeenth century, even members of the English clergy were accepting New Year's gifts. Not surprisingly, England's Puritans strongly opposed giving gifts, regarding the custom as yet another diabolical pagan rite countenanced by the Anglican Church.[27]

In colonial America, the earliest record of gift-giving comes from German Moravian immigrants in Bethlehem, Pennsylvania. A December 25, 1745, diary entry notes: "Some received scarves, some a handkerchief, some a hat, some neckerchiefs, and some a few apples." Dutch custom dictated giving gifts on *Nieuw-jaar* as "omens of success for the ensuing months." Thus children and sometimes adults, especially in the middle colonies, might receive a small token on the first day of the year. Puritans, Quakers, and Separatists, like their European counterparts, usually refrained from gift-giving. In fact, few colonists, north or south, regardless of religion, commemorated either Christmas or the New Year with presents.[28]

Increasingly, however, exceptions could be found, particularly on New Year's. For example, in 1720 Puritan Judge Samuel Sewall recorded that he had made a gift of a book to Colonel Dyer and that Mrs. Sewall received a "Present of Oranges and a Shattuck." Ten-year-old Anna Winslow, described by Alice Morse Earle as a "vain little Puritan devotee" sent to Boston to be "finished" in 1772, wrote in her diary that she had kept Christmas at home that year and worked. However, on January 1, although she had "bestow'd no new year's gift, as yet," she received a handsome "History of Joseph Andrews abreviated. In nice Guilt and flower covers."[29]

By the nineteenth century, gift-giving had become more prevalent, and some reciprocal giving was in evidence. Meriwether Lewis presented William Clark with "fleece hosrie Shirt Draws and Socks" on December 25, 1805, while at their winter camp on the Columbia River. He received "a pr. Mockersons" and a small Indian basket from his men, and "two Dozen white weazils tails . . . & some black root" from Indians. In most cases, though, giving tended to be "one-way," and the presentation of gifts continued to reflect status relationships. Those of higher rank gave gifts to those of lower status; servants, and sometimes children, most often benefited.[30]

In the South, masters and house slaves played a game of surprise at Christmas that reinforced status lines. Whoever was the first to greet another with the phrase "Christmas gift" got as his or her due a gift in recognition of quickness. Nearly always the master took the role of the good loser and presented a gift kept ready for the occasion. New Yorkers played a similar game. Whether on Christmas or New Year's, wrote Gabriel Furman in 1830, the family or friend greeted for the holiday was "expected to make a present to the person who greets him or her." Usually the younger of the participants could count on winning.[31]

Workers often chose New Year's to remind patrons of status obligations. On that occasion, newspaper carriers presented their subscribers with "a New Year's Address," a short poem about the old and new year for which they expected, and got, "a douceur." One of these verses, written by "Evens," appeared as early as 1762. Watchmen anticipated similar treatment. Bakers' boys gave each of their masters' regular customers several "New Year's Cakes," and received recompense. Givers were rewarded in another way. "I love to make a cheerful heart," noted Thomas Cope of Philadelphia. "The awkward scrape of the leg, the smile of satisfaction & the thankee sir, thankee, are a rich regard for the trifle bestowed."[32]

As American social and economic structure began to change during the antebellum period, so too did old patterns of gift-giving. The formal, one-way dispensing of duty gradually yielded to rituals of exchanging gifts among family, friends, and neighbors. Christmas, rather than New Year's, became the primary occasion on which to give presents. The popularity of the custom widened. Of course the marketplace, charged with an unprecedented abundance of goods and the money to buy them, played a crucial part in broadening the appeal of giving gifts. Equally powerful, however, was the importance the antebellum middle class placed on the sanctity of home and family and the role that gifts played in promoting its ideals. Along this unstable connection between market exchange and family solidarity, Americans began to shape new meaning for old gift customs.[33]

To shopkeepers the meaning was "profits." Noticing a heightened involvement in giving, they soon learned to anticipate a growing need for holiday gifts. Late in December their stocks of unique, useful, clever, and thoughtful items to be purchased and then given away swelled. As early as 1830, John Pintard commented on the "endless variety of European Toys that attract the admiration & empty the pockets of parents friends & children" he found in New York City that December. "Our shops," wrote a Bostonian in 1842, "are so filled at this season with every kind of tasteful article to attract one that it is hard to refrain." About the same time, a woman visiting New Orleans noted that "the streets and shops display the most attractive & beautiful articles," adding, " —how little do I want."[34]

Almost seamlessly, this expansion of holiday sales built upon social rituals of Christmas and New Year's shopping. Early in the 1830s, one New York visitor wrote that "during the evening until midnight, these places are crowded with visitors of both sexes and all ages, some selecting toys and fruit for holiday presents; others merely lounging from shop to shop to enjoy the varied scene. . . . " In 1858, George Templeton Strong described a similar scene: "Shops are full of business, streets are thronged; every other pedestrian carries a parcel or two, or escorts one or more eager, expectant children with big eyes fixed on the gorgeous succession of shop windows." In Albany, New York, on December 24, 1855, Edward S. Johnson reported the streets "alive with People. . . . Thousands are out buying Christmas Presents." St. Louis stores were "crowded with people buying Christmas things," William Paisley wrote. "The toy & funny goods houses particularly are doing a big business."[35]

Merchants, however, did not pay much heed to the particular holiday they supplied. They tended to advertise wares for the "winter holidays," New Year's, or, sometimes, Christmas. Rarely did they advertise solely for Christmas. For instance, the *Augusta* (Georgia) *Daily Chronicle & Sentinel* ran an advertisement for "Presents for the Holidays" in 1843 that made suggestions for "Chrismas [*sic*]," New Year's, and even St. Nicholas Day. Unfortunately, the adverstisement appeared on January 3, well after each of the gift days it promoted. In the 1850s, the *New York Times* made numerous offerings for "holiday gifts," but seldom designated any for Christmas.[36]

Despite signs that the incidence of gift-giving was increasing, many Americans, whether because of social or religious practice, kept an allegiance to New Year's giving. Mary Austin Holley sent her daughter a barrel of sugar and oranges as a New Year's present in 1830. In 1837, Samuel Rodman's children "had a day of excitement in rec'g and making New Years presents." Lydia Maria Child wrote one friend that, for her New Year's gift, she "wanted a thermometer badly, to regulate the heat of my room." (She did not receive one.) Another year she gave a friend "a little seal" for her desk, and asked for "six cents worth of the seed of the Hyacinth Bean" for herself.[37]

New York City's elite turned New Year's giving into a particularly immoderate event. "New Year's presents have abounded this year," Philip Hone wrote in 1847. "This is the Parisian mode of celebrating *le jour del'an*, and we are getting into it very fast." The houses he had visited the day before gave "the appearance of bazaars, where rich presents were displayed, from the costly cashmere shawls and silver tankard to the toy watch and child's rattle." That same New Year's Thomas Robbins observed "a great deal of visiting and giving gifts" in Hartford.[38]

Some religious groups—Quakers, Congregationalists, and other Calvinist denominations—continued to discourage followers from participating in Christmas gift-giving. As late as the 1890s, one Presbyterian woman returned a Christmas parcel to her relatives, writing tersely: "You know we don't like Christmas presents[,] won't give any or accept any." Social custom often reinforced religious belief. Pennsylvanian Robert Blair Risk remembered that although "the legend of Santa Claus was told in every household and believed in by every child" at mid-century, "[t]here was little or no exchanging of gifts between members of the family, or with neighbors or distant relatives."[39]

The association of Christmas gifts with servants and slaves both in the antebellum South and North may also have restrained people from exchanging Christmas gifts. The *New York Herald* in 1856 told its readers that it had been the custom in New York City and Albany "for the servants of gentlemen, particularly if they were blacks, to go around among their master's friends to receive Christmas boxes." It claimed that "this practice led genteel families not to give or receive presents themselves on that day." For at least one prominent Washington, D.C., resident this seemed to have been the case. In 1868, Orville Hickman Browning recorded in his diary that he had given a silver cake basket, silver butter dish, and silver goblet to his personal servants, but he made no note of any gifts to his family.[40]

When compared with the importance that Americans had begun to attach to gifts, such social opinions and religious practices mattered less and less. Increasingly, families incorporated the custom into their home celebrations, and this turned attention to Christmas giving. One diarist, for example, noted in midcentury that her grandparents made no fuss over presents. "They say," she wrote, "when they were young, no one observed Christmas or New Years, but they always kept thanksgiving day." Her holiday was different, though, for she recorded having received several gifts from her cousins.[41]

Antebellum Americans found that gifts and the act of giving fit well into the concept of Protestant home religion. Giving joined two potent elements of the domestic ideal, those of family and religion, together. In the context of religion, a gift symbolized God's gift of Jesus to Man, and the emphasis rested on giving rather than receiving. In a social context, the custom signified a bond between giver and receiver, and again stressed giving over receiving presents. Within the family and among friends, the ritual of gifts strengthened such important, intangible qualities as amity, affection, appreciation, generosity, and mutual dependence, qualities that held no monetary value in the world of commerce.

The material gifts exchanged around a family's hearth or between friends at Christmas encoded relationships that were at one and the same time the most cherished and basic and the most vulnerable. Indeed, ethnographic studies suggest that ritualized gift-giving in any society is a method of expressing relationships that are important but insecure, whether between family members and generations or through one-way giving, such as gifts to children. The transaction as well as the gift itself joined giver and receiver and defined their relationship. According to sociologist David Cheal, "transfers of gifts from one individual to another must be understood mainly as a feature of the institutionalization of social ties within a moral economy." Trading worldly items as a currency of sentiment provides a "symbolic media for managing the emotional aspects of relationships." If one fails or refuses to respond to a gift by giving one, Marcel Mauss asserts, the "pattern of spiritual bonds" breaks. At Christmas, the getting and giving of material things symbolically represented social intercourse and moral obligation. The rational absolutes of the day-to-day commercial world became secondary. One could request or hint at one's wishes, but it depended on another's willing generosity to make any object truly a gift. For his or her part, the giver chose a fitting present not to keep, but to offer in friendship, admiration, or love.[42]

As a symbol or substitute for the nurture traditionally associated with home, gift-trading within a closed circle of family testified to the home's protective role and to the importance of its members to each other. Parents rewarded children and spouses accorded respect and affection to each other. Presents made to friends gave definition to the interlocking small worlds of sociability and cooperation that individuals relied upon in lieu of or in addition to family. This exchange of Christmas presents in American households resembled, in some ways, the potlatching of Northwest Native Americans. In looking at modern custom, Claude Levi-Strauss suggested such a parallel. The seasonal flurry of interclan feasting, goodwill, and especially the ceremonial divestiture of personal possessions kept tribal economy flowing (just as holiday buying helped circulate money through the marketplace). As important, the potlatch trading of goods altered status relationships among clans. Some became richer, others less so.[43]

The gift ritual engaged in by middle-class Americans had a similarly festive bustle, but the presence of a market economy and the fairly static condition of the middle class endowed gift-giving with a related but essentially different purpose. In a true potlatch, individuals and clans provided the items to be given away. However, participants in the Christmas custom increasingly turned to the marketplace as their source of goods. Thus, by using the gifts bought and given through the medium of shops and stores, Americans engaged in a "potlatch" of magnification, not reallocation, of personal goods. One member of a family "clan" could raise the status of other members by adding to the collective material wealth of the entire family. At the same time, the gift provided the individual a palpable expression of attachment to and sentiment toward a single individual. Such acts did not (at least directly) work to the detriment of those outside the family. That is to say, Christmas presents added to a family's material possessions and gave discernible proof of affections, but had no effect on the accumulation of wealth and declarations of affection in another family.

Whatever its social implications outside the household, giving gifts spun a complicated web of meanings and associations for those within a family. Much of the burden fell on the mother, who more often than not shopped for or created the gifts and orchestrated the ceremonies of giving. Yet each of the family members took part in the ritual in ways that revealed cultural assumptions and hierarchies.[44]

Husbands and wives often exchanged gifts, but the two sexes seemed to have different ideas about their nature. Husbands, probably because of their role as breadwinners and their absence from the everyday workings of the home, seemed inclined to bestow gifts more sentimental, less practical, and frequently more expensive than those their wives gave them. "Mother received from Father a handsome silver tea and coffee service," one girl noted. George Templeton Strong, after resolving to be "parsimonious" and spend no more than twenty dollars on his wife, became "inflamed" by a $200 cameo brooch displayed in the window of Tiffany's. With little hesitation, he went inside and bought it with money he had withdrawn that morning to pay bills. Mrs. Strong surprised her husband with "a very carefully finished and colored cabinet picture of herself." ("Considered as a likeness," Strong wrote, "it is a libel.")[45]

Women, who often lacked the personal monetary resources their husbands may have enjoyed, tended to give their spouses personal, sensible, and time-costly gifts, such as slippers they had made. And even when women tacitly equated a gift's suitability with its monetary expense, their magazines might assign an additional, practical dimension. Giving a gold pen to a young gentleman intimated "mental power and moral improvement . . . refinement of thought, and progress in civilization." "[N]ewly-married people who live in the country, might appreciate a practical gift," ran another piece of advice, such as "Spear's anti-dust, Gas-Consuming Stoves."[46]

Children remained largely the recipients of gifts, although trading among themselves and even giving presents to parents was not unknown. In this regard, as in so many others, the German example inspired the practice of some. George Ticknor's stay in Dresden in 1835 awakened him to the idea of trading gifts within the family. The children's gesture of giving especially impressed him. On Christmas Eve, he wrote, "we witnessed some of this very peculiar national feeling and custom; that, I mean, of the children giving presents to the parents and the parents to the children on Christmas Eve." His German host had summoned family and guests into a room "where the presents which the children had secretly prepared for the elder members of the family were placed under the tree." There "was nothing very valuable or beautiful in what was given, yet it was all received with so much pleasure by the parents and elder brother, that the children were delighted, and kissed us all round very heartily."[47]

Parents, of course, usually gave much more to their children than they received. Advice literature encouraged responsible parents to supply their children with toys in order to make pleasurable their experiences in lesson-learning. When translated into the language of domesticity, toys became a useful adjunct to the rearing of children. In the 1830s, members of the Baptist Maternal Association asked of *Mothers' Monthly Journal*, "Is it proper to supply our children with toys?" The editor replied with an unwavering "yes," and followed with detailed lessons about how to use toys to teach good work habits.[48]

Horace Bushnell heartily endorsed the value of children's toys. "One of the first duties of a genuinely Christian parent is, to show a generous sympathy with the plays of his children; providing playthings and means of play, giving them play-things," he asserted. "Happily there is now such an abundance of games and plays prepared for the entertainment of children that there is no need of allowing them in any that stand associated with vice." Noah's arks enjoyed particular popularity, especially in homes where strict Sabbath observance limited entertainment to religious instruction. Spinning tops, dolls, candies, books, and other favors could also be made to serve useful ends, and Christmas provided an appropriate time at which to present these treats and diversions.[49]

The joining of religious instruction and material acquisition was a unique characteristic of Protestant home religion. Although ostensibly home values provided a retreat from the pressures of the commercial and industrial world, they paradoxically echoed and endorsed these profane realms. Children who expected gifts from Santa and parents learned from an early age "to take and to receive," a custom that folklorist Alan Dundes has suggested is "important training" for life in a capitalistic society. John Pintard's gift to his grandchildren demonstrated this dual role. In 1820, he sent them a "beautiful diamond Bible, so called from the type," plus money, a firkin, and half Eagles ($5 gold coins). Money made a fine, instructive gift. One woman who grew up in Ohio at the beginning of the nineteenth century remembered that each of the children in her family always received a gold piece, but they were never allowed to spend it. "It had to go right into the bank," she said.[50]

The ideal gift combined an appreciation for the material, objective worth of an object with an appreciation of values loftier than the money that purchased it. This required that a gift be morally or aesthetically instructive. Consequently, in addition to brooches and other feminine finery, items such as Bibles and books served as lucrative mainstays of the gift trade. A particular sort of book, the gift annual, exemplified the double criteria. Similar to contemporaneous annuals published in England, they began to appear in the 1830s and could be found for sale at Christmas and New Year's time. They were expensively and beautifully bound. Some were oversized. Others were small and exquisite, with tooled leather binding, gilding, or mother-of-pearl inlay. Fragile ones might be "inclosed in a sort of pasteboard coffin," one editor recalled, to be "extracted by the aid of a strip of ribbon which it was a fearful joy to handle."[51]

Poetry, prose, and fine steel engravings filled these books, which bore such titles as *Keepsakes, Atlantic Souvenirs, Landscape Annuals, Gems, Oriental Annuals, Books of Beauty, The Pearl,* and *The Amethyst.* American writers and others of note, including William Cullen Bryant, Edgar Allan Poe, Henry Wadsworth Longfellow, John Greenleaf Whittier, Catherine Sedgwick, Nathaniel Parker Willis, and President John Quincy Adams, contributed to them and sometimes found their first audiences and profits there. Although the literary merit of these offerings varied and often slipped into what Douglas Branch has called the "flabby narrative" of love, sympathy, and virtue, mixed with self-indulgence, their givers invested them with moral and aesthetic worth. *Godey's,* for example, hoped that "some thousands" of *Kris Kringle's Book*, ornamented with "gilded covers and coloured pictures," would "find their way into the stockings hung up in chimney corners in anticipation of Kris Kringle's annual visit." "The moral tone of the stories," the article emphasized, "was as commendable as the beauty of the execution."[52]

As middle-class American Protestants began to establish a new Christmas during the first half of the century, the notion that money and commerce might taint the holiday was significantly absent. This was in part because Protestantism itself used financial success as an indicator of faith. The Rev. Dr. Dewey of New York, for example, published a series of sermons in 1838 that, to his mind, illustrated that "there is an object, in the accumulation of wealth, beyond success; . . . and that is virtue." Another minister reasoned that "the desire to possess more property than is sufficient for our maintenance . . . *is* a law of human nature, its purpose must be wise and benevolent. . . . From this common desire," he asked, "may it not be presumed that it is a duty to be rich?"[53]

In a time that could see success as God's reward for virtue, Christmas gift-giving became an exercise in religious training. A cornucopia of goods available in stores, "virtuous" money to buy them, and the ways in which gifts reinforced domestic ideals insured that commerce and values of home intertwined to encourage consumption—for oneself and to give to others. The tantalizing array of trinkets, toys, mementos, and more substantial treasures stowed beneath an imposingly decorated Christmas tree created a powerful icon of the emerging American Christmas. Antebellum Americans eagerly entered into its whirl. And while these traditions remained isolated mainly in the city homes of the new middle class during the first part of the nineteenth century, their importance and meaning to Christmas had begun to change customs nearly everywhere.

CHAPTER 6

Christmas in the Slave South

In 1845 the southern writer William Gilmore Simms published *Castle Dismal or The Bachelor's Christmas*. Declaring it to be "illustrative of the traditions of the Southern States," Simms opened his story as Carolinian Ned Clifton pondered where to spend Christmas. "No doubt," said Clifton, he could "find pleasure enough, in any one of the old haunts," that is, among his relatives, but, yawning, he declared them "old and I have been there so often already." He wanted "novelty — change — change." So, with an irony befitting the modern age in which he had grown restless, Clifton decided to visit Castle Dismal, the home of an old friend who "had the fancy of doing things as they did of old."[1]

There, Clifton found the essentials of what he and his friend Frank Ashley took to be a "traditional" southern Christmas. At "holiday times we must look for visiters [*sic*] of all classes," Ashley proclaimed. "The Christmas log must be burning when they come, and Christmas cheer must smoke upon the table. There must be mince pies, of course; and for the drink, Ned, see you yon pile of eggs! We'll have a noggin, to night, or I'm no sinner." Ashley admitted that the holiday had its excesses, but as quickly excused them. "What then?" he asked. "It fed the poor, — it filled the hungry. It encouraged the humble. It brought men together, even as benefactor and dependent, and they grew glad and parted with all their doubts and difficulties for a season." To him, such a Christmas seemed "to be far better than the niggardly reserves of modern times, where we have

75

the stiffness but not the parade—the formality without the feast,—or the feast without the fun."[2]

The relationship of past to present, the importance of tradition, and the harmony of classes concerned Simms as much as it had Washington Irving. Irving had tried to find in the Christmas traditions at Bracebridge Hall a solution to the seeming characterlessness of modern life and the dissolution of the social order. He discovered instead that the Squire's fussy attention to ancient ritual yielded more of an historical showpiece than a true holiday. As a Carolinian, Simms wrote from different circumstances. Largely unshaken by the stresses of urbanization and industry, the South experienced less tension between old traditions and the new world of the nineteenth century. Indeed, southerners enjoy a fairly continuous history of Christmas celebration, at least among the plantation elite.

In many ways, the spectacle of the antebellum plantation Christmas exemplified a seamless passage of past into present. It had changed little from the rounds of fox-hunting and balls Fithian described in eighteenth-century Virginia. In good part, this continuity of tradition owed to the general influence of Episcopalian religion and the region's abiding favor of English custom. But it also related to the timing and uses of Christmas in the South. In the warmer climes of the southern states, the holiday arrived soon after harvest rather than in the middle of fallow winter. It marked the end of a period of exhausting physical work and emotional stress and supplied the restorative benefits of a festival. Its days of leisure afforded time to renew social bonds among plantation residents and between inhabitants of other plantations. Traditionally, Christmas was also an occasion to take stock of financial affairs, a time when planters recorded their year's profits and losses, reviewed and renegotiated contracts, and hired or leased out slaves for the next year.[3]

Preparations began weeks before the actual holiday. Besides bringing in the cash crop, slaves had to shuck corn, butcher hogs, render lard and smoke hams, stuff sausage-casings, make mincemeat, and bring in wood "cut and stacked high in the wood-house and on and under the back porticos, so as to be handy, and secure from the snow which was almost certain to come." For the feasts of Christmas, nuts, raisins, citron, and currants had to be procured and readied for the days of baking, and the woods invaded for turkey, duck, partridges, and an ample supply of evergreens. Stores of alcohol and dairy products were laid in for the endless bowls of songaree, sack posset, syllabub, or egg-nog. The Yule log had to be selected and brought to the firegrate. Masters and mistresses planned games, balls, hunts, and other amusements. "Gentlemen . . . make account of it as a time to be spent [merrily?] among friends," noted a visitor from the North in 1816. "Ladies & gentlemen, especially the latter, form parties, playing, [dining?] &c. are the order of the day. Boys are dismissed from school, indeed, all is sport or idleness."[4]

Yet the South was not immune to change. As slavery spread westward, economic competition intensified. Sectional differences became more pronounced, and, after 1820, criticism of slavery sharpened. By the 1840s, southerners had begun to forge a "cavalier" myth to define and defend themselves and their institutions. Christmas became a key element in expounding the southern ideal, one in which the perceived virtues of the plantation system could be symbolized and ritualized. In the boldest ways, the southern Christmas provided a picture of harmony amid increasing tension.

Nowhere was the romantic evocation of southern noblesse oblige, uncalculating generosity, and the bond of paternalism more persuasively and self-consciously evident than in "Maize in Milk. A Christmas Story of the South" (1847), also by William Gilmore Simms. Simms set his story at Maize in Milk, a prosperous Carolina plantation owned by the benevolent Colonel Openheart. Openheart had fallen on hard times. His crops had failed in recent years. He had recently purchased an additional tract of land. And to save the slaves on the old Butler plantation from being sold down river, he had bought them all, despite the fact that most were old and infirm.

As Christmas neared, Mrs. Openheart suggested that the family visit her uncle for the season. Well aware of the precarious financial situation, she tactfully sought to avoid the cumbersome expenses of their traditional and generous Christmas that family, neighbors, and slaves had come to anticipate each year. Openheart would not hear of it. Her idea was "only too ridiculous," he said. Hard times made the keeping of custom even more important. "We must make our hearth-fire brighter," the story's narrator advised, "and gather our friends about the warming, and make merry within while all is melancholy without; and show to one another how cheerful everything may be, though the tempest blows never so angrily against the shutter."[5]

Christmas, then, would go on at Maize in all its glory. As neighbors began to arrive on December 24, the women and girls arranged myrtle, bamboo, holly, and cassina greens over the windows, doors, mirrors, and antique family pictures, "giving to the spacious walls and rooms a charming aspect of the English Gothic." The men and boys, with their horses and dogs, surveyed the surrounding woods and fields, then went down to the river to fire a Revolutionary fieldpiece three times as they did every year. When they returned, a new Yule log was kindled from the old. In the evening, the Openhearts and their guests danced to the music provided by "the sable fiddler" and "an urchin with a rude tambourine," finally stopping for a drink of eggnog, "that luscious draught not to be foregone." Then the eligible young daughter Bessie sang "another of her ancient Christmas carols," the signal that the evening had ended.[6]

The same relaxed pace continued on Christmas Day. It opened early, with an inventory of the gifts Father Christmas had left the children in the night. For the boys there were, among other toys, spurs, "a buck-handled knife and very pretty flagelet," "a bag of marbles, an India-rubber ball," and "a joint-snake." Only young Tom got hickory switches. The girls received gifts "of less doubtful taste" — a common-prayer book, a gold watch, music-box, chess pieces, and a copy of *Pilgrim's Progress*. The loud report of the old blunderbuss fixed at the front of the house interrupted their examinations and awoke the rest of the household. Amid cries of "Merry Christmas," and "I've caught you, — I've caught you!," Col. and Mrs. Openheart distributed gifts of their own to the children and to expectant house servants. Meanwhile in the kitchen, house servants separated, whipped, sugared, and combined more eggs with wine for another batch of eggnog, "the necessary preface to a Christmas breakfast, after the old fashion in Carolina." Breakfast followed, "then all parties sallied forth, in several groups, to ride, to ramble and to hunt."[7]

Toward the end of the morning holiday rituals, "a new collection of shining faces," the field slaves, assembled at the porch to greet "old maussa" and to receive their gifts. They numbered about eighty, and included those Openheart had just bought and those who were old, lame, mute, one-armed, and half-witted. Some said "God bless you, maussa," or "Merry Christmas, old maussa," or "Hoping you live tousand merry Christmas more." Others recited rhymes, such as:

> Christmas come but once de year,
> Da's wha' mak' we come up yer.

and

> Enty dis da Christmas come?
> Yer's de nigger look for some!

Openheart expected them. On a recent trip to the city, he had purchased knives, scissors, shawls, caps, kerchiefs, razors, hatchets, tobacco, and cases of pins and needles to divide among them. He gave no money. Any judicious master knew it would be "spent perniciously at some neighboring groggery."[8]

Openheart believed Christmas to be a season in which "High and humble should equally show gratitude. . . . The high was to be high only in the exercise of an ability to make the lowly glad and happy; the humble was to exult in gratifications which showed them consciously in possession of bounties bestowed, in the first instance by the Lord of all. . . . " His uncomplaining generosity with his slaves illustrated one aspect of this philosophy. Christmas dinner, the high point of the holiday at Maize in Milk, showed another. When guests entered the great hall that had been "dressed in a deep Gothic garment of green boughs and branches, sprinkled with red berries and blue, with candles distributed between, and a great oak wood fire blazing at the extremity," they "felt themselves transported to the old baronial domains of our Anglo-Norman ancestry, and their minds were naturally elevated with the moral sentiments which grow out of their recollections of history." The effect doubled as the feast appeared. Guests savored "the 'boar's head,' done after the ancient Saxon method, dressed in rosemary and with a huge lemon in its open mouth," complemented with every variety of meat, spirits, ("Madeira that had been walled up for thirty years, and sherry that had grown pale, indeed, from weight of years," and "natty English ale, – a potation which did honor to the British breweries"), and desserts ("fruits of Cuba and the north, nuts and figs, not forgetting pindars, groundnuts, or peanuts," mincemeat pies, and plum puddings).[9]

"Day slipped away unconsciously while the parties were still at the table," Simms wrote. Then, once again, the violin was taken up and the younger people began to dance. Colonel Openheart and the older members of the dinner party, though, went to the "Negro Quarter" where the slaves had not one, but three violins. "Such wholesale *abandon* as they showed – so much recklessness of care, and toil, and vexation of spirit – would delight a philanthropist from Utopia. . . . [T]he grounds between their several cabins were filled with jigging groups – tossing heads, kicking shins, rompings and rollicking – with the rare impulse of so many happy urchins just let loose from school. They had their supper too . . . " – a veritable feast of "a good-sized barbacued steer," hogs, 'possum, bread, "and some fifty gallons of *persimmon* beer."[10]

The Christmas that Simms extolled was not pure fiction. Diaries and reminiscences also recorded similar holidays replete with feasts, music, greetings, preparations, and other rituals. Emily Wharton Sinkler recalled slaves knocking on her door and saying, "Merry Christmas Miss Emily, long life and *Crosperity to you*!" A northerner observed in 1849 that "[A] Southerner had rather be robed [*sic*] of his reputation than miss of his Christmas dinner." "We rushed around like wild to complete the preparations for the coming ball guests," Eliza Ripley wrote of Christmas on a Louisiana plantation: "Miles and miles some of them drove in carriages," while others arrived in skiffs, each accompanied by "champagne baskets . . . and, like as not, a dusky maid. . . . " Meanwhile, the plantation's musicians ("our own negroes") assembled with "two violins, a flute, a triangle, and a tambourine. A platform had been erected at one end of the room, with kitchen chairs and cuspidors, for their accommodation."[11]

Christmas quite naturally also became a focus of nostalgia in the many memoirs of Old South life. Stately rituals and innocent celebrations dramatized by images of happy slaves created an apotheosis of southern grandeur. On the Smedes's plantation, house servants typically called out "Christmas griff!" One Christmas morning, Susan Smedes wrote, she heard the quietest and lowest-voiced of them booming, "Hi! ain't dis Chris'mus?" As soon as Henry Benjamin Whipple rose, "the servants were all waiting with laughing faces to wish us a Merry Christmas, expecting to receive a bit or so as a contribution." Thomas Nelson Page, writing in the late nineteenth century, recalled bygone southern Christmases for the "beautifully dressed church," dinner, apple-toddy and egg-nog, games, dances, "negro parties, where the ladies and gentlemen went to look on," and the almost certain occurrence of "a negro wedding during the holidays." "[A]ll times and seasons paled and dimmed before the festive joys of Christmas," he wrote. "It had been handed down for generations; it belonged to the race. . . . Time was measured by it. . . . "[12]

The realities of slave life and slave Christmases, of course, were hardly as simple or benign as pictured in such accounts. In fact, the holiday experiences of slaves varied widely, and the celebrations allowed by masters were shaped not only by paternalistic affection but also by their fears of insubordination and calculation of work time lost. If Christmas was a ceremony of symbolic harmony, the power of the master and hard lot of the slave shaped the experience of both.

Not surprisingly, many ex-slaves harbored fond memories of the holiday, taking joy from any rest time their masters might permit. Custom had grown to allow them relative freedom not only on Saturday afternoons and Sundays, but on Christmas and other special occasions. Plowden C. J. Weston, for example, banned slave work on Good Friday, three days at Christmas, Sundays, and the first Saturday after threshing, planting, hoeing, and harvest were finished. Only "half task" was to be done on Saturday, except during planting and harvest or punishment. Former Georgia slaves George Caulton, Caroline Ates, and Arthur Carlson noted Christmas and the Fourth of July as their holidays. Ex-slave Harriet Jones had special memories of Halloween and Christmas. Others remembered corn-shucking, hog-killing, and Easter as the best times.[13]

These memories rested on the simple pleasures that a little free time might bring. Where Sara Crocker worked, the slaves "would lie around under the trees in the morning, resting and sleeping" on the Fourth, eat a big dinner prepared by the whites, then play games and dance. "Lawd I kin' member dem holidays, what times we had," recalled another former slave. The men built "a gra' big platform an' brung it to de house for to dance on. Den come de music, de fiddles an' all dem other things. . . . Sech a dancin' you neve seed befor'." Surrounding them were "dem big demi-johns of whiskey what marsa done give us. An' de smell o' roas pigs an' chicken a-comin' outer dat cabin."[14]

Of all the holidays, Christmas loomed largest in memory. Some ex-slaves recalled the holiday almost as romantically as the whites. "Slaves lived jus' fo' Christmas to come round," commented Mrs. Fanny Berry, an ex-slave. Beginning with "de fus' snow fall," they would "commence to savin' nuts and apples, fixin' up party clothes, snitchin' lace an' beads fum de big house." For all it was a time of "general celebratin' . . . 'cause husbands is comin' home an' families is gittin' 'nunited agin. Husbands hurry on home to see day new babies. Everybody happy." "Christmas sho was handsome time," another said. Prince Johnson, of Yazoo, Mississippi, called Christmas "de time o' all times on dat old plantation." A fourth remarked wistfully: "If I could call back one of them Christmas Days now. . . . Lord, I was so happy!"[15]

On many plantations, masters freed slaves from their normal work routines for several days or even as much as a full week. Many granted passes to visit nearby plantations or to take a trip to town. As George Fleming recalled, "Marse jes' sort of turned 'em [slaves] loose." Some slaves were lucky enough to have a little spending money or credit, from cotton or other produce they had been allowed to raise in small garden plots or for some bit of handiwork. One exceptionally lucky slave usually received fifteen to twenty dollars each Christmas.[16]

As at Maize in Milk, slaves on many plantations received gifts of some sort. At the Elms, they got "turban-handkerchiefs made by the white women and woolen caps and other articles." "Marse Jim," in New Orleans, summoned his field hands to the back porch of the main house, where he "distributed the presents—a head handkerchief, a pocketknife, a pipe, a dress for the baby, shoes for the growing boy . . . etc., etc., down the list. . . . Then after . . . everyone had a comfortable dram" of whiskey, the hands "filed off to the quarters, with a week of holiday before them and a trip to town to do their little buying."[17]

Slaves valued these tributes. "Christmas time Mars Charles gived us lots er things," remembered Levi Pollard. "Sometimes dey wo[u]ld be a little extra, but us always got a peck er flour, a whole ham, 5 lbs. real cane sugar." The master also gave out winter clothing. "Every man gits two workin' shirts, one coat, one pair pants, one jacket, en one pair shoes. De women git near 'bout de same I reckon. . . . " Extra rations of meat, sugar, coffee, "great quantities of sweet potatoes," flour, salt, rice, and molasses counted as gifts, as did such delicacies as "plum pudding and gingerbread, apples, oranges, currants, and other fruits, and heaping plates of ham, turkey, and goose."[18]

Many slaves remembered best the Christmas feasts. Caroline Ates remembered the "big dinner up in marster's back yard; one table for the little niggers an' one for the big ones," with "Barbequed chicken, pork, coffee, cakes an' pies." Solomon Northrup, author of *Twelve Years a Slave*, wrote of an open-air Christmas table loaded with roasted chickens, ducks, turkeys, pigs, and maybe a wild ox, varieties of vegetables, biscuits, preserves, tarts, and pies. The tired staples of bacon and corn meal were nowhere in evidence. "Unalloyed and exulting happiness lights up the dark faces," Northrup wrote; "a multitude of eyes roll in ecstasy." He also took note of the "white people [who] in great numbers assemble to witness the gastronomical spectacle."[19] Liquor was almost always a prerequisite, although some plantations were dry. "Marse always send a keg of whiskey down to de quarters by old Uncle Silas, de house man," remembered Mrs. Berry. "Ole Joe would drink all he kin long de way, but day's plenty fo' all. Ef dat don' las' old Marse Shelton goona bring some mo' down hisse'f." On another plantation, "about thirty bottles of wine" were distributed to the slaves. "Warm punch or egg-nogg circulated freely" where Charlotte Gilman lived. Charley Hurt, a Texas slave, said that on Christmas Day, the master "puts a tub ob whiskey, or brandy, in de yahd ob de qua'tahs, an' hangs tin cups 'round de tub. Den de cullud fo'ks he'ps demse'ves." Male and often female slaves were expected to get drunk, recalled Booker T. Washington. In fact, masters made alcohol so readily available at holiday time that, as Frederick Douglass noted, "[n]ot to be drunk during the holidays was disgraceful."[20]

Behind the merrymaking lurked the masters' anxiety over possible insurrections, fears at times expressed in private and in law, and resentment of labor time lost. As early as the late seventeenth century, the General Assembly of Virginia had become so uneasy with slave gatherings that it authorized the militia in each county to disperse "all unusual concourse of negroes, or other slaves" during the holidays lest "great danger . . . happen to the inhabitants of this dominion from such unlawful concourse." On his own plantation at Sabine Hall, Landon Carter took his own steps in 1774 to institute control over his servants and the holiday. "I can't but fancy that I have been quite happy in not letting my People keep any part of Christmas," he wrote in his diary.[21]

Even in the late days of slavery, some planters cruelly denied any Christmas break. "We didn't know but one holiday, that was Christmas day, and it was not much different from any other day," remembered an ex-slave from Virginia. For another, Christmas "was just lak any other time wid de slaves." "We never had anything extry. Marster Barrows allus had big dinnah but dey never done us any good." Bennett Barrow (probably not the same "Marster Barrows") used the occasion of Christmas to sharpen punishment. He chained two of his slaves during Christmas in 1836, one "for general bad conduct" and the other for "bad conduct during cotten picking season." In 1839 he wrote: "intend Exhibiting Dennis during Christmas on a scaffold in the middle of the Quarter & with a red Flannel Cap on."[22]

As for the matter of lost work time, David Golightly Harris complained in 1856 that "the negroes or most of them [had] gone on a frolic and no one to do anything." It is the "[l]ast day of the negro holiday & thanks for it," wrote another planter in 1857. Bennet Barrow reflected in his diary on December 29, 1845: " . . . getting tired of Holidays, negros want too much, Human nature." However, most owners and overseers well understood that withdrawing such privileges would be difficult. "We are in the midst of the Christmas vacation. Considering the work to be done, four days is rather much," one planter protested, "but Mr. Fredericks [the overseer] said it was customary to give that time and it was given."[23]

Indeed, slaves had come to regard off times and holidays as their due and in many places created their own distinctive traditions. They made

Christmas a time to sing, socialize, dance, feast, and dress up—a moment of freedom. Each plantation's slaves seemed to develop their own form of celebration. On one place in South Carolina, "the young people sometimes bored holes in trees, filled them with powder and set-off by fuses." In Galveston, in 1845, blacks organized a formal ball, "the music of which resounded late into the night." At the Elms, Charlotte Gilman's character Cornelia Wilton recalled, slaves were allowed to fire a small field-piece at dawn. Neighboring Roseland had no cannon and so "commenced a salute with the combination of every noise they could make by the agency of tin and brass, aiding their rude music."[24]

Similar revelry awakened Henry Benjamin Whipple in St. Mary's, Georgia, at midnight. He had never seen a "more motley group of dark skins," all dressed in their finest and "full of joy and gladness at the return of their annual holidays." Throughout the South dancing to tambourines, fiddles, and other instruments began soon after daybreak and, as Gilman indicated, was not "suspended a moment by the presence of the whites." "Such music as these darkeys will make for a few days cant be beat with 'tin horns,' goard shells & or beans," a visitor to Baton Rouge wrote.[25]

In North Carolina, a highly ritualized form of Christmas celebration developed among slaves that seemed to set their revelry somewhat apart from those in other states. Disguising themselves, sometimes as animals, they danced, paraded, and begged for money or food. These rites were known as John Canoeing, John Kunering, Koonering, or other related terms.[26]

In 1830, the Rev. Moses Ashley Curtis observed that the blacks in Wilmington, North Carolina, had "a singular custom . . . of dressing out in rags & masks, presenting a most ludicrous appearance imaginable" on Christmas Day. Attended by "a troop of boys singing, bellowing, beating sticks, dancing & begging," "[t]hree or four of these John Cooners as they are [called] made their appearance":

One of them was completely enveloped in strips of cloth of every color which depended in the most ragged confusion from every part of his ebony hip. Over his face was drawn the nether part of raccoon skin from the center of which hung the tail. . . . On each side of the tail appeared two holes through which shone the whites of his eyes. . . . Then dancing & his rags flying & his flexible nose gamboling about his face, singing with a gruff voice in concert with his satellites, I was ready to burst with laughter.[27]

A doctor witnessed a similar occasion, a Kooner parade at Somerset Place, about 1855. A "ragman" dressed in scraps of fabric, jangling bells, a headpiece of raccoon skin and oxhorns, sandals made of "the skin of some wild 'varmint,'" and carrying a "short stick of seasoned wood," led the way. A second man "simply arrayed in what they call his 'Sunday-go-to-meeting suit'" followed, holding "a small bowl or tin cup." Then came "half a dozen [other] fellows, each arrayed fantastically in ribbons, rags, and feathers" and bearing "several so-called musical instruments or 'gumba boxes.'" A "motley crowd of all ages, dressed in their ordinary working clothes, which seemingly comes as a guard of honor to the performers," brought up the rear. [28]

Upon reaching the front door of the "great house," the men "beat their gumba-boxes violently" as their leaders danced with "a combination of bodily contortions, flings, kicks, gyrations, and antics of every imaginable description." The wild crowd gleefully joined in, shouting, clapping, and demanding gifts from their master. Receiving them, they bowed low and shouted: "May de good Lord bless old massa and missus, and all de young massas, juba!," then proceeded to visit each of the other houses on the plantation, "wind[ing] up with a grand jollification."

The origins of these rituals are not known. They may have first appeared in the Bahamas as an imitation of European colonial traditions, then spread to other slave domains such as North Carolina. One scholar argues that, rather than being a cultural mutation, the John Canoe festival came directly to the busy seaport of Wilmington on slave ships arriving from the West Coast of Africa. [29]

In any case, slaves performed versions of Koonering throughout the American South. At Eutaw Plantation in South Carolina, wrote Emily Wharton Sinkler, they "went to every door in the house and made some such speech. One went to her brother James and said 'Merry Christmas, Massa, may you live t'ousand year and have to drive you hosses all de time.'" Henry Benjamin Whipple, in Georgia, watched slaves as they "march[ed] up & down the streets in great style," led by "a corps of staff officers with red sashes, mock epaulettes & goose quill feathers, and a bank of music composed of 3 fiddles, 1 tenor & 1 bass drum, 2 triangles & 2 tambourines." These were followed by others dancing, walking, hopping, and singing. "They levy contributions on all the whites they see & thus find themselves in pocket money," he noted. [30]

Mary Austin Holley saw a similar sight in Louisiana, finding it "grotesque and amusing beyond measure." For three days following sugar harvest and coinciding with the onset of Christmas, the slaves "came up in procession . . . with every sort of noisy instrument of their own manufacture in the way of music. . . . Violins, kettle drum, tambourine, and triangle made their bow and they played and sang with great glee." The last day of their festivities "exceeded all the rest. It was a sort of jubilee." Field slaves "marched up enmass" to be joined by house servants, "making such a din as you never heard." "Some very old congo men performed with great agility," Holley reported, "coming up to their master on one knee, then on the other, then prostrate, with other exhibitions of homage all in time to the music. The music, though laughable, was also affecting." In response, onlookers threw "hand-fuls of money which they would scramble for" from the gallery where they looked on. "Madame would throw among them colored handkerchiefs which they are very proud of and which they lost no time in decorating themselves."[31]

These lively productions of singing and dancing presented for tribute suggest obvious comparisons to the modifications that other Americans had made of European mumming traditions. They were almost exclusively male (although there are hints that women "on occasion" participated), and played on the dual powers of intimidation and amusement. In the North, working-class mumming brought with it a distinct spirit of defiance, which was read by the middle classes as something more dangerous than diverting or useful.[32]

In the South, plantation managers often actually encouraged these holiday antics. "During the Season of Christmas our Slaves . . . have been in the habit of enjoying a State of comparative freedom; of having dances & entertainments among themselves; & of celebrating the season in a manner almost peculiar to this part of the world," explained one Dr. Norcom in 1824. "These festivities are not only tolerated by the whites, but are virtually created by them. . . ." One pamphlet, titled "Management of Servants," explained that "During this *jubilee* it is difficult to say who is master. The servants are allowed the largest liberty."[33]

In this sense, Koonering and other Christmas rituals were similar to the many instances of ritual role reversal that Sir James Frazer located in English society. English noblemen had been known to relinquish their places at the Christmas groaning board to the peasants who served them the remainder of the year. By allowing the lower classes temporary access to authority, the gentry intended to maintain their own position and perhaps strengthen it. Robert Chambers compared the occasion to a Roman Saturnalia "in which the relations of master and servant were for a time reversed, and universal licence prevailed."[34]

The plantation Christmas, whether or not it involved Koonering, fell short of any "universal licence." Always denied the privilege of outright reversal, the slaves celebrated at Christmas only to the extent that owners felt they could maintain sufficient control. If in Christmas celebrations slaves found a way of expressing a distinctive culture and acting out a symbolic reversal, masters gained the use of a relatively harmless safety valve for slave dissatisfaction and therefore useful insurance for their invest-ment. Indeed, black abolitionist, Frederick Douglass thought "those holi-days were among the most effective means in the hands of slave holders of keeping down the spirit of insurrection among the slaves." Ira Reid reached a similar conclusion in his study of Koonering, calling the ritual an "avenue of psychological release for the controlled emotions of the subjugated blacks."[35]

In fact, the demonstrable happiness of slaves at Christmas reinforced the masters' own belief in the benevolent character of their paternalistic rule. Nancy Williams, an ex-slave from Virginia, remembered her master's de-light in the slaves' holidays. "Ole marsa stan off wid his arm folded," she said, "jes' a puffin on dat pipe an' a sayin! 'Look at my niggers! Ain' my niggers havin' a good time?'" Then the mistress would reply, "'I b'live you lak yo' niggers better'n you do me.' To which Marsa say, 'Sho I lak my niggers; dey's money to me. You gwan back de house. Ise gwan stay watch my dance.'"[36]

The image of happy slaves magnified in importance as abolitionists stirred sentiment against slavery and provided additional justification for the slaves' brief winter holiday. One observer on a Georgia plantation noted: "It would make a northern abolitionist change his sentiments in reference to slavery could he see as I have seen the jollity & mirth of the black population during the Christmas holidays. Never have I seen any class of people who appeared to enjoy more than do these negroes. . . . " Another, after seeing the slaves in holiday attire, noted that slaves in New Orleans were freed to do as they pleased until January 1, "and as I listened to their pleasant salutations and jovial conversation, I changed my opinion in regard to the condition of the down-trodden slave."[37]

Still, slave celebrations were not solely, perhaps not even primarily, a drama between master and servant. Robert Dirks, looking at the case of eighteenth-century "slave saturnalias" of the Indies, which were similar in many respects to those of the antebellum American South, discerns a more complex meaning at work in the phenomenon. Dirks, as have others, asserts that owners and overseers, for their own purposes, cultivated a spirit of unity and order; "everyone involved leaned over backward to make the rites appear as frivolous and profane as possible."[38]

Dirks suggests this was something of an illusion. Through begging, disguising, dancing, and demands, slaves acted out divisions, alignments, and common experiences among themselves. Their unbidden calls on the master, made with "impudent vivacity," were not the acts of individual slaves in direct interaction with the master, but usually the actions of groups, separated by rank and tribe, "clamoring competitively." In other words, rather than being an exercise in "letting off steam" against slavery and slave conditions, the Christmas saturnalia encoded underlying tensions over conditions, behaviors, and social relations of the plantation as a whole community. "Against the background of the plantation's otherwise uniform facade and lockstep order," Dirks notes, "all of this appeared disturbing."

Historian Charles Joyner emphasizes a different aspect of ritual meaning, arguing that the free time, including Christmas, that slaves took as their own allowed those of diverse African cultures to practice, share, and even create new folkways that could unite them and be passed from one generation to the next. Holiday and leisure time "was not *leisure* time, in the usual sense, but part of the moral economy of the plantation time."[39]

In short, as Eugene Genovese has noted, "slaves developed a sense of community among themselves and, to a much lesser but still vital extent, a sense of community with their white folks" during the holiday intervals. "White folks" tried to foster the feeling of community. At Christmas (and probably almost always) they strived to instill in slaves a sense that the welfare of slave and plantation were the same.[40]

The holiday rituals that whites shared with blacks, even though it remained clearly evident who was master and who was servant, probably made an even stronger bond of loyalty than did the permission whites may have extended for riotous dancing or the sobriety they may have exacted through religion. Harriet Jones's memories highlight the way in which the celebration of Christmas joined slaves and whites together. Christmas, she said, "meant a lot ter bofe de niggers an' de white chillun. Dey so excited dey say, 'Christmas comin' ternight,' whilst dey dance all ober de place." The slaves helped carry in the Christmas tree, holly and evergreens, put candles on the tree, "an' hangs de stockin' up fer de chillun, an' fer my chillun, too."

The next morning, black servants and white children rose before daybreak to find what Santa had brought them. "Dere is sumpin' fer us all," including the men, since sometimes Master Johnny put a keg of cider or wine on the back porch "fer dem all ter have a little Christmas speerit." "De nex' thing dat day has is de dinner. . . . [A]n' dat dinner!" When the whites finished theirs in the dining room, they moved into the kitchen to watch the slaves eat theirs. In the evening slaves had their own Christmas. They feasted on "maybe wild turkey or chicken an' udder good things" laid out on a long table set in the yard of the quarters. In the main cabin, a dance with "fiddlers an' de banjo an' guitar players" would follow. The master, mistress and children, after having finished their own singing, would go down to watch, "ter see de niggers have day dance."[41]

While the festive saturnalia stood at the heart of many southern Christmases, the region's celebrations could not remain totally isolated from the force of evangelical piety sweeping the rest of the nation. After the 1820s, themes of Christianity and domesticity played an increasingly important role in shaping communal experience. Whites worried especially about the paganism that they saw lurking in the black's masking and dancing. "I dont know what the religionists of Lexington would have thought of the ushering in of this holy day here," wrote Mrs. Holly from Louisiana in 1830 after she had witnessed the wild mirth of the plantation slaves. Josiah Collins hired an Episcopalian minister to live at his plantation and convert his slaves. The minister took as his challenge the eradication of such heathenish practices as the saturnalia. When "strict religion" reached the slaves on Burleigh plantation, singing and dancing at Christmas were forbidden. "The whole workforce joined the church and 'henceforth, not a musical note nor the joyful motion of a Negro's foot, was ever again heard on the plantation.'" Charlotte Gilman remarked that even in antebellum years, some slaves "seemed to recognize the sacredness" of Christmas, a result of the increase of "religious observances and facilities of late years."[42]

Along with a new Christian piety came other features of the new national Christmas. Santa, Christmas stockings, and Christmas trees dominated the recollections of many ex-slaves. The master of the South Carolina plantation where Junius Quattelbaum lived called the slaves together on Christmas, and made all the children sit around the Christmas tree. The adults "jined hands and made a circle 'round all" and waited for "marster and missus" to call each individually to receive a gift. "After all de presents was give out, missus would stand in de middle of de ring and raise her hand and bow her head in silent thanks to God. All de slaves done lak her done. . . . I sees and dreams 'bout them good old times, back yonder to dis day." Lucendy Griffen's master would "instruct old Santa Claus to bring us a big sack [of] nuts[,] candy and some big old red apples to eat. . . . Master would have just as much fun as we negroes," she said. Mandy Hadnot's master gave her a Christmas tree trimmed with popcorn each year.[43]

The southern Christmas also began to center more directly on children. On Christmas in 1856, Edmund Ruffin's guests adjourned to "the basement to see the shades of the Magic Lantern. . . . The young children, & the negroes, are delighted," he reported in 1859, "– & all the grown persons, except myself, are there to enjoy the joy & pleasure of the children. . . ." One ex-slave recalled that nearly every year they received a Christmas tree from the "white folks," after which they would sing, "Chris'mus kums but once a year, everybody ought to git his sheer." But in the event that they failed to get a tree, the "chilluns would hang dere stockin's up an' in de mawnin' git up a three an' four o'clock to see what ole Santa brung dem." At a plantation in Mississippi, "Every child brought a stockin' up to de Big House to be filled." (For the occasion, Prince Johnson said, they all tried to get one of the mistress's stockings, "'cause now she weighed nigh on to three hundred pounds.") On one Louisiana plantation no one had ever seen a Christmas tree until the Civil War. Since no cedars or pines were available, "a tall althea bush, hung [with] presents" became the tree for "all the house servants, as well as for the family and a few guests." Not everyone understood its purpose, however. One woman overheard one of the "little negroes" remark, "'all us house niggers is going to be hung on a tree.'"[44]

By the 1850s, the plantation South's Christmas celebrations reflected not only the rich and harrowing contradictions of slavery and two cultures of white and black, but also the region's simultaneous separateness from and connection to the rest of the nation. A world of its own, still it slowly assimilated customs from its rival region. A region under siege, it cleaved to and gloried in the traditions that symbolized its own special and doomed way of life.

CHAPTER 7

⚜

A Holiday for the Nation

D uring the first forty years of the nineteenth century, Americans
adopted and shaped Christmas celebrations that reflected a broadening sense of regional and cultural identity. At the same time, they elevated
the holiday to new prominence. Beginning early in the 1840s and continuing through the Civil War and into the 1870s, Christmas underwent yet
another transition. Similarities eclipsed differences, and the festival began
to acquire a distinct profile as a national holiday.

The consolidation and nationalization of Christmas emerged from more
general trends and events of the period, ones as benign as the expansion of
national media, as relentless as the development of marketplace and industry, and as cataclysmic as the Civil War. In all these, the North led the
way. Whether as a center of publishing, manufacturing, and trade, or as
the war's victor, it defined much of the "national" culture that appeared in
the 1850s and solidified in the aftermath of the war. Under its primacy,
Christmas acquired a more unified set of rituals, symbols, and meanings, a
pattern for a nationally celebrated holiday.

The first signs of this process at work appeared in several magazines in
the 1850s, where writers expounded on a theme that once had surfaced
only in personal diaries: the relative lack and shallowness of holidays in
America. "It has often been a subject of remark by some . . . that our
country can boast of no festivous customs, or old merry making days,"
observed *United States Review* in 1854. Compared with America, another

writer remarked, European "life is profusely decorated with holidays. It is an easy skip from one to another." A wag writing for the *Washington National Intelligencer* made a more direct assessment: "There is little danger that the popular mind may be dissipated or the popular energy softened by the too frequent recurrence of days devoted to rest and relaxation from the burden of daily life." Moreover, the anticipation of those few holidays Americans traditionally celebrated had dwindled. "We all dread the coming of the Fourth of July now," the editor of *Harper's Monthly* wrote in 1854. Enthusiasm for it "has long since flown away in villainous saltpetre." The next year, in 1855, he again addressed the issue. "[O]ur fairest festivals languish," he commented. Even Valentine's Day had grown too common.[1]

Critics did not simply bewail the absence of holidays. They sensed that holidays provided a crucial key to the unity of the nation. The many customs immigrants brought to America from their ancestral homes, especially from Great Britain and Holland, along with "some others originating in our own land," had been "domesticated among us, and of right, form part of our history as a people," one author wrote. Yet, he conceded, "we cannot go back into the dusty ages of antiquity [as could Europeans], and trace many which may be strictly called *national customs*." "In a day of general change," the editor of *Harper's* wrote, "we sigh for conservative elements and wonder how we may more closely attach the country to its best hopes and traditions." The answer was holidays that stressed unity. Thus, Orville Hickman Browning declined to attend a supper commemorating the Pilgrim's landing at Plymouth Rock. Such anniversaries "tend to keep us mere sectional distinctions and divisions," he reasoned. He proposed instead that "National days should be observed, for instance 4th July, 22nd. Feby, thanksgiving &c. In these," he argued, "all can participate and each feel that he has an equal share with every other, and they contribute to the growth and development of a healthy sentiment of patriotism."[2]

The Fourth of July offered the most promising and logical holiday around which the nation might rally. Since Revolutionary days the sense of nationhood had hinged on shared values exemplified by the battle for independence and a veneration of its heroes. *Harper's* thought "this reverence for 'the fathers'" the "most beautifully conservative of all influences" as it presented "the common sacred ground on which all political parties, all sectional divisions, and all religious denominations can heartily unite." The editor believed that "every such difference ought to give way . . . in the presence of the healing spirit that comes to us from the remembrance of those old heroic times."[3]

Yet "old heroic times" held little importance for many Americans. And Independence Day failed to deliver the expected infusion of patriotic fervor. Recent immigrants and even the children's children of the nation's founding generation learned Revolutionary ideals second-hand. Pioneers settling the western frontier were at work creating their own heroic times. Southerners were creating a separate history. Only some Americans, it would seem, had the temerity to recall the Founding Fathers without acknowledging how modern times differed from Revolutionary days.

Part of the difference lay in a shifting locus for the practice of virtue. The Revolution and its promise had envisioned a public life marked by public virtue in government and marketplace, one that would justify and fulfill the brave battles fought in the War of Independence. By the 1840s, however, it had become painfully clear to middle-class Americans that the public stage was hardly the place for invoking or inspiring republican and Christian ideals. As home became in their minds the center of morality and order, they left the rousing public ceremonies to politicians and the rowdy fringe of "lower" elements.

At the same time, discomfort with public festivals led to an assertive campaign for instituting holidays appropriate to the new moral world of the home. Few thought to domesticate Independence Day, which by its very nature had been a public celebration. However, especially in New England, some touted the advantages of a more frankly spiritual exercise in the form of a national Thanksgiving. What once had been a central day in the Puritan calendar some saw as a partial cure for what ailed the nation.

Significant opposition to the Puritan feast, stemming primarily from differences in religion and region, had existed since colonial days. New Englanders failed in their attempts to persuade the Revolutionary congress to declare a general Thanksgiving. Their efforts, wrote Charles Francis Adams, had "foundered upon the church-state and federalist-antifederalist conflict." Despite objections raised by the likes of South Carolina's Representative Thomas Tucker, who said the designation of a thanksgiving was "a religious matter" and "not the business of Congress," George Washington, at the prompting of Congress and Alexander Hamilton, had appointed several days of national thanksgiving during his tenure as President.[4]

In New York, politicians attacked Governor John Jay, claiming he sought to incur favor among religious groups when he proclaimed Thanksgiving Day a regular state holiday in 1795. Pennsylvania's newspaper editors, writes a modern folklorist, "sneered" at Thanksgiving, ridiculing it along with other New England customs "as Yankee importations which had no real reason for existing on Pennsylvania soil." Southerners displayed little inclination to institutionalize what many saw as a New England, Calvinist, and, later, abolitionist holiday. Even some New Englanders rejected the idea of a civil declaration of what, at least at its American roots, was perceived as a religious holiday. "The appointment . . . of a thanksgiving by a civil officer, is strictly a union of Church and State," wrote William Lloyd Garrison in 1835. Even so, by 1830 civil law in a number of New England towns and states had legitimated the old Pilgrim religious feast.[5]

Thanksgiving also failed to fulfill many personal expectations. Themes of reverence, family, and giving thanks often proved secondary to the main task of the day—eating. "The time passed pretty much as such time has often passed before, in the demolition of eatables which were given to us in fair quantity and quality," wrote Charles Francis Adams in 1831. William Lloyd Garrison reported of his Thanksgiving in 1835: "Almost every body got punished, more or less for slaying and eating so pitilessly; for the conglomerated fragments of fowls and puddings and pies, which were ravenously swallowed, soon united in getting up an insurrection in the stomach. . . . " A seventeen-year-old put it another way: "A heart disposed to set apart a day for thanksgiving and praise [did not need] to have its powers and feeling quickened by gormandising."[6]

Ironically, these "abuses" of the spirit helped popularize Thanksgiving and dissipate its associations with Calvinist austerity. According to Charles Francis Adams, this home holiday was "gradually making its way as a festival into States which have but a very small infusion of the Puritans, and setting up a sort of independent existence against its more ancient form." One Minnesotan, writing in 1854, thought it the best legacy of the "old Pilgrims." He presumed that the fact that it had become more a social than a religious festival was "quite as agreeable to God as his creatures." In 1848, Texas becomes the first southern state to declare a Thanksgiving. Virginia followed in 1855. On the eve of the Civil War, five southern states, all the New England and middle states, and all the western territories observed a Thanksgiving holiday.[7]

Sarah Josepha Hale, the New England-bred editor of *Godey's*, had been a strong force in bringing Thanksgiving to this level of participation. As a widely read and influential spokesperson for homemaking and an articulator of the bridge between home and nation, she aspired not only to join together the nation's populace through such a day, but also to reinvigorate the nation with the virtues of domestic life. Thanksgiving, she believed, gave a unique opportunity for ritualizing traditional republican ideals that found little practical expression in the day-to-day world of modern life. To her, the holiday symbolized an idyllic sense of community, family, and natural (as opposed to manufactured) wealth that emanated from the work of women and the timeless rhythms of daily life. Thanksgiving, she wrote in 1857, created a time "when the noise and tumult of worldliness may be exchanged for the laughter of happy children, the glad greetings of family reunion, and the humble gratitude of Christian heart."[8]

Hale first applied her tireless energy to promoting a national day of thanksgiving in 1827, while editor of *American Ladies' Magazine.* When in 1837 she took charge of *Godey's,* her efforts continued. She perfected her case during the 1850s, addressing ongoing concerns over the paucity and meaning of American holidays and recommending the feast as a solution. "To make a national festival," she reasoned, "the time of holding it must be fixed by circumstance, by custom, or by statute." Americans had only "two national holidays, Washington's birthday, and Independence day . . . both settled by circumstances; one in midwinter, the other in midsummer." Without so much as a nod to Christmas, Hale argued for "a third festival, hallowed by custom or by statute, for autumn," and endorsed setting aside the last Thursday in November for it. She deemed that date "best suited when the people . . . might sit down together . . . and enjoy in national union their feast of gladness, rendering thanks to Almighty God for the blessings of the year." "We believe," asserted Hale, "the people would be gratified to have this union of sentiment carried into effect."[9]

Hale pressed the nation's Presidents and the state's governors to adopt her idea. She urged readers to "[c]onsecrate the day to benevolence of action, by sending good gifts to the poor, and doing those deeds of charity that will, for one day, make every American home the place of plenty and rejoicing." Biblical injunction underlined the importance of just this sort of holiday. "A day yearly rejoicing and giving of gifts was not only sanctified but enjoyed, by Divine authority, on God's chosen people," Hale held, citing Nehemiah 8:10. "Let this day, from this time forth, as long as our Banner of Stars floats on the breeze," she wrote in 1857, "be the grand THANKSGIVING HOLIDAY of our nation. . . . "[10]

Even as Hale called upon Americans to make Thanksgiving the nation's holiday, Christmas continued to gain popularity among the descendants of New England's Puritans. In 1841 George Templeton Strong reported that in New York City Christmas had "been verily well observed." He especially noted "a lachrymose paragraph in the 'Presbyterian' headed 'Times are Changed.'" Henry Wadsworth Longfellow detected "a transition state about Christmas here in New England" in 1856. "The old puritan feeling prevents it from being a cheerful, hearty holiday; though every year makes it more so." In Reading, Pennsylvania, a newspaper remarked in 1861, "Even our Presbyterian friends who have hitherto steadfastly ignored Christmas – threw open their church doors and assembled in force to celebrate the anniversary of the Saviour's birth." And the First Congregational Church of Rockford, Illinois, "although of genuine Puritan stock," was "preparing for a grand Christmas jubilee," a news correspondent reported in 1864.[11]

One indicator of Christmas's growing significance was the lengthening list of states that set aside December 25 as a legal holiday. Louisiana was the first to declare it an official holiday. In 1837, it designated December 25 along with January 1, January 8, February 22, July 4, Sundays, and Good Friday as "Day[s] of public rest and days of grace." However, the "grace" to which the law alluded was not heavenly, but the small "grace" from having to pay bills on a certain day. Arkansas passed a similar law, "An Act concerning days of grace on commercial paper," in 1838, that named Sundays, Christmas, and the "fourth day of July." Other state legislatures created comparable calendars as part of their banking codes. By 1860, fourteen states – California, Connecticut, Delaware, Georgia, Maine, Minnesota, New Jersey, New York, Ohio, Pennsylvania, Rhode Island, Tennessee, Vermont, and Virginia – had joined the list, often naming the Fourth of July, Thanksgiving, and New Year's as well. And although, as Charles Francis Adams noted, "as yet a large part of the puritan stock still hold off from the observance of it with some distrust," even Massachusetts set aside a day for Christmas.[12]

These laws enforced at least cursory general observance of Christmas and a few other festivals, but they clearly served the requirements of business, not those of the spirit. Officially, they commemorated nothing. They did not require that businesses close or that commerce halt. Neither religious nor social interest motivated their passage. Indeed, by designating as a legal holiday only the most common and least controversial days, the state laws tacitly limited the number of holidays and thereby circumscribed the varietal richness of traditional calendars.[13]

Nonetheless, the wide circulation of magazines, a result in part of cheaper printing costs and a better mail system, increasingly drew American attention to the celebration of holidays. Christmas especially made a perfect subject for countless news items, poems, stories, and illustrations. At first, these appeared only sporadically and during seemingly odd times of the year. *Harper's Monthly*, for example, made its first reference to Christmas in a poem, "The Approach of Christmas," in its August 1850 issue. "Christmas Hymn," *Godey's* first literary tribute to the holiday, ran in February of 1841. The magazine's first serialized Christmas story, William Gilmore Simms's "Maize in Milk: A Christmas Story of the South," appeared throughout the spring of 1847.[14] However, within a relatively short period of time, the popular print media had consolidated an array of information about the festival's associations, emotions, and rituals into December issues. In *Godey's*, December titles included "The Christmas Party," "The Christmas Gathering," and "The Ingle Nook: A Simple Story for Christmas." Soon recipes for plum pudding, mince pie, and other "seasonable receipts" began to appear on an annual basis.[15]

Additional December pieces related in detail the customs of other nations, especially Germany. In 1848, for example, *Godey's* reported that on Christmas Eve German parents led their children into a darkened room to await Christkindel and ponder what delights "the little infant Jesus" might bring them. They then repaired to where a Christmas tree, "a large *evergreen* with many branches, fantastically lit up with tapers and lamps, with its branches gilt or silvered over, as in fairy tales," awaited them. Suspended from its branches they found their "beautiful presents, all inscribed with the names of the donees."[16]

Harper's provided its readers with a similar account of "authentic" Christmas customs—"a regular old-fashioned, German, family Christmas festival" in Hamburg. After a week of public festivities, "a regular bazar . . . —a Crystal Palace—with a universal exhibition of trinkets from all parts of the globe," the family gathered to dine, waltz, and tell a "Christmas tale, tradition, or legend." They then joined in a noisy procession to the nursery to drive out witches. "[F]or a fortnight past," this room had "been locked against every body but the parents," but once opened, it revealed "a novel and interesting sight . . . a fir-tree, about ten feet in height, illuminated by something like one hundred and fifty little wax-tapers fastened to the branches, which latter were also literally loaded down with toys, grapes, golden apples, dolls, and gew-gaws of every possible and impossible description." When the excitement abated, everyone retired to the dining-room to discover what presents had been secreted beneath their napkins.[17]

While these articles gave readers a deeper familiarity with Christmas, they also carried in them associations comparable to those of the Thanksgiving holiday hailed by *Godey's*. Both elicited nostalgic memory, emphasized children and familial bonds, and firmly embraced the importance of tradition. Charles Francis Adams saw so much similarity between Thanksgiving and Christmas that he predicted in 1857 that the two would eventually be merged into a single holiday, as it seemed "superfluous to have them both."[18]

Instead, Christmas prevailed. It suggested none of the strong regional connections that linked Thanksgiving with New England. As important, Christmas, coming into the popular culture as the nation tensed for civil war, held within it a rich reserve for grappling with issues of absence, discord, misunderstanding, forgiveness, and regeneration. It beckoned men and women past earthly travail into an idealized domestic haven that was neither particularly northern nor southern in its origins or biases.

The yoking of domestic imagery with national interest revealed itself in a number of places. The tree standing in at least one American household, that of George Templeton Strong, had been surrounded by a flag and adorned with a banner on which "Mrs. Ellie" had written with "great care and labor . . . 'THE UNION FOREVER!'" Even more striking were the magazine fiction, editorial comments, illustrations, and even political cartoons which linked peace with the family home and discord with the impending war. A short story published in *Godey's* in 1860 illustrated the lesson. "The Christmas Tree" told the bittersweet tale of Marion, who had fallen in love with the son of her father's sworn enemy. On Christmas Eve, the anniversary of her mother's death seven years before, Marion pleaded for forgiveness from her father. Then she presented her lover to her father "from behind the tree." The sentimental parable ended happily. "Christmas was surely not a time for quarrels. . . ."[19]

It was, in fact, during the "quarrel" that followed—the Civil War—that Christmas developed a definitive profile as the principal American holiday. Northerners and southerners, civilians and soldiers alike attempted to create in it the peace and well-being that eluded the nation. Their aspirations could be found in nearly all aspects of the festival, from nostalgic yearnings posted in a letter home to times for makeshift Christmas dinners stolen from the bloody and endless conflict. "Christmas is a great institution, especially in time of trouble and disaster and impending ruin," wrote George Templeton Strong in 1862, adding, "*Gloria in Excelsis Deo et in Terra Pax* are words of permanent meaning, independent of chance and change, and that meaning is most distinctively felt when war and revolution are shaking the foundations of society and threatening respectable citizens like myself with speedy insolvency."[20]

For many who had already come to associate Christmas with family gatherings, abundant food, peace, and good cheer, the war derailed the home rituals of Christmas. In one place, turkeys for holiday dinners sold at $11 each. The next year sugar shortages raised the price of candy to "$8 per pound," making sweets too expensive to hang on the limbs of the Christmas tree. In summary, a Confederate clerk noted, "It is a sad Christmas. . . . " The mood was no different in the North. A Union woman wrote to her sisters in Europe that she was neither "making a time over Christmas presents this year" nor receiving New Year's callers. "People are so depressed about the times." At least one Tennessee family postponed Christmas until January, "the yankees seeing fit to spend Christmas with us. . . . " Mary Boykin Chesnut sat down to a Christmas dinner served on "everything . . . that a hundred years or more of unlimited wealth could accumulate as to silver, china, glass, damask—&c&c." In 1861, she knew that her old life as a wealthy plantation mistress was irrevocably gone.[21]

Whether civilians or soldiers, many attempted a holiday escape from carnage and conflict. Some avenues were imaginary, some actual, but all were fleeting. The efforts of field soldiers to enjoy Christmas showed a particularly nostalgic and almost reflexive search for comfort from wartime reality. "Christmas!" wrote Captain Henry A. Chambers, "What a crowd of bye-gone associations crowd upon the mind upon this almost universal holiday!" A Confederate nurse left an equally philosophical note: "What visions of cheer does not the sound of 'Merry Christmas' bring in review— happiness, plenty, and the forgetting of a few short hours the cares of this weary world!" For many soldiers, the feelings were more personal. Wilder Dwight wrote to his mother on Christmas Morning, 1861: "'A merry Christmas,' said I to *myself*, for want of a larger family-circle." "[F]amily ties," he mused a few days later, "are never so close as in these days of separation and trial." The "thought of home and the loved ones there" made Amos Stearns, a prisoner at Andersonville, "sad to think that I was not among them." Another prisoner hung his Christmas stocking "for habit's sake if nothing else."[22]

Some soldiers were lucky enough to find a bit of unexpected entertainment at Christmas time. "Some half dosen darkeys came down to our camp with their fidles temboureans and banjoes and they had a publick negro show," wrote a Union soldier. Another recorded that his "jolly German neighbors" were making such noise behind his tent that he had gone to investigate. He soon found that they had "a row of Christmas trees through their camp, all a-twinkle with candles, and hung with 'hard-tack' [ship-biscuit] curiously cut into confectionary shapes, and with slices of salt pork and beef." Yet the war was never far away. A rebel, having met the Yankees on Christmas, 1862, "gave them a Christmas greeting in the shape of a few shell," a decidedly emphatic reminder of reality.[23]

Many gauged their Christmas by its dinner. The groaning board of the old English Christmas, its capacity to bear weight tested by sumptuous quantities of goose, game, puddings, and pies, set a standard that few met. "Dined with McIlrath's company—sergeant's mess; an eighteen-pound turkey, chickens, pies, pudding, doughnuts, cake, cheese, butter, coffee, and milk, all abundant and of good quality," wrote Rutherford B. Hayes from his post in Fayetteville. A prisoner at Belle Island ate "corn bread and butter, oysters, coffee, beef, crackers, cheese, &c." At Andersonville, another had turkey and plum pudding. One southern soldier's Christmas dinner "was composed wholly of beef with gravy and corn bread." Wounded soldiers at a hospital in Maryland ate "[f]ifty roast turkeys . . . sixteen large loaf-cakes iced to perfection and decorated with the most approved filigree work, pies without number, cream puffs, cranberry sauce, puddings of all sorts, etc., etc. . . . " J. B. Jones, a southerner, succinctly wrote of his holiday meal: "I have no turkey today and do not covet one. It is no time for feasting."[24]

In general, the attempts Americans made to keep Christmas during wartime had a temporary and incomplete feeling. The holiday, for all the intent of its participants, often had to be celebrated among strangers and frequently with little ritual. As it was cast in the popular magazines of the day, the festival relied as well on novelty and simplicity rather than elaborate meals and ceremony. A magazine might provide the recipe for plum pudding, not directions for an entire feast. An unpretentious diversion, such as the suggestion in *Godey's* of a game called "Gypsies," might satisfy the needs of a Christmas party. It required that three preselected callers, disguised as gypsies, mingle among the Christmas crowd, telling fortunes and, finally, inviting themselves to stay for dinner. The fun of the game was the feeling of shock the guests would feel at being thrown together with gypsies.[25]

"Ella Moore's Letters from the City," published in 1861, encouraged innovation, not custom, in planning Christmas celebrations. Her family annually held a party at Grandmother Moore's, "with of course a little variation in the gifts, mottoes, and tableaux." One year, Ella Moore wrote, she had decked the front parlor with evergreens, boughs, red berries, and a banner reading "A Merry Christmas," providing a pleasing backdrop for "the moving tableaux of 'A Visit from St. Nicholas,' and 'Kriskringle's Call'" performed for the forty guests. Having broadly sketched the scene of her Christmas fete, Moore narrowed her focus to the details of its success. Realistic icicles for Kriss Kringle's beard and fur, she advised, might be made at home by melting a small amount of alum, then sprinkling it over his faux beard. "[I]t cools in the most beautiful crystals." The conclusion to Moore's letter left little doubt that her intended mission had been to teach. Her final, enthusiastic wish was that she had given "Dear Suzie" (or any of the magazine's 150,000 readers) at least one suggestion for a Christmas entertainment. If she had been successful, her letter would "not have been written in vain."[26]

While much of the wartime experience of Christmas involved a conscious escape from the war and its issues, its symbolic language had become enough a component of the experience of Americans to be of partisan use. *Harper's Weekly* printed a timely selection of the young Thomas Nast's drawings for holidays. A fervent Unionist, Nast often fused political allusion to his illustrations for Thanksgiving, New Year's, Independence Day, and other holidays. "Palm Sunday" paired Biblical imagery with Union triumph, and "The Savior's Entry into Jerusalem" with "The Surrender of Gen. Lee and His Army to Lieut. Gen. Grant." But Christmas elicited the most affecting metaphors. "The Union Christmas Dinner" showed Lincoln inviting the "Prodigal Son" in from the snowy cold to dine with him and the Union states.[27]

Nast did not rely solely on the combination of God and Union to promote the northern cause, but enlisted the venerable Santa Claus on the side of the Union as well. Nast already had some experience with Santa. In 1862 he had supplied thirteen color lithographs for an edition of "A Visit from Saint Nicholas," one of them a delicately colored rendering of Nicholas in a suit of light tan. In 1863 he illustrated J. M. Gregory's *Christmas Poems* with drawings of Santa and his reindeer and sleigh. However, the war called for a different sensibility. In 1863, Nast drew the saint visiting the Union army troops. "Santa Claus in Camp" depicted Santa in striped pants and a starred jacket, distributing toys and boxes to good (that is, Union) soldiers. In the foreground, Nast posed two uniformed youngsters, seated on copies of *Harper's*, examining a jack-in-the-box. The following December, Nast transferred Santa back home, but kept him in service to the Union. "A Christmas Furlough" showed a soldier returning to his happy wife and family, and to a Christmas tree loaded with gifts. In a cameo to the left, Nast sketched Santa, burdened with a full sack of toys, bending over two sleeping children. [28]

Less explicitly sectional renditions of Christmas also appeared during the war. In 1863, *Godey's* opened its December issue with five scenes of "Christmas." They provided something for everyone and offended few. "Sledging through the brisk, snowy atmosphere," a "joyful company of merry lads" collecting pine branches, a "happy, loving family gathered to hear the Christmas story of the wondrous Babe of Bethlehem, and of the bright angels that came" with "good-will to men," "the little pet of the family . . . with arms full of the treasures brought by Kristkinkel," and grandma's photo album—these scenes, explained the editor, portrayed "very truthfully the different pleasures of the Christmas anniversary." [29]

Faced with the widening popularity of Christmas and its centeredness on northern interests, not even Sarah Hale could sustain her old zeal for Thanksgiving. To be sure, she continued to urge presidential declarations of thanksgivings and even had some success. Following victories at Gettysburg and Vicksburg in 1863, President Lincoln named August 6 of that year to give thanks, overcoming a general tendency of Presidents to sidestep the church-state issues raised by the holiday. Hale continued to lobby, suggesting in September 1863 that Lincoln's proclamation be made annual. A month later, on October 3, 1863, Lincoln proclaimed a general day of Thanksgiving for the last Thursday of November. The following year, he declare two thanksgivings, one each for the victories at Atlanta and Mobile. To the second of these, the *New York Times* gave its editorial support: "This custom of the New England Pilgrims, at first confined to a few states, has at last, in 1864, assumed the scope and standing of a grand national holiday, which it is hoped, will be permanent and universally observed." [30]

Yet Hale's increasing favor of sentiment and an expanding national enthusiasm for Christmas had already begun to rechannel her energies. By 1865 she had fused onto the patriotic and pious tones of her earlier Thanksgiving arguments images and meanings that were also those that many associated with Christmas. "Even sober-minded elderly folks catch glimpses of their own childhood's happiness through the vista of past Thanksgivings," she wrote, "which make life more sweet, and their own soul more thankful for the good gifts God's love has bestowed in our favored land." [31]

More telling than her addition of nostalgic musings to the Thanksgiving holiday was Hale's assessment of Christmas itself, made only a month later. "Should not the American people become, on this Christmas, like little children in their feelings of love and gratitude to our Heavenly Father, for his great gifts of peace and good-will to our family of States?" she asked in her December editorial. "Shall not the blessed day draw closer the bonds of brotherly and sisterly affection of all classes, and elevate the minds of our citizens to the task—and the triumph, which now seem to be set before them—of leading the world in the way of prosperity and good works?"[32]

In these two commentaries, published within a month of each other in 1865, Hale displayed a subtle understanding of the relative strengths of each holiday. She did not mention Pilgrims or New Englanders in her November column, but appealed to the nostalgia of a nation whose very union had been tested in fire. Thanksgiving was a day to look back to simpler times of childhood and before the Civil War and to be thankful. In Christmas, however, Hale uncovered an interaction of past and present more dynamic than that in Thanksgiving. The December holiday, like November's, required giving thanks to God, but Hale specifically listed "peace and goodwill to our family of States" as a Christmas gift. And rather than looking back at past Christmases, she took the holiday as a time to recapture a child's tender feelings and to put them to use in perfecting the fellowship and good will in the contemporary world.[33]

Where once parallels might have been drawn between Thanksgiving and Christmas, such was no longer the case. In Christmas could be found more broadly inclusive humanitarian and familial ideals. "Religion, family happiness, childlike mirth, and pure generosity," *Godey's* asserted in 1866, "all unite to make it the day of all the year most filled with pleasant memories." *Harper's Monthly* echoed the sentiment: "Apart from the feelings which the sacred relations of the festival awaken, and the religious duties which it involves, Christmas is a day peculiarly connected with the associations, the pleasures, and the obligations of social and domestic life."[34]

As Christmas flowered, Thanksgiving began to fade somewhat. Falling later in the year, Christmas coincided more closely with the cities' slowed production schedules of winter than did the Thanksgiving harvest feast. More important, Christmas emanated from a diversity of sources, making it a holiday potentially more inclusive and democratic than Thanksgiving. By contrast, the custom of giving thanks by feasting (as well as it obverse, fasting) traditionally emanated from church and civil authority. This continued to be so, as Hale urged governmental authorities to declare such days. Nor did Thanksgiving command dedicated advocacy or confirm American historical tradition to the extent that Christmas did. In fact, because of its origins as a folk festival, Christmas thrived independent of official declaration and history. Thus, although it potentially raised the issue of church and state separation more directly than Thanksgiving, Christmas's grounding in folk culture prevented the concern from coming to the fore.

Even Sarah Hale conceded the primacy of Christmas among the nation's holidays. In 1867, for the first time, she ranked it above the "American national Thanksgiving-Day" in importance among "the household festivities." Christmas, she argued, "is the root from which spring all the good seeds of our civilization, it is the great agent by and through which the best fruits of our national resources are developed and ripened." To compare "our three national holidays with Christmas, would be like comparing water, earth, and air with the sun," she wrote. "Christmas holds the celestial magnet of brotherhood that should draw all who enjoy its blessing into that feeling of National Union." [35]

By the late 1860s, the softening of Calvinist attitudes toward Christmas, media recognition and exploitation of the wealth of Christmas imagery, especially those with sentimental and indistinct religious allusions, and the war's dramatic backdrop against which the silhouette of Christmas sharpened, fixed Christmas in the national imagination. Its associations with home, comfort, and transcendent verities had been baptized in blood. A telling though more prosaic endorsement could be read in state law books. By 1865, 31 states and territories officially recognized Christmas as a legal holiday, 13 more than in 1860. On June 26, 1870, for the first time in its history, the United States Congress declared Christmas a federal holiday. Although the act's stated purpose was the regulation of fiscal matters on several holidays, the law nonetheless formally endorsed the importance of a holiday that had been developing in the homes and sensibilities of the nation's citizenry for half a century. [36]

CHAPTER 8

A Traditional
American Christmas

"WW e have saved out of the past nearly all that was good in it," wrote
Charles Dudley Warner in 1884, "and the revived Christmas of
our time is no doubt better than the old." In a sentence, Warner had
grasped a truth about the holiday. By the 1880s Americans had reinvented
Christmas. They culled a pastiche of customs and rituals from the past,
originated modern traditions, and placed upon the entire holiday a meaning and order fit for their own times. In this Christmas they found a retreat
from the dizzying realities of contemporary life and a lens through which
to envision, as a people, from whence they came and whom they had
become.[1]

This national Christmas came of age in the last quarter of the nineteenth
century, an era Mark Twain christened the "Gilded Age." Adding to the
trauma of the Civil War and Reconstruction, the disorienting innovations
and dislocations of a second industrial revolution had wreaked unprecedented change on society. Urbanization, mechanization, and the power of
commerce and industry transformed American life at an ever-increasing
rate, leaving old values and even the idea of constancy behind. Great
poverty and phenomenal wealth existed side by side in the major metropo-
lises. Laborers faced job insecurity and low wages. Farmers struggled
against drought and debt. And the vast frontier, the mythic safety valve of
American life, quickly vanished.

As important, even the physiognomy of America's citizenry changed under the double onslaught of emancipation and massive emigrations from such previously underrepresented places as Eastern, Central, and Southern Europe, as well as Asia. As new immigrants, freed blacks, common laborers, and farmers faced change, the more established Protestant middle class, where the American Christmas had taken earliest and firmest shape, looked to new sources for understanding its past and present.

The pressures and challenges of the modern age made many long for earlier times. Thus, in the latter half of the nineteenth century, culturally powerful Americans exercised a growing enthusiasm for premodern ceremonies and rituals. They hoped to find in the intense experience of them not salvation and substance, but an alternative to the vagueness of liberal Protestantism and the sterility of positivism. The Christmas that these well-educated and comfortably middle-class or wealthy Americans embraced as a national holiday also reflected this leaning toward ceremonies that imagined simpler times when spirituality and community had once existed.[2]

Americans struck by anti-modernism did not simply borrow from the past, but rather varied old themes and wove new symbols into the received fabric, creating something definitively their own. Their sending of Christmas cards, decorating evergreen trees, caroling, hanging Christmas stockings, and exchanging gifts did not flow from ancient custom and belief, but constituted a collage of ritual adapted to conditions of the late nineteenth century. Rather than venture into the snowy woods to cut Christmas trees, Americans bought them from tree dealers. As quickly as they adopted the tree custom, they abandoned the tradition of homemade ornaments, toys, and gifts and went shopping for them. They sent Christmas cards with ready-written sentiments in place of handwritten letters to friends, and sang Christmas carols created only years before. Taken together, these acts and rituals made the modern Christmas seem a timeless tradition of American home life.[3]

Something that is so enduring nonetheless must have a history, and Americans implicitly understood the need to square their new but ancient festival with the past. Commentators on American life enhanced the impression of the holiday's timelessness by searching for, and writing frequently on, the origins of the nation's Christmas. In most instances, they defined it as a European hand-me-down, and often suggested that Americans still had not grasped an authentic feeling for the festival. "Christmas has never been fully observed" in America, "was never celebrated with an approach to old English heartiness except in the South" a Lancaster,

Pennsylvania, newspaper reported in 1866. A *Harper's* editor thought Americans had derived "much of our poetic feeling for the holidays" from the English, and the "German Christmas-tree we have transplanted . . . flourishes wonderfully in Yankee soil." But he missed "the burlesques and pantomimes which we associate so strongly with an English Christmas." "The American Christmas," affirmed another writer, "is a modification of the English." "Of Christmas in the New World," the *Nation* wrote in 1883, "we need not speak at all, since its customs, for the most part, have been transplanted from the Old."[4]

In many cases, writers charged American Puritans with thwarting the nation's celebration of Christmas. Their indictment carried an implication that Puritan influence on New England had somehow dampened all of America's participation in the festival of Jesus' birth, and certainly that it had made an indelible mark on New England celebrations. "[S]ome of our solemn progenitors," George McWhorter wrote, had attempted "the abolition of Christmas and its pleasures." However, he added that "Nature and reason were against the attempt, and it failed." "In New England the grim spirit of the Puritans prevailed so long that until lately little notice of the feast was taken," noted *Catholic World* in 1871. George Curtis went so far as to suggest that "[t]he Puritans frowned on Santa Claus as Antichrist" and a relic of "popery." He reminded readers that colonial Massachusetts had levied fines against anyone who observed Christmas. "And Peters, the old historian of Connecticut," he added, "says that one of the blue-laws of Connecticut forbade . . . keeping Christmas or saints' days, [or] making minced-pies. . . . "[5]

Harper's Monthly did not stray from the theme of condemnation. Believing that "[t]he Puritan element of this country long held old Christmas at bay," the editor recounted a story to illustrate his point. In New England, "one little fellow" had discovered in "some old book in the public library" with "glowing descriptions of the ancient [English] customs." But when Christmas arrived, he found "no sign of Christmas in the little town—no peal of chimes, no generous expectation of Santa Claus." Not only did a personal sense of grief oppress the boy, but also "a feeling of something exceptionally wrong and monstrous in such disregard of such a day." His mother, "to whom Thanksgiving was the high feast of the year," then gave him "a purse with a bright silver piece," which he took to the confectioner, an old Frenchman, saying, "That's my Christmas present." "'Christmas! Christmas!' exclaimed the old man, impatiently. 'No, no; nobody know[s] Christmas here!'" In the Frenchman's "depth of scornful repudiation of a community that knew not Christmas," the writer concluded, the little boy "felt that his deep longing for some due observance of the day had been satisfied. . . ."[6]

Ironically, these same writers often attributed improvements on the old Christmas to Puritan sway. "[A] better influence has at last triumphed," wrote McWhorter. Now Christmas was kept "more as a social than a religious holiday, by all those who are opposed to such observances on principle." Curtis felt that, in the end, the Puritans had performed the great duty of stripping the old Christmas of its excess, thereby allowing the emergence of a better holiday. "The purifying spiritual fire, historically known as Puritanism, has purged the theological and ecclesiastical dross away, and has left the pure god of religious faith and human sympathy," he asserted. "Even the New England air, which was so black with sermons that it suffocated Christmas, now murmurs softly with Christmas bells." Curtis judged that Christmas "could not be the most beautiful of festivals if it were doctrinal, or dogmatic, or theological, or local. It is a universal holiday because it is the jubilee of a universal sentiment, moulded only by a new epoch, and subtly adapted to newer forms of the old faith."[7]

The reality observed by Curtis was that the nation's Christmas encompassed the quintessence of American beliefs and values. By restructuring the connection between the holiday and Puritanism, Americans modified the standards of Biblical truth insisted on by Calvinists and also rescued the holiday from the excesses of folk custom. Unmoored from either extreme, Americans could recreate Christmas in the symbols and language appropriate for their time. Thus, the holiday enveloped the often contradictory strains of commercialism and artisanship, liberal Protestantism and spirituality, and nostalgia and hope that defined late nineteenth-century culture.

Surely, though, this American holiday did not evolve by collaboration or design. It disclosed itself by parts, through fundamental traditions that had been recaptured or newly invented. Christmas carols, for example, originated as pagan round dances, which became popular as "occasional entertainments" throughout Europe well before 1020 C.E. For centuries, authorities of the Catholic Church had issued, in the words of one folklorist, a "formidable series of denunciations and prohibitions" against them, but in London and elsewhere, as early as the thirteenth century and as late as the eighteenth, street hawkers sold carol sheets to passersby at Christmas time. By the sixteenth century, the songs had become an intrinsic part of Christmas throughout Europe.[8]

These carols were of two sorts. Chorus-boys or bands of waits usually sang the religious sort. Hired minstrels or full complements of guests sang the festive ones. During Cromwell's rule, Puritans, who objected to all caroling just as they denounced the unrestrained revelry and popery of Christmas itself, briefly stopped the singing. With the Restoration, the heartier carols quickly regained their old popularity, but as quickly waned, causing Englishman William Hone to predict in 1822 that in a few years carols would be heard no more. However, by the mid-nineteenth century, Christmas carols showed the same clear signs of revival as Christmas itself. In England, William Sandys published his *Selection of Christmas Carols, Ancient and Modern* in 1833 and J. M. Neale published an edition of old carols, *Carols for Christmastide*, in 1852.[9]

While borrowing from England, Americans also wrote their own Christmas songs, creating what Reginald Nettle has called "the best Christmas hymns of the nineteenth century in the English language." Edward Hamilton Sears, a Unitarian minister in Wayland, Massachusetts, wrote the words to "It Came Upon a Midnight Clear" in 1849. A year later, Richard Storrs Wills, an organist from New York, wrote the melody for it. John Henry Hopkins, Jr., rector of Christ's Church in Williamsport, Pennsylvania, wrote "We Three Kings of Orient Are" around 1857. In 1863, Henry Wadsworth Longfellow wrote "I Heard the Bells on Christmas Day" as a poem and later set it to an existing tune. In 1865, Episcopal rector Phillips Brooks wrote "O Little Town of Bethlehem" while en route to Bethlehem, and three years later his organist, Lewis Redner, put it to music. Both events reputedly occurred on Christmas Eve. The authorship of "Away in a Manger" remains unknown, but possibly a German Lutheran in Pennsylvania wrote it. It was first published in Philadelphia in 1885.[10]

Secular Christmas music also appeared. A Unitarian clergyman, Rev. John Pierpont of Boston, wrote "Jingle Bells" in 1856. *Godey's*, in 1863, announced a sheaf of new music "appropriate to the season." Copies of "Christmas Chimes, a splendid new nocturne by that favorite composer, Brinley Richards; Happy New Year's Schottische, by Ascher; Around the Fire . . . ; Under the Mistletoe . . . ; and Kris Kringle, a charming divertimento" would be "ready by the first of December. It will make a splendid Christmas present," advised the editor, "and thousands of copies will no doubt be sold for that purpose alone."[11]

These Christmas songs and carols developed out of the nation's own music preferences. Colonial Puritans had allowed no musical instruments, but they did sing psalms. Other seventeenth- and eighteenth-century colonists favored country fuging and shape-note singing. Among the elite, Haydn, Handel, and other musicians of the classical tradition dominated religious music. In fact, parts of Handel's *Messiah* had been first heard in America, on January 16, 1770, in the music room of the New York City Tavern, two years before its premiere in Germany. Following the Civil War, huge choruses sang *Messiah* each year in a New York armory. As Protestant churches adopted more ornate liturgies and settings, their congregations sang more, but the highly evangelical hymns of the early century hardly seemed appropriate for the day and age. Nor did the newer English tunes, which were usually dedicated to moral and social reform, hold appeal. Instead, late nineteenth-century American taste made Martin Luther's Christmas hymns and traditional English carols such as "First Nowell" and "Good King Wenceslas" popular. [12]

The Christmas songs Americans liked revealed a wholly American perspective. Simply arranged and heartily sung, the carols straight-forwardly interpreted religious and human sentiment. They transcended time and change (in much the same way that Americans envisioned Christmas itself), and characteristically avoided the earthly issues of poverty, irreligion, or revelous high spirits. For example, "O Little Town of Bethlehem" did not teach the lessons of moral responsibility and charity that the English sang in "Christmas is Coming, the geese are getting fat. . . . " It skipped past recent histories and took the singer to Biblical times in its description of the setting of Jesus' birth. Pieces that had no specifically religious content betrayed similar penchants for the ideal and mythic. "I Heard the Bells" spoke of peace on earth. "Jingle Bells," while catchy and without lesson, evoked an earlier moment when time paced itself to horses and sleighs, not trains and clocks.

In the 1890s and 1900s, the trend toward reviving older hymns and carols and writing modern songs in the older manner continued. Americans also began caroling, an old English tradition of carol singing by bands of roving waits. Specifically, one Frederick W. Briggs, of Newtonville, Massachusetts, after "spending a merry and musical evening in an English town," introduced the custom to Bostonians of Beacon Hill. By the late 1890s, caroling had become an annual event in a number of communities. Some 150,000 wandering singers toured Boston's streets in 1895. Hackensack, New Jersey, saw a similar venture. Within another twenty years the tradition had spread throughout the United States. A 1918 survey by the National Bureau for the Advancement of Music found thirty cities with community carol singing, but by 1928, 2000. [13]

Just as caroling revealed the nation's, and especially its ministers', aptitude for creating music that resonated with strains of American optimism and avoided the mire of history and social condition, the popularity of the Christmas tree illustrated the way in which the same culture modernized and reinterpreted "foreign" traditions to make them its own. As trees and ornaments became more widely available in the marketplace, their "German-ness" receded, to be replaced in many cases by a complete acceptance of the tree and rituals associated with it as "American."

The familiar presentation of the Christmas tree provides one illustration of this transition. In diaries and letters home, American travelers recorded their fascination with the way German families assembled on Christmas Eve to admire their lighted and bedecked evergreens. Increasingly, similar scenes could be found in America, but with no reference to Germany or to Germans. One diarist described how "Emily" had spent the entire day decorating the family Christmas tree. In the evening, after a bell had rung, "we were all ushered into the parlor, which was beautifully lighted up with small wax candles placed among the branches of the cedar which stood on the table, with the presents all arranged round it." Patience Price's "Sketch" in *Godey's* explained women's role in staging a proper tree presentation. On Christmas Eve "under the pretence of secrecy," she wrote, "[t]he folding doors [to one parlor] are closed. . . . Only the mother and the eldest daughter are suffered to enter into that sacred and private apartment. . . ." These accounts and others echoed closely the pageants that the Ticknors and Storys had witnessed in Germany and similar descriptions that had appeared in magazines such as *Harper's*. However, they made no self-conscious nod to the foreign antecedents of the rituals. They stressed instead the immediate effect of the tree's unveiling.[14]

Probably most responsible for the "Americanization" of traditions associated with Christmas trees was the growing commonness of the evergreens. By the 1880s, New York City's Washington Square bristled with trees cut upstate and hauled to town for seasonable profits. The *New York Tribune* estimated in 1881 that 200,000 trees had been supplied to the city's markets. By 1900, one American in five was estimated to have a Christmas tree. In some places, nearly everyone did. In the South and West, however, trees were less common, in many cases not used until the twentieth century.[15]

The absence of a Christmas tree often meant only that one could not be found, not that the custom was unknown or had been found wanting. One plantation mistress recalled having to put up an althea bush because no evergreens were available. On the tree-bare American plains the under-taking proved even more difficult. None of the children in North Madison, Iowa, saw a Christmas tree until 1872, when a townsman charged each $1 per viewing. Citizens of Westport, Missouri, saw their first full-sized Christmas tree in 1882, and then only with the aid of Oswald Karl Lux, a cabinet-maker and recent German settler. He had tried to purchase a tree both in Westport and Kansas City, but could not find one over a foot and a half tall, and its branches were too flimsy to hold ornaments. Undaunted, Lux built a tree using a broomstick for the trunk and the curved staves of a barrel keg for the branches, which he wrapped in red paper, tipped with rolled tinfoil, and draped with evergreen branches. In any case, by 1930, Christmas trees were nearly a universal sight throughout the United States. [16]

The decorations that made a tree of any sort a Christmas tree and set it apart from nature reflected the same American willingness to improvise if necessary. Nuts and popcorn, the staples of tree ornamentation, gave way to more sophisticated homemade items or imported ones, the old form overtaken by the urge to make the tree a showpiece for the artistic arrange-ment of "glittering baubles, the stars, angels, &C." A resourceful hand might add beads, oranges, lemons, or candies to the homemade trinkets used to decorate a tree. Even the casual reader could easily find tips for further improvements. *Godey's* "Work Department," for example, displayed "Articles for Christmas Trees, Easily Made at Home" in its 1874 December issue. It included bags for sweets, pincushions, and ornamental pen wipers. A small Pennsylvania paper reported that "[c]otton-wool dipped in thin gum arabic and then in diamond dust makes a beautiful frosting" for tree branches. [17]

Import trade afforded even greater possibilities for creating a stunning tree. Around the mid-1860s, Germans introduced the first glass ornaments and icicles into the nation. The description, which appeared in *Harper's Bazaar* (1869), of the fragile glass ornaments that Santa Claus unpacked from his bag gives a clue to why they became so sought after. His treasures included "globes, fruits, and flowers of colored glass, bright tin reflectors, and innumerable grotesque figures suspended by a rubber string." He also took out "clowns with cap and bells, funny little men concealing their faces behind funnier masks . . . Bismarck leaping up Napoleon's shoulders, exaggerated seraphim with flapping wings, and strange-looking old women with heads larger than their bodies." [18]

American businesses quickly perceived the profit potential in selling tree ornaments. As early as 1870 they had begun to import large quantities of all kinds to be sold on street corners and later in toy shops and variety stores. Often these trimmings only replicated home designs of icicles, pine cones, and sweet treats. Doily-lined paper cornucopias, brimming with nuts and candies, became a favorite, but angels and numerous designs in tin also had their partisans. Toy wholesalers such as Amos M. Lyon and Erlich Brothers, both in New York, listed glass beads and balls in assorted bright colors, glass ornaments in all imaginable shapes, tinsel, candleholders, transparent gelatin lanterns, wax angels with spun glass wings, gilt paper, small silk and puffed-satin candy boxes, and even white cotton batting for snow in their Christmas gift catalogues. "So many charming little ornaments can now be bought ready to decorate Christmas trees that it seems almost a waste of time to make them at home," an advertisement in the *Pottsville* (Pennsylvania) *Miners' Journal* declared in 1881.[19]

As tree ornamentation changed to reflect international trade, American taste, and modern invention, the illumination of the tree advanced from a few wax candles to a fine art. One guideline recommended 400 candles for a 12-foot tree. The spectacular effect of all those lighted candles, though, was dangerous. Trees bought at city stands were seldom as fresh as the ones newly cut from nearby woods, and the wooden houses they graced proved to be flammable tinder. Each year newspapers reported lurid details of deaths caused by the flames of unwatched candles. Fiction writers added accounts of tree blazes to their tales. Consequently a set of informal rules came to govern tree lighting. In one family, for instance, each member stood ready with a bucket of water as grandfather lit the candle wicks. Other kept blankets near to smother flames should the water prove inadequate. Candles burned but a few minutes, enough for the sensation of their light to be registered, and then were quickly snuffed.[20]

One way to lessen the danger of fire was to find an effective way to fasten candles to a tree's branches. They needed to be upright and steady so that they neither dripped on the floor nor ignited the tree. Originally, candles had been wired onto branches or put in tin holders with sharp points that stuck into the wood. Neither method really worked, giving rise to many ingenious improvements. In 1867, American Charles Krichholf patented a counterweighted candleholder. A weight hanging decoratively below the branch balanced the candle above. Unfortunately, his invention doubled the heaviness of the candle and caused tree branches to droop dangerously. Frederick Arzt, a New Yorker, solved the problem in 1879 with his invention of a spring-clip holder. It did not keep candles as straight as Krichholf's, but they stayed on, and the gadget remained popular until the 1920s, when candles finally went out of fashion. [21]

Despite efforts to make candle light safer for Christmas trees, none of the measures proved reliable. Fires became so common and costly that finally, in 1908, a number of insurance companies announced that they would no longer pay for fires started with candles and trees, and began invoking a standard clause that invalidated a policy if the holder took "knowing risks." [22]

The real solution to the fire problem, of course, was electricity. At least among those wealthy enough to afford their own generators and those who lived in districts served by Edison Electric, electric lights quickly replaced common candles. Edward Johnson, who lived within the first square mile of New York City to have electricity, claimed in 1882 to be first to add electric lights to his tree. As vice president of the newly formed Edison Electric, he had small bulbs hand-blown and hand-wired in the company laboratory. Not long after, in Reading, Pennsylvania, "big-hearted Robert H. Coleman and his many employees," enjoyed a 25-foot tree lit with "220 two-candle power electric lamps. . . . A dynamo run by water-power in the basement of the building," reported the local paper, supplied electricity for it. By then, Edison Electric had taken up the manufacture of light bulbs, the rights to which it sold to General Electric in 1890. And by 1895, electric lights had even replaced candles on President Cleveland's White House tree. [23]

Electrical wiring, imported glass balls, tinsel garlands, and fancy needlework did not define the tree for all Americans. Ultimately its interpretation depended on individual creators. The heavy concentration of Pennsylvania Dutch in Pennsylvania, for instance, made the local standard for tree decoration quite different from that enjoyed by the Edward Johnsons and J. P. Morgans of New York City. In the 1880s Pennsylvania farmers, whether because of the scarcity of trees, their own thrift, or some idea of vogue, stripped their Christmas trees of needles and stored them for the following year. When the "evergreens" appeared again in parlors, their branches looked snowy in new cotton batting. After the holiday, the trees would again be returned to the attic, this time in a swath of protective newspapers. [24]

In this same region, many households created elaborate landscapes beneath Christmas trees, a fashion that existed throughout the late century and at least into the first decade of the twentieth. Some went so far as to transform their front rooms in bowers, abundantly decked with greenery.

Others made "landscapes, . . . a succession of hill and dale, rustic bridge and charming rivulet. This last," one contemporary news article noted, "is rarest and prettiest of them all; rarest because few people have the proper room and requisite degree of artistic taste to form one, and prettiest because most like nature." It was not uncommon for these showpieces to feature earthen hills, three to five feet tall, covered with snow or moss. One house had a mountain, achieved with an estimated half ton of rocks, in its front room. Some boasted streams, waterfalls, and miniature fountains that required a cistern to be temporarily erected in the room above.[25]

Through such extravagance of design and dedication, Christmas trees ceased to be solely (if they ever had been entirely) objects of private delight. Many of their creators constructed them for public display, albeit in a private setting. John Lewis, an Englishman who spent Christmas 1875 in Philadelphia with his son, took this as a characteristic of the entire nation. "The usual arrangement in this country," he wrote, was to place in the parlor as "large & fine a tree" as could be found and cover it "with every conceivable shape into which coloured & gilt paper & card can be cut, and little pictures, glass balls, chains, garlands, etc., anything to make a gay and imposing display." As fancy dictated, other attractions might be added. At one place Lewis visited, the owners proudly illuminated a complicated scene that included a tree plus a "very handsome," three-foot-long river steamboat made of white, colored, and gilt cards and carrying "about 50 passengers (these last small pictures cut out)" and a "beautiful fire hose carriage."[26]

Owners kept window blinds raised and brightly lighted their elaborate scenes, allowing the passersby a full view. "Frequently people would knock at the door to be admitted to a closer inspection." Lewis had heard that in two hours' time, 75 spectators had toured a single house. Women, it seemed, were particularly interested, a fact attested to by one Pennsylvanian. Over one hundred people had called to see his tree. "These visitors were almost equally divided between women and children — the men forming a very small proportion. Squads of ladies — as high as ten in number — are to be seen daily going their rounds 'among the trees.'"[27]

Adopted into many households and trimmed according to the dictates of local fashion, the Christmas tree had been Americanized. Its adoption also became an index of cultural assimilation. Christmas trees "bloomed" even in the homes of "the Hebrew brethren," noted a Philadelphia newspaper in 1877. "[T]he little ones of Israel were as happy over them as Christian children. One of them said: 'Oh, we have the trees because other people do.'" In other cases, the tree as much revealed a lack of integration into American culture. A newspaper reporter took an amused and patronizing look at a tree he had discovered in New York City, in the section known as Little Germany. He had spied a tree as tall as a house. It proved to be a butcher's sign, complete with flashing lights, showing off holiday stock. "Pine branches were fastened to the naked limbs of a tree, and rabbits, poultry, links of sausage, and torches were hung all over it."[28]

In 1898, the *New York Times* distinguished between the ways of rural ethnic populations and the sophistication of the city. "Finery," it reported, had "but little place on the country Christmas tree." On farms near Reading, Pennsylvania, they could be found decorated with "[h]uge honey cakes, ginger cakes," some of them "several feet square and made attractive by sprinklings of red, white and blue sugars," and resembling "great fat hogs, sheep, rabbits, cats, horses, cows and other farm life." Stuffed squirrels and chipmunks perched on the branches, "while grouped around the base of the tree are opossums, raccoons, and occasionally, a large red or gray fox." All were trimmed with "brilliant-hued home-made taffy, large red apples and Winter pears, with a sprinkling of shell barks, chestnuts and other productions of the farm."[29]

Few people voiced serious objections to the place of the Christmas tree in the holiday, however. Indeed, whatever reservations remained seemed to have narrowed to a point of preference for hanging Christmas stockings over putting gifts beneath trees. A *New York Times* editorial had called the Christmas tree "a rootless and lifeless corpse – never worthy of the day," and predicted that stockings would replace the evergreen. But a Pennsylvania newspaper reported in 1874 that Christmas trees had "ruled the hanging up of stockings out of order." Another asked, "Is it more stylish to have Christmas trees for the children than to let the little creatures hang up their stockings as their grandmother did?" "No, no," it answered. "We all do as we please in the matter. The high fashion authorities are silent here." And so it seemed to remain a matter to be settled within the family. In 1893 a Brooklyn woman, questioned as to whether she celebrated Christmas with a tree or with her children hanging their stockings, replied, "My husband's people always have a tree, but I was brought up to celebrate in the other fashion, and so we hang up ah – er – We hang up our hosiery."[30]

Some families still arranged their holiday rituals around the old Dutch custom of hanging Christmas stockings. One Connecticut family began Christmas Eve by tying a short rope between two doors in the sitting room. Then, according to one of the youngsters, each of the nine children "brought out, our largest pair of stockings, not forgetting two extra pair, intended for Father and Mother," and pinned them together on the rope. The task completed, the family climbed into the double carriage and, "in spite of wind and snow, all of us went down town, through the crowded streets, and afterward the brilliantly lighted stores, to buy our last gifts, and see the many dazzling sights, of a large city on Christmas Eve." Returning before midnight, each placed newly purchased gifts in the various stockings, and went to bed. "Next morning, early, we went down stairs. . . . [U]nderneath on the floor, were many boxes and bundles with strings tied to each, and the other end of the string fastened to the stocking belonging to the one for whom it was intended. The tips of Ollies stockings rested on this firm foundation, but nothing of the other's could be seen below the ankle, they being packed away among the numerous packages."[31]

While decorating a Christmas tree and hanging a stocking in anticipation of Santa's visit had antecedents in the past, these rituals also reflected the capacity within many American families to adapt customs to conform to their needs and expectations about the holiday. Thus, a family's tradition could be at one and the same time novel and old. Sending Christmas greeting cards, however, was an almost entirely new idea. But Americans approved the practice with the same zeal they did other Christmas traditions.

Christmas cards became essential to fostering friendships and business acquaintanceships. Senders often resorted to them instead of honoring the old customs of writing Christmas letters or making personal holiday visits. Carrying a full supply of ready-made sentiment, a card could lighten one's own workload and free the sender to claim (or disavow) the sentiments written on a greeting card as solely his or her own. Cards also substituted for gifts. "[W]ornout from choosing gifts" for old friends and school mates, one writer noted, "we usually fall back on Christmas cards, which constitute one of the most precious and at the same time inexpensive contributions of these latter days to the neglected cause of sentiment." A new emphasis on formality and manners added to the importance of Christmas greeting cards.[32]

Moreover, increased geographic mobility sometimes made sending cards the only way in which families and friends remained in contact. Following the Civil War, as Congress standardized delivery, mail traveled more rapidly, dependably, and cheaply than it ever had before, taking huge quantities of Christmas cards throughout the nation. "I thought last year would be the end of the Christmas card mania, but I don't think so now," the *Washington Star* quoted one postal official as saying in 1882. "Why four years ago a Christmas card was a rare thing. The public then got the mania and the business seems to be getting larger every year. I don't know what we will do if it keeps on." By the mid-1890s, publishers had begun to print Christmas greetings on their view cards, either as an over-print or as part of the design. These novel and cheap postcards only accelerated the frenzy of sending holiday messages. [33]

The cards that Americans preferred to send came from the printing presses of Louis Prang. Born in Breslau, Germany, in 1824, Prang left Germany after the 1848 revolution, arrived in New York in 1850, and soon moved to Boston. After several years of working first for himself and then as a wood engraver in the art department of *Gleason's Pictorial*, he entered into a partnership with Julius Mayer to become a lithographic and copper plate manufacturer. An astute reader of public taste, Prang became sole owner of the business in 1860, renamed it L. Prang and Company, and became known as a printer of business cards, announcements, mailing labels, and forms of small advertising. He also ventured into a new area— album cards and pictures. From this came a series of four oversized cards, "Prang's Illuminated Christmas cards," which Prang intended to decorate homes and Christmas trees. [34]

By 1868, Prang owned perhaps half of the steam presses in America and, by 1870, two-thirds of the total, a success that reflected Prang's business acumen and dedication to the art of printing. He already had improved significantly the quality of his prints by using an expensive new multi-color lithographic printing process that he himself had perfected. He seldom used fewer than eight colors and sometimes as many as twenty to produce some of the finest color "chromo" prints to date. In 1873, he made another improvement on the process, switching from stones to zinc plates. [35]

Having created a thriving business, Prang was ready to enter the international market. He printed a good supply of his own business cards, decorated them with flowers, and went to the 1873 Vienna International Exhibition. So popular were his cards that by the end of the visit he had distributed over 20,000. The following year, on the suggestion of the wife of his London agent, Prang added a Christmas greeting to the cards. He introduced these illustrated Christmas greetings into the United States in 1875, where they proved such a hit that he could not meet demand. The second season found Prang much better prepared. His work force of 300 people began printing over 5 million cards yearly, many for export. [36]

A family at Christmas, from the sketchbook of Lewis Krimmel, c. 1810. Courtesy, The Winterthur Library: Joseph Downs Collection of Manuscripts and Printed Ephemera.

"The Christmas Tree," by F. A. Chapman.

Santa Claus paying his usual Christmas visit to his young friends, *Harper's Weekly,*
December 25, 1858. The Institute of Texan Cultures, San Antonio, Texas.

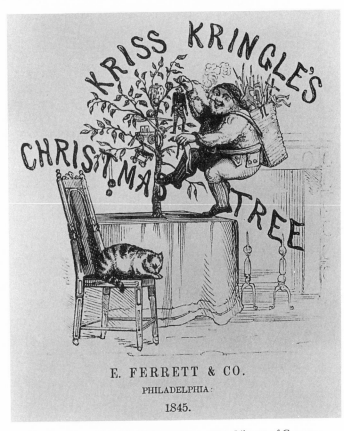

Title page, *Kriss Kringle's Christmas Tree,* 1845. Library of Congress.

"Santa Claus and His Works," by Thomas Nast, *Harper's Weekly*, December 29, 1866.

Center illustration from "Santa Claus and His Works."

"The Children's Corner at the Centennial Exhibition of Dolls and Toys," by Theodore R. Davis, 1877.

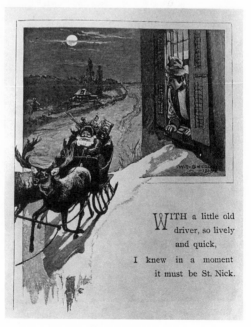

An illustration by William T. Smedley for The Night Before Christmas by Clement Clarke Moore, published by Porter and Coats, Philadelphia, 1883.

WITH a little old driver, so lively and quick,
I knew in a moment it must be St. Nick.

"A Wintry
Christmas Greeting
to You. The cherished fields
put on their winter robe
of purest white."
Christmas card printed by
Prang and Co., 1883.

"Childhood's Faith in Santa Claus—The Christmas Letter," *Frank Leslie's Illustrated Newspaper*, 1887.

Christmas tree with gifts stacked beneath it in downtown Austin, Texas, near the beginning of this century. Austin History Center, Austin Public Library, Austin, Texas.

Workmen receiving their pay on the construction site of Rockefeller Center, New York, N.Y., Christmas Eve, 1931. Photo courtesy of Rockefeller Center. © The Rockefeller Group, Inc.

Although new, Prang's Christmas cards hailed from along line of greetings. Egyptians and Romans apparently sent messages along with their New Year's gifts. As Christianity took hold, these messages became religious. The practice in general declined during the sixteenth and seventeenth centuries, but a version of the old custom resurfaced in the eighteenth century, minus the religious element, in the form of a card offered to announce a visitor. If the intended recipient was not at home, the called scribbled a message on a card, thereby making it a token of good wishes and obviating the need to call in person. Especially in Austria, Germany, and France, industries specialized in extravagant calling cards ornamented with lace, silk, and engraving.[37]

Illustrated visiting cards, along with widely popular advertising quodlibets, illustrated notepaper, Christmas letter headings, Valentines, and other paper goods, inspired the format of the earliest Christmas cards. However, the actual invention of the Christmas card, according to the claims of an English historian of the subject, took place in England. One, perhaps the first, bore a handwritten note, "A Happy Christmas to my dear mother 1839." The best-known of the "first" cards was that of painter and illustrator John Calcott Horsley. About the size of a lady's calling card, his featured a portrait of a happy family. Smaller pictures of the poor and hungry banked it on both sides. "A Merry Christmas and a Happy New Year to you" overarched the scenes.[38]

R. H. Pease, an engraver, lithographer, and variety store owner who lived in Albany, New York, distributed the first American-made Christmas card in the early 1850s. As in the Horsely card, a family scene—parents and three children with their presents—dominated the small card's center. In the background a black servant set the table for Christmas dinner. But, unlike its English forerunner, the images on each of the card's four corners made no allusion to poverty, cold, or hunger. Instead, pictures of a "small, rather elf-type Santa Claus with fur-trimmed cap, sleigh and reindeer, a ball-room with dancers, the building marked 'Temple of Fancy,' and an array of Christmas presents and Christmas dishes and drinks" suggested the bounty and joys of the season. The two lines of text only emphasized the contrast between the English and American cards—and made Pease's card what some might call typically American. Where the English one wished the season's greetings, the American card added a self-promotional "Pease's Great Varety [sic] Store in the Temple of Fancy."[39]

None of the early makers of Christmas cards, whether English or American, had the vision or inclination to exploit the market. To them, writes one historian, cards "appeared to be merely ephemeral business . . . a temporary vogue." It fell to Prang to create a highly profitable Christmas card industry that catered to American preference. His first Christmas cards did little more than repeat the conventions of Victorian decorativeness and symbolism. Printed on only one side, an elegantly scripted couplet or prose greeting complemented arrangements of flowers, birds, trees, and, occasionally, robin's eggs or butterflies. Only the message was "Christmas-y." A summer flower might appear beneath a winter-barren tree to reflect Christmas's association with the solstice. A red rosebud meant "Pure and Lovely." A red double pink meant "Woman's Love." Sometimes birds were incorporated into the design. Robins had at least two meanings. According to one legend, a bird, trying to ease Christ's suffering on the way to the cross, pulled a thorn from his crown and a drop of blood fell on the robin's chest. Another held that a wren flew to Hell to obtain fire for man, and when he returned, he himself was in flames and a robin rushed to his rescue, scorching his breast.[40]

Prang soon found that Christmas pictures and larger sized cards brought even better returns than the small Victorian ones. Christmas themes edged in seasonal greenery became increasingly evident. In the iconography of Victorian flora, the greenery had special significance. Ivy denoted constancy. Holly, whose sharply pointed leaves were said to frighten away witches and other bad spirits, was considered especially good luck. Because it remained glossy green in winter, holly also symbolized life. It had decorated Episcopal churches since colonial times and had become common in the latter half of the nineteenth century. Santa often wore a sprig of it in his hat. At midcentury many still regarded mistletoe, with its pagan and English connection, a curiosity at best. Nathaniel Hawthorne, while living in Liverpool in 1855, had noticed branches of it throughout his rooming house, and discovered that the maids "did their utmost to entrap the gentlemen boarders . . . [in order] to kiss them, after which they were expected to pay a shilling." Before the century ended, mistletoe twined gracefully with holly leaves on Christmas card borders. Poinsettias appeared not much later. The red-crowned plants could be found in select greenhouses as early as the 1830s, but in 1870 New York shops began selling them at Christmas. By the turn of the century they had become fully associated with the holiday.[41]

As Prang added Christmas details to his cards, he also enlarged them to 6″ × 8″ and 7″ × 10,″ made the verses longer, and decorated both sides. The larger and more detailed could be purchased with or without wide silk fringe, the hallmark of an elegant greeting card. His artists, many of them women, drew children in snowy sledding scenes, girls with gift dolls, penguins on ice, and mishaps of skaters. One card depicted a little girl, beautifully drawn, kneeling in front of a fireplace, praying. Above her, Santa Claus with hand to ear, listened to every word. Underneath it read: "Good Saint Santa, grant, I pray, / To All a Merry Christmas Day." Another, in sepia monochrome, showed six children and two white doves framed by holly leaves and berries and a bit of mistletoe. Each dove carried a blue streamer, one inscribed "Joy!" and the other "Mirth!" For these cards, Prang charged from a dime to a dollar, depending on how lavish they were.[42]

Prang did not see his cards solely in terms of their profitability. Far from ordinary, his work exhibited a strong dedication to aesthetic values and set a standard of perfection. English critic Gleason White conceded late in the century that "it is doubtful if any designs this side of the Atlantic [in Europe] were better printed." Prang also refused to make tasteless comic cards or produce trick or mechanical ones. His humorous cards, writes George Buday, "were of the arty, caricature type as opposed to the crude jocularity." Indeed, Prang saw his cards as small works of art, affordable to nearly anyone. He had designed his "Illuminated Christmas cards" (in 1864) as a way to introduce Americans to well-known works of art at reasonable prices, an idea that apparently took his fancy while on a trip to Europe in 1864.[43]

With greeting cards, Prang's plans for the democratization of art expanded. Starting in 1880, Prang sponsored annual competitions for Christmas card designs. Through them he hoped to obtain the best art for his cards, educate public taste, and stimulate an interest in original decorative art among art students. He encouraged entrants with promises of large prizes and a chance to be included in an exhibition at the American Art Association Galleries in New York. Competitors ranged from the ambitious but untrained and untalented to some who would later become important figures in American art, Thomas Moran and J. Alden Weir among them.[44]

Many regarded the contest as the top event of the New York art season, and for artists, it brought recognition and employment. If Prang used an entry for a card, he added the initial of the card's designer and details of the contest on the finished greeting. However, the competitions did not meet Prang's expectations. He thought that they "call[ed] forth a good deal of original talent" but that they resulted "to a great extent . . . [in] very crude efforts."[45]

Nonetheless, Prang's determination to use cards as a vehicle of public art education persisted. In the third contest (1882), he approved a two-part competition limited to American artists. Artists and art critics awarded $2000 for the category "Artist's Prizes." Popular vote determined the winner of the "Public Prizes," which carried a second purse of $2000. By the fourth competition, Prang had all but abandoned his idea for promoting the public's talent and decided instead to concentrate on an appreciation of artists. He commissioned twenty-two well-known American artists to design cards and also invited them to enter their same designs in his competiton. [46]

While Prang's card competitions may have failed in their original purpose, they had an unintended effect. They so popularized Christmas cards that other card manufacturers entered the market. "[A]fter 3 or 4 years," wrote Prang, the competition of European imitators "began to press upon me." (Charles) Goodall & Son, Marcus Ward, Joseph Mansell, and Dean & Sons emerged as the best-known English producers of Christmas cards. James A. Lowell and Company of Boston printed cards noted for their fine steel engravings during the 1880s. In the 1890s, German stand-up cards and trade-card greetings dominated the field. Low wages and cheaper materials, Prang declared, "made it impossible to battle successfully against foreign competition in the same line." So, in 1890 Prang withdrew from the card business entirely and turned his attention to the promotion of the "Prang method of education," which focused on developing an artistic awareness in the young, and to the manufacture of art supplies. [47]

When Charles Dudley Warner had written that Americans had rescued the best of Christmas from the past and made Christmas "no doubt" better than the old, he had observed an essential truth about Christmas, but it was only part of the story. What made the "revived Christmas of our time" seem so much better than the old was that it had been entirely Americanized and therefore felt more comfortably familiar. Americans had rewritten its history. Rather than seeing Puritanism as an impediment to the survival of Christmas, the nation's media credited it with refining the holiday. The German influence on Christmas trees faded to a mere footnote once Americans dragged the evergreens into their parlors and decorated them with tinsel and baubles. Christmas carols and Christmas cards also reflected this American penchant for reclaiming customs and traditions as its own. And so, whether an example of "innovative nostalgia," an exercise in "evasive banality," or, perhaps better, a multi-faceted episode of American cultural invention, Christmas in the late nineteenth century became that old-fashioned holiday to which nearly everyone looked forward.

CHAPTER 9

Gilding Christmas:
Gifts, Charity, and Commerce

"Christmas won't be Christmas without any presents," Jo March grum-
bled to her sisters. It had been a hard winter for everyone, and Mrs.
March suggested that the girls not spend money for pleasure when others
suffered while fighting the Confederate army. On Christmas morning each
cherished her only present, a small book found beneath her pillow, and
surrendered the idea of receiving a wealth of gifts. Instead, the March
women took armloads of food and clothing to a needy family—a "poor
woman with a little newborn baby" and six children, who were "huddled
into one bed to keep from freezing, for they have no fire," nor anything to
eat. [1]

These events, which open Louisa May Alcott's *Little Women*, illustrate
the key place that gift-giving had taken among America's Christmas rituals
and allude to the place charity held in it. Through gifts, Americans mediated the fragile relationships of an increasingly unsettled society. Through
charity, they sought at least symbolic solutions to the problems of extreme
economic inequality that threatened social peace and conscience.

Perhaps more than any other element, the rise of commerce and consumerism as a central feature of the American economy determined the
customs of Christmas charity and, more obviously, gift-giving. Earlier in
the century, especially in rural areas and along the frontier, gifts had been
of necessity usually simple and homemade (although youngsters regarded
"store-bought" candy with particular fondness). Commonly, children re-

ceived most of them. Mothers knitted, tied, stuffed, laced, stitched, or baked special treats. Fathers whittled and carved toys. [2]

As the nation became more market-oriented, such homey pleasures sometimes seemed inadequate. Stores and shops throughout the nation offered the consumer an ever-growing feast of choices, nearly any of which might be made a gift. Among those described in nineteenth-century diaries and letters were: a "silver slop basin," a breast pin, a gold pencil, the complete works of Robert Burns, a pocket book, a writing desk, a "beautiful box with writing materials of all kinds," a "case with scissors, thimble etc.," a work box, a knife, slippers for everyone but especially for fathers, a camp chair, "a large bottle of colongne [*sic*], a bottle of liquid court plaster," match boxes, pen wipers, a bonnet, a "beautiful copy of Shakespeare," carbuncle sleeve buttons, a "pretty basket card," a pencil case, a paper case, a velvet bag embroidered with gold, books, marbles, "a morocco case with silver working implements," gold spectacles, camel's hair scarf, a "magnificent silver tea urn," and a "pair of boots worth seven Dollars." No child could resist "Napoleon's Old Guard, the elephant with the moveable head," a train set, a big doll, or "a little chair." [3]

By late century, the definition of gift had broadened to include every category of practical housewares, novelty items, greeting cards, money, extravagant oddities, and simple mementos. There was, in a phrase, something for everyone. Beginning in the 1880s and lasting for many years, cheap and useless novelties known as "gimcracks" enjoyed a vogue. Those seeking more tasteful, but still relatively inexpensive, tokens of goodwill gave Prang Christmas cards. These could be framed, displayed on Christmas trees or on special racks, or made into wallpaper appropriate for home china cabinets. Others turned their attention to more prosaic and efficient wares; household work savers became acceptable gifts for mothers and wives. Parents, aunts, and other well-meaning elders could always rely on a gold piece or a $2 bill as a gift intended to encourage a child's habit of saving. [4]

Meanwhile, gift lists scrolled longer and longer. One young girl covered several pages of a letter to a friend detailing all the treasures she and her family had exchanged and laid out for display. In 1882 President Hayes jotted in his diary that his wife, Lucy, had given presents "to all of her Sunday-school scholars, to all of the servants, and to many friends. Also presents enough to us. . . . " "People are making smaller presents to more persons," one store manager observed. "Where a man would come in years ago and say, 'Give me twenty-five yards of $4 silk,' and sent it to his favorite maiden aunt for a present, he'll buy twenty $5 presents for all his sisters and cousins as well as his aunts."[5]

It would be erroneous to assume, however, that the new marketplace alone determined the importance of Christmas gifts. Several studies of gift-giving in the twentieth century suggest that the custom helps chart and establish hierarchies of social relationships. Gifts act as tangible evidence of ties between and among individuals. Those who participate in a gift trans-action determine the worth of an item. David Cheal, for instance, writes that the choice and presentation of gifts "is in fact constitutive of a differen-tiated gift economy." He demonstrates this point by noting "that the most valuable Christmas gifts are given to close family members, especially spouses; and that women are more active in all forms of gift giving than are men." He interprets women's greater involvement in the process as a "consequence of their participation in a discourse of relationships," not their experience as homemakers. Mihaly Csikszentmihalyi and Eugene Rochberg-Halton concentrate on objects rather than people, but derive a compatible conclusion. They assert that kinship is a major theme in deter-mining the value of an object. Cherished objects, they write, "provide continuity in one's life and across generations." Michael Schudson's work on advertising confirms the power of material objects to preserve intangible relationships. He argues that "we consume materials very often to preserve families." In what he calls our "materials-intensive way of life," a gift often serves as a "social statement."[6]

In addition to materialism, then, it may well have been the need to demonstrate more vividly kinship ties and communal bonds that insured the importance of Christmas gifts. The Gilded Age was a time of particu-larly challenging social and economic upheaval. Immigration, poverty, and urban crowding, the growth of titanic business organizations and massive personal fortunes, graft, political corruption, labor unrest—all part of the era's history—made personal relationships and associations of home and family all the more dear because of the stability they implied.

Gifts symbolized and helped secure these ties. In an 1875 story in *Godey's*, "The Holly Wreath," Ino Churchill commented that gifts made "invisible chaplets . . . a 'mystical cordage' wherewith to bind heart to heart." *Harper's* had expressed a similar sentiment in 1856: "Love is the moral of Christmas. . . . What are the gifts but the proofs and signs of love?" And because social structure had become as complex as the world around it, gifts helped distinguish the nuances within that structure. Thus, Christmas presents became an important language through which to express, maintain, and differentiate a hierarchy of personal association.[7]

The expansion of gift-giving, what has too often been seen as a one-sided "hype" of a traditional holiday by commercial interests, resulted from the closely connected, reciprocal, and always escalating relationship between consumerism and Christmas. Evidence suggests the transition to a Christmas economy in many instances happened only gradually, as demand crept up on merchants. Starting in the mid- to late 1850s, during the take-off phase of that economy, some imaginative importers, craftspeople, and storekeepers began consciously to reshape the holiday to their own ends even as shoppers elevated the place of Christmas gifts in their home holiday. A brief look at F. W. Woolworth's life illustrates the way in which savvy and innovative business people profited from Christmas.[8]

At the beginning of his career, Woolworth had coaxed a small Philadelphia factory owner to sell him his entire stock of gold tinsel garlands and tree ornaments (which had already been contracted for by other buyers). Bigger Christmas profits awaited him when an importing firm persuaded him to stock some German-made glass ornaments. "[T]he first thing they did," Woolworth remembered, "was to drag out a lot of colored glass ornaments the like of which I had never before seen." When the importer explained that they were "oh, such fine sellers," Woolworth laughed. He acceded only when the company guaranteed his sale of twenty-five dollars' worth of them. With "a great deal of indifference," Woolworth put them on the counter of his small store. In two days they were gone and, as Woolworth said, he "woke up."[9]

So well did the glass balls sell that Woolworth began to make trips to small towns in the Thuringian forest of Germany to buy the fragile decorations. There, Woolworth boasted, he was "pointed out on every corner of the street as the big buyer of tree ornaments and they tackle me everywhere trying to sell me more. . . ." On his visit to Germany in 1890, Woolworth placed an order for 1500 gross of Christmas tree ornaments. These rapidly sold in America, making Woolworth even richer than before.[10]

Woolworth would not have met with such success had Americans not been ready for and demanding the wares he had to sell. Of course, advertising and an increasing variety of stores and services tailored to holiday shopping helped create the milieu in which he could benefit. As early as the 1820s, '30s, and '40s, merchants had already noticed the growing role of gifts and laid in additional wares to be sold during the holiday-rich winter season. In the postbellum era, these efforts changed in magnitude and intensity. What had been the interest of individuals became an under-taking of commerce and industry, and what had been a somewhat modest reaping of December profit spiraled to a windfall as merchants increasingly became more organized, competitive, and aggressive in their bid for the Christmas dollar. They created new schemes for expanding the Christmas market. They opened new stores, advertised new wares, and extended special attention to holiday customers, for, as *Godey's* pointed out in 1866, "Christmas brings profit and pleasure to the vast world of dealers in beauti-ful futilities."[11]

Merchants had begun to advertise some seasonal goods in small newspa-per notices early in the century (although news text only rarely mentioned holidays or gifts even as late as the 1840s). Intermittently throughout the 1820s, New York and Philadelphia papers advertised New Year's and holiday presents. By the mid-'30s, even frontier Missouri papers carried holiday sales notes. In 1849, the weekly *Fort Smith* (Arkansas) *Herald* listed raisins, almonds, horehound, and ketchup for sale as "Christmas and Holliday Articles." St. Louis companies offered silver snuff boxes, earrings, finger rings, breast pins, and "fancy inkstands."[12]

As the nation's market economy grew, larger advertisements, illustrated and adjective-laden, overshadowed modest two- and three-line notices. The *Augusta Chronicle* printed one of its first major holiday advertisements the day before Christmas in 1845. A three-column, six-inch engraving, displaying unusually large type, announced that F. Lamback's Lafayette Hall would be open that day to offer "Christmas and New Year's presents. . . . A variety of rich and fancy articles, suitable for the holidays." In 1859 the *Wilmington* (North Carolina) *Daily Journal*, which had carried only one or two advertisements for holiday presents each season in prior years, ran an outsized pitch for a "Beautiful and appropriate Christmas gift"—a Singer sewing machine—and illustrated it with a picture of a woman at work.

In December 1856, *Godey's* canceled, for the first time, its usual domestic discourse. "Our business friends demand some of our space . . . and as [Christmas] is the season most favorable to their business, we are glad to lend a helping hand," it explained. Therein, Tyndale & Mitchell's promised "every variety of China-ware." Brodies' advertised "Mantillas, Talmas, &c." E. W. Carryl suggested housekeeping items. C. Oakford & Sons offered "Furs, caps for children, hats for gentlemen." White & Co. tendered fashionable clothing. Upon receipt of a letter, George Fischer promised he would "pick out such toys as will suit" the needs of parents for their children.[13]

All the while, commerce was becoming more dependent upon Christmas sales. Toy stores, which had multiplied rapidly since the 1850s, offered playthings from all over the world. Christmas was their busiest time. Music supply houses and commercial Sunday-school houses issued Christmas "services," that is, songs, recitation pieces, and inspirational cantatas, to turn themselves a profit. The holiday, reported the *Democratic Review* in 1854, had "recently become a great harvest for the booksellers, in enabling them to dispose of large numbers of their books . . . during the Holydays."[14]

By late century, store owners had developed a number of strategies that made the Christmas season more enjoyable for buyers and, not incidentally, more lucrative for themselves. For example, they raised Christmas-dressed store windows to an art form that enchanted thousands. "One of the signs of the approach of Christmas," reported the *New York Tribune* in 1882, was the crowds of "sidewalk spectators" that gathered around the windows to watch mechanical toys. Lydia Maria Child noticed that one Boston store owner kept up his "frantic competition for popular favor" by transforming his display window into a snowy fairyland complete with a stout Santa Claus "in a carriage drawn by stuffed rein-deers." Early each December Macy's installed a Christmas exhibition of hundreds of mechanical toys and dolls and in 1883, apparently for the first time, added the novelty of steam-powered, moving figures. Santa Clauses also made their appearance in shop windows. D. M. Williams & Co. advertised that "A Real Live Santa" appeared daily at its store or in its show windows that recreated his workshop. F. W. Woolworth directed the clerks and managers of his chain of variety stores to give their emporia a "holiday appearance." He suggested they hang Christmas ornaments and perhaps put a tree in the window. "Make the store look different. . . . This is our harvest time. Make it pay."[15]

Many businesses kept late hours in order to make holiday shopping easier. In 1867 Macy's stayed open until midnight on Christmas Eve, taking in over $6000. "Such a crowd as I never before saw in a store," wrote Macy's partner, Abiel T. LaForge. The store continued to stay open until ten or eleven o'clock each season, later if the crowds warranted. In Atlanta, Rich's did not lock its doors until nine in the evening. Bloomingdale's, boasting that its "assortments and facilities [were] equal to the greatest task of the year," took out a full-page advertisement in 1894 to announce that it would stay open late for holiday buyers. One could shop at Barrios Diamond Company anytime, since it planned to be "Open All Night" on Christmas Eve. Package delivery improved too. By 1888 Macy's was guaranteeing that purchases made on December 24 would be delivered within the city on the same day or, if desired, on Christmas Day. The following December their messengers took 162,624 gifts to doorsteps throughout New York City. [16]

For all the efforts of businessmen to exploit and shape the season to meet profit goals, or perhaps despite them, Americans persisted in their attempts to separate the influence of commerce from the gifts they gave. Within the gift economy, handmade gifts ranked above purchased ones. Nearly every December *Peterson's*, *Godey's*, and other magazines supplied detailed instructions for knitting comfortable bedroom slippers and cozy shawls, fabricating pen wipers, and creating other homey or useful items. At least in the abstract, hand-worked items epitomized the care and loving thoughts of the giver and were therefore thought to be superior to manufactured ones. They had the bonus of revealing a woman's conscientious use of her own time and saving of her husband's money. Well into the twentieth century, such efforts continued to be held in high regard. As A. L. Gorman asserted in 1908, in *Harper's Bazaar*, "Gifts which are the product of one's own handiwork are generally the most highly prized for they carry with them the sweet assurance of many moments of painstaking effort and loving thoughts with every stitch and stroke." [17]

Yet the effect of commerce even on handmade gifts could hardly be avoided. By the 1880s it had become fashionable to purchase partially assembled goods to which givers applied their personal, finishing touches. Handkerchiefs that needed hemming, furniture that needed assembling, and patterns still to be colored with embroidery stitches became mainstays of many cottage industries. These so-called "halfway" gifts effectively combined the appeal of mass-produced goods. They did not take too much time to complete, but displayed attributes of a hand-worked gift. [18]

Another way in which Americans moderated the relationship between commerce and giving was by wrapping the gifts they gave. The custom had once been merely to give a gift unadorned and uncovered, a straightforward tribute to the bonds of amity and obligation. A present hidden in paper or some other guise heightened the effect of the gesture, helping to fix the act of giving to a moment of revelation. Children thrilled to find their gifts tied to a tree, tucked beneath their dinner plates, or jammed in the toes of stockings. Alice James recalled her disappointment when, with the encouragement of her father, Henry Sr., she and her brothers annually searched out the hiding places of their Christmas gifts before the 25th. In 1902, Wells-Fargo Company made this excitement of anticipation a staple of the American Christmas when, to lessen the usual crush of business the week before Christmas, it supplied printed labels reading "DO NOT OPEN UNTIL CHRISTMAS."[19]

The drama of surprise led to proposals that gifts might be made better by more elaborate ruses. At one point, *Godey's* suggested burying wrapped presents in a tub filled "with either bran or sawdust." Allowing the children to "dip" for the gifts, the editor argued, would "afford as much amusement, and give far less trouble than a Christmas tree." (The tip might have been especially appealing to women for, as the editor pointed out, the time consumed in preparation would be much less than for a Christmas tree.) By the 1880s givers had begun routinely to enfold their treasures in white paper, fastened with sealing wax and straight pins. Indeed, the romantic and decorative impulse of the late Victorian era favored the practice of covering nearly everything in a household. It decreed, for example, that lace, velvet, and fringes be draped fashionably over every stick of furniture. Understandably, this criteria applied also to gifts and demanded that even they should be shrouded.[20]

Wrapping also helped designate an item as a gift. As increasingly gifts came from stores, factories, and homes of cottage laborers, paper and string helped redefine an object to meet its social use. Their presence indicated that the item no longer belonged to the realm of the marketplace, but now functioned as a gift to be given. The commercial world also comprehended the importance of this symbolic transformation of goods. The grander stores began to wrap gifts purchased from their stock in distinctive colored papers, tinsel cords, and bright ribbons as part of their delivery service. Thus, while paper might have blurred a present's association with commerce in some cases, in others it advertised a material status associated with patronizing the "right" store.[21]

The dual role of gifts as material evidence of personal ties and as an important source of revenue for commerce and industry did not evolve without conflict and confusion. To choose a gift that appropriately reflected—in value and presentation—the relationship of giver to receiver was an increasingly baffling, costly, and time-consuming task. *The Nation* pinpointed one aspect of the dilemma. Christmas, it noted in 1883, brought "so much mingled hope and dread—hopefulness over dreams of what we may receive, and dread at the thought of what we shall have to give. . . . " Charles Dudley Warner identified another pervasive concern. Believing that "all holidays, the Christian no less than the others, [tended] to go to excess," he predicted that Christmas would "soon become as burdensome as it formerly was by reason of excessive gifts and artificial social observances." "One-half the populace seems possessed of a wild desire to purchase all the things the other half has for sale," a cynical newspaper editor succinctly wrote.[22]

Such quantities of money were expended on Christmas gifts that the *New York Tribune* repeatedly advised its readers not to spend what they did not have. Pay the bills owed the shoemaker and butcher before buying gifts for rich friends, it counseled. Even as early as 1861, a character in "Auntie's Merry Christmas" had paired the problem of paying bills and giving expensive gifts: "'No Christmas presents this year' — every dollar must be saved for that unfortunate debt to Mr. T– –. . . . "[23]

Toward the end of the century, the mad pace and material excess of Christmas had started to wear noticeably on the American public. "The Christmas time I have had 'beggars description,'" John Holmes reflected in January 1889. "Somehow or other Christmas . . . does n't allow you any rest, what with one thing and another. I feel as if I had just returned from a tour on foot to the Rocky Mountains." To him, people seemed "too distracted with sendings and receivings and answerings to enjoy any peaceful satisfaction." The *New York Tribune* concurred, declaring, "[T]he modern expansion of the custom of giving Christmas presents has done more than anything else to rob Christmas of its traditional joyousness. . . . [M]ost people nowadays are so fagged out, physically and mentally, by the time Christmas Day arrives that they are in no condition to enjoy it. . . . As soon as the Thanksgiving turkey is eaten, the great question of buying Christmas presents begins to take the terrifying shape it has come to assume in recent years." In summary, the paper wrote, "the season of Christmas needs to be dematerialized."[24]

The call to "dematerialize" the holiday emphasized the relationship between affluence, which many saw as a reward from God, and Christian duty. Mixing traditional Protestant and American doctrines of individualism with the newer vision of Social Darwinism, many in the Christian community felt that American prosperity was proof and extension of God-ordained success, a link confirmed by lavish Christmas giving. Ministers often used their pulpits to support consumer gain. Rev. Russell H. Conwell, known for his sermon "Acres of Diamonds," and Bishop William

Lawrence, who claimed that "Godliness is in league with riches," pressed home the congruence of virtue and success in the commercial world. Significantly, the liberal minister Edward Everett Hale preached an 1880 Christmas sermon entitled "Christ the Giver." In it he listed the Declaration of Independence, the Constitution, and "modern commerce" as Jesus' gifts to the congregation and mankind.[25]

However, the growing disparity between rich and poor, and especially the heart-rending scenes of urban poverty on the streets amid the riches of Chicago or New York City, also drew concern. Especially ministers and laypersons who proclaimed their loyalty to the Social Gospel thought that individualism had its limits, and that the gulf between the affluent and the impoverished threatened to destroy American society. "What can be done to bring these scattered, diverse, alienated, antipathetic groups of human beings into a real unity?" asked Washington Gladden, a leading proponent of the Social Gospel. "How can all these competing tribes and clans, owners of capital, captains of industry, inventors, artisans, artists, farmers, miners, distributors, exchangers, teachers, and all the rest, be made to understand that they are many members but one body . . . ?" "The business of the Christian Church," he stated, "is to preach and realize here in the earth the Kingdom of Heaven . . . a kingdom of peace and good-will." This kingdom would come when man realized his obligations to his fellow man.[26]

The Social Gospel never significantly transformed the deep, individualistic current in American Christianity into a force to salve the nation's social ills. However, its sentiments combined with more general Christian social themes to redirect a portion of the nation's materialistic leanings toward the less fortunate at Christmas and, at least on a symbolic scale, to earmark gifts as a form of charity. As the *New York Tribune* observed, Americans widely felt "a vague sense that our religion is involved in this matter of trees and stockings. . . . This fever of generosity [to friends, family, and charities] breathes through the paper; it is contagious; the coldest-blooded man begins to glow."[27]

For many Americans, the turn toward others meant only a cheerful holiday interchange with associates or a greeting to strangers on the street. "Certainly no week is so charming as Christmas week," *Harper's* noted in 1864. People wore "a pleasanter expression" because they now had "an interest for others, and not for themselves. They are hastening to spend money, not to make it. . . . It is in giving gifts that the 'good-will' of the Christmas season reveals itself most clearly." *Godey's* noticed a similar phenomenon. "[W]e know nothing more enlivening than a walk through the streets where at this time the show of 'happy human faces' is quite equal to the shining wares in the shop windows."[28]

Although charity and gift-giving clearly emanated from different kinds of social situations and personal motivations, they had comparable effects. Both types of giving acted as cathartic exercises in selflessness. It would not far overreach historical reality to speculate that the same social changes that highlighted gift-giving as a means for reinforcing kin and social bonds at the private level also inspired charitable gifts as a means of, if only symbolically, declaring a unity and safety in society that extended to even the most impoverished.[29]

It was but one more large step to extend those good feelings and generosity to the homeless, hungry, and unemployed and to target Christmas as the time for the amelioration of these conditions. In earlier days, church stewardship had seen to the needy throughout the year, but since the 1830s and '40s the numbers of poor and indigent had multiplied. Ministers might remind their flocks that Jesus preached faith, hope, *and* charity, but the ability of their churches to tend to such fundamental human needs as food and shelter had faltered in the face of growing demand and a qualitatively different sense of relation to the poor and needy. The growth of cities, impermanence of employment, and separation of communities within urban areas made direct aid from individual churches impractical. The clergy extended sympathy, but had begun to see poverty as a social problem of class-divided communities. An emerging sense of a distinct middle-class order further separated the poor from others, in custom and culture as well as geography.[30]

Increasingly, the call for relief emanated from the public pulpits of the media and from local officials, reformers, and state legislators. Magazines, newspapers, pamphlets, and broadsides served as secular agencies for expounding the obligations of the wealthy to help individuals who lived in poverty. And they generally delivered their sermons at Christmas time. In 1848 the *Raleigh Register* encouraged the wealthy to visit the city's sick and destitute, "administering from your abundance to their suffering and wants." "Edward," a character in "Christmas Presents" (1848), posed the challenge in a slightly different way: "How many hundreds and thousands of dollars are wasted on useless souvenirs and petty trifles that might do a lasting good if the stream of kind feelings were turned into a better channel?"[31]

During the antebellum period, stories of compassion and action, while not so difficult to find, did bring to mind the patrician concerns that prompted charitable gestures. "The out of doors public in general are inebriated – in honor of Christmas Eve," George Templeton Strong had written on that day in 1841. Yet he was reluctant to "scold our poor day labourers . . . the 'scum of the Earth'" for their behavior. "If we were in their shoes," Strong wrote, "as devoid of comforts – as inexperienced in all Enjoyments but those of sense – as ignorant – as uncared for – as homeless – as they are," he only hoped that "we should yet be as respectable as moral as decent & as temperate as we are now."[32]

Lydia Maria Child, who longed to have children of her own, had been so moved by one ragged and homeless waif she had encountered at Christmas in 1843 that she became his benefactor. "The watchmen," she wrote to her friend Anna Loring, had "picked up a little vagabond in the street . . . [and] put him in the tombs." He was about ten, too old to go to an orphanage, and "too dirty and disgusting to describe." He said he had lost his way. He had neither father nor mother; his mother used to get drunk and sleep in the streets, but he had not seen her for five years. Child and her husband rescued him. She scrubbed him and gave him new clothes and boots with which he was delighted – "it seemed as if the sun had shone out all over his face." She reported him saying that he would "remember *this* Christmas the longest day I live."[33]

"Unfeeling obtuseness," a phrase from Walter Bagehot's history of the Victorian era, probably more aptly described the general attitude toward the poor in the early nineteenth century than did Child's kindness. But in the latter part of the century, he notes this feeling "was to be corrected by an extreme – perhaps an excessive – sensibility to human suffering. . . . The tradition of benevolence reached its peak and added its powerful influence to that of moral earnestness in promoting Victorian charity and social legislation." In America, media, individuals, and private social agencies, as well as churches, became key to poor relief after the Civil War. Often they premised their calls for sympathy and action on the obligations accrued with wealth. "Does it occur to you as you walk up and down Broadway, in the best of all days of the year, the Christmas days, that actual happiness is for sale in those bright shops – happiness, that is, for those who can enjoy it?" *Harper's Monthly* asked. The text beneath an engraved scene of a Christmas party that appeared in *Godey's* underscored the illustration's visual message as it directed the reader to "Mark the contrast between the guests entering the brilliantly lighted hall and the poor woman and her child at the door."[34]

A sense that there were those who were worthy of relief and those who were not qualified the attention devoted to poverty relief, though. Children almost always deserved aid, as did honest women. Seldom did the same plea go out for men. A seasonal article in the *New York Tribune* implored the public to provide for poor children. In 1877, it reminded readers that most Americans were "Christian people," and advised them to try their best to keep children from being deprived at this time "when they think that all good gifts and gladness come straight from Him whose birthday it is." At the same time, the paper advised the sympathetic to ignore plain street beggars.[35]

When popular stories engaged the topic of charity, they revealed a similar inclination to rescue women and children from poverty. "Christmas for the Rich and Poor," by Annie Frost, told the tale of a woman who on Christmas fifteen years earlier had married against her father's wishes and been disowned. Fate treated her cruelly. Her husband died, leaving her with two children. She fell ill, and her little family's poverty forced the children to beg for whatever warmth and sustenance they could find. On Christmas Eve their quest took them to a prosperous street, where one household took them in. As it turned out, the home belonged to their mother's wealthy father. Upon seeing first his grandchildren and then his daughter, the father forgave the wayward daughter and took them all back into the family.[36]

The sentimentalization of "worthy paupers" at Christmas time, whether in fact or in fiction, did not bring into question the essential structure of the market economy that had, if only indirectly, produced their poverty. Instead, it imbued destitute women and vagabond children with admirable qualities that existed apart from materialism, perhaps even as substitutes for tangible wealth. It also aroused the sympathies of readers by giving a face to poverty, and placed the means of solving the problems of hunger and homelessness in the hands of individuals.

Although the dramatic deliverance from financial poverty figured prominently in Christmas pauper tales, the stories often carried another theme, that of the rescue of a wealthy man from a moral poverty expressed in his cold-heartedness. In the case of "Christmas for the Rich and Poor," the wealthy father/grandfather, who had disowned his own daughter and thereby disowned his grandchildren, won, through the simple act of forgiveness, a much fuller life. The mother and two children, although they suffered from cold and hunger, had never relinquished their warm and sustaining love for each other.

Perhaps more than any other single work, Charles Dickens's *A Christmas Carol* provides the paradigm for the moral attitude and obligation that Americans adopted toward Christmas charity. In 1867, the same year that Sarah Hale declared Christmas the "celestial magnet of brotherhood," Dickens made a second tour of American cities. He needed money and believed that since his work had been widely published and read by Americans, often in editions that had been pirated and for which he had received no royalties, he could realize sizable reward by giving readings. He was not disappointed, and found Americans especially responsive to his recitation of *A Christmas Carol.*[37]

Dickens had written *A Christmas Carol* in 1842, the winter after he had returned from his first visit to America. A "small, bright-eyed, intelligent-looking young fellow, thirty years of age, somewhat of a dandy in his dress," according to one description, he had enjoyed a lavish welcome from Americans already familiar with his stories. For part of his visit, he stayed in the home of Henry Wadsworth Longfellow, who allegedly imparted to Dickens a strong sense of the country's spirit and customs. This included Christmas. Prior to then, Dickens had apparently shown no interest in the holiday. "Although he was constantly organizing entertainments for all times and occasions, it never occurred to him to celebrate Christmas. It was New Year's Day, apparently, that held the first place in his affections," reported the *New York Tribune* in 1900. Only after his visit to America did Dickens begin to give large Christmas parties.[38]

When Dickens returned to England in the summer of 1842, he was desperately short of money. He quickly dreamed up a Christmas story (possibly drawing on his new appreciation for the holiday) and dashed it off just in time for a London paper to serialize it in mid-December. *A Christmas Carol, in Prose, Being a Ghost Story of Christmas* went on the stands on December 19. An immediate and resounding success, the full edition of 6000 copies sold out on the first day.[39]

At first, Americans were less enthusiastic. Dickens's *American Notes for General Circulation* (1842) had wounded national pride. Americans were also smarting from his treatment of them in *Martin Chuzzlewit*, which was currently being serialized. But *A Christmas Carol* proved too compelling to be ignored, and by the end of the Civil War, copies had circulated widely. "Dickens," noted the *New York Times* in 1863, "brings the old Christmas into the present out of bygone centuries and remote manor houses, into the living rooms of the very poor of to-day." The *North American Review* asserted: "His fellow-feeling with the race is his genius." John Greenleaf Whittier thought it a "charming book . . . outwardly and inwardly!"[40]

With the publication of *A Christmas Carol*, Dickens articulated the essence of Christmas in strikingly new terms. Previously, he and others had glorified the past in their telling of Christmas tales. In the Bracebridge stories, Washington Irving had explored the way in which the staging of a nostalgic English Christmas might restore a social harmony and well-being ravaged by modern times. Dickens himself had once approached Christmas in a similar manner. "A Christmas Dinner" in *Sketches by Boz* (1833) pointed out that some people "will tell you that Christmas is not to them what it used to be. . . . " (Dickens, however, advised: "Never heed such dismal reminiscences.") In the *Pickwick Papers* (1837), he idealized the Christmas of eighteenth-century England at Dingley Dell, making it the focus of fond memories, "companionship and mutual good-will," a "season of "hospitality, merriment, and open-heartedness."[41]

But that Christmas no longer existed, if it ever had, especially not for Americans. Irving had realized as much by the time he had finished his Bracebridge stories. George Templeton Strong, the observant New York diarist, recognized the same truth. "O for the times of old England & the Christmas day . . . of three centuries ago," he wrote in 1837. "Those times are most glorious to write about & to dream about—whatever their real character was." But Strong knew that the holiday many imagined Christmas to have been could not exist in his time. If it had, compromises would have to have been made. Merchants would have to keep open house as they used to and in would rush "a mob of promiscuous loafing—Rahag Tahag, & Bohob-tay-d—," breaking glasses and spitting tobacco everywhere. The Yule log would have to burn in the kitchen range or some other "scientific uncomfortable contrivance." No, declared Strong, "Christmas in the glorious antique style" was "irrecoverably gone." Dickens knew that too.[42]

In its place, Dickens provided *A Christmas Carol*. Although it incorporated the familiar feast and conviviality of the "traditional" Christmas, Dickens set his tale of Ebenezer Scrooge's conversion to humanity in the unheated walls of commerce, on dreary city streets, and around the warm hearths of urban homes, away from the baronial countryside: One Christmas Eve, seven years to the day after the death of his partner, Jacob Marley, three Christmas ghosts visit Scrooge. The first takes Scrooge on a journey into distant memories, where the old merchant's tenderer emotions are rekindled. The second spirit, the ghost of Christmas present, transports Scrooge from his cold and dreary bedroom to the homes of Scrooge's nephew and his humble employee, Bob Cratchit, where their families have gathered for Christmas dinner. The third spirit gives Scrooge a glimpse of what his future will be like if he does not learn and act upon what he has just witnessed. [43]

In this tale, past and future affect the most important time, the present. In order to redeem his future, Scrooge has to face his past and repent. His past is hardly a repository for nostalgia, but it is crucial to and even a part of his new self. It is a source of regeneration and salvation. So, on Christmas Day Scrooge rises a new man. He orders the largest turkey delivered anonymously to the Cratchits. To the man who had solicited money from him the day before on behalf of the poor and indigent, he makes a sizable donation. He attends church and then visits his nephew's house, where all have a "wonderful party, wonderful games, wonderful unanimity, wonderful happiness!" The next day Scrooge raises Cratchit's salary and promises to help him with his struggling family. Tiny Tim, Cratchit's lame little son, does not die, as the ghost predicts, and Scrooge becomes "as good a friend, as good a master, and as good a man, as the good old city knows, or any other good old city, town, or borough, in the good old world." [44]

The salvation of Scrooge recalled that of the United States as it emerged from war. Hale, using the language and imagery of family and brotherhood, had pointed out that Christmas symbolized a time of regeneration, when the nation could recapture its past and rededicate itself to the future. In many ways, Dickens sent a similar message; the spirit of Christmas Present accentuated the emotional safety of home. As darkness fell and it began "snowing pretty heavily," Scrooge and his spirit departed from the Cratchits'. In windows along the streets, they saw peaceful domestic scenes, the wonderful "brightness of the roaring fires in kitchens, parlors, and tall sorts of rooms." They observed the "cosy dinner" and the curtains ready to be drawn against the cold and night. Children ran out of houses and into the snow to meet their arriving "married sisters, brothers, cousins, uncles, aunts." These scenes and feelings provided the foundation for redeeming both Scrooge and society's futures. [45]

The redemption of Scrooge underlined the conservative, individualistic, and patriarchal qualities of what came to be known as Dickens's "carol philosophy." It depended on the willingness of a more fortunate individual to look after a less fortunate one. It did not call forth the power of government or any agency to effect changes in an economy that created extremes of poverty and wealth. Instead of offering an antidote to modern depersonalization and greed, the personal patronage that Scrooge bestowed on the Cratchits delineated a narrower interpretation of old forms of noblesse oblige. Where he might have suggested a broader and more tolerant social morality, Dickens relied on a highly personal moral conscience and emphasized individual action. So, after being haunted through what must have seemed to him a nearly interminable night, Scrooge provided the turkey for the Cratchits' Christmas dinner and raised Bob Cratchit's salary. But Cratchit and Tiny Tim had first to demonstrate that they were worthy objects of Scrooge's new found charitable attentions. Moreover, Dickens gave no sign that any other of Scrooge's employees besides Cratchit received an increase in salary. Nor did he indicate that Cratchit's miserable working conditions might improve in other than monetary ways. [46]

However, Dickens's message in *A Christmas Carol* was not simply, or only, "Give to the worthy poor." It involved a significant exchange between giver and receiver. True, Scrooge alleviated Cratchit's dire poverty. But Cratchit, who actually did nothing, gave Scrooge a gift, too, albeit one less concrete; the example of Cratchit's life helped Scrooge realize his own humanity. In fact, the story's message had more to do with Scrooge's rescue from a solitary and miserly life than it did with the Cratchit's poverty of hard currency. The story's real patron proved to be Cratchit, and the wealthy, miserable Scrooge, the recipient. At the story's end, we believe Scrooge to be a better man for being blessed by Tiny Tim and raising Bob Cratchit's wage. Scrooge's reward, as it were, was an intangible calm that he could not find in dreams or in his warehouse, but only in joining the ranks of humankind. Scrooge had undergone a secular spiritual conversion.

In their comprehension of poverty and its solutions, most Americans moved little beyond Dickens. They believed their Christmas generosity praiseworthy. Charles Dudley Warner thought the present American Christmas to be "fuller of real charity and brotherly love, and nearer the Divine intention" than earlier Christmases. The *New York Tribune* found the holiday "hearty and generous-minded, [full of] good-cheer and open-handed hospitality." "Nowhere in Christendom," it contended, "are the poor remembered at Christmas-tide so generously as they are in American cities, especially in our own." [47]

In this glow of self-congratulation, Americans persisted in seeing poor relief as a matter of individual action to be undertaken on much the same terms as gift-giving within the circle of family. That is, Christmas was the time to give. The best and largest gifts went to those closest to the circle's center. The lesser gifts, in descending order of value, went out to relatives and acquaintances of decreasing importance. The worthy poor, as the outermost members of the larger community family, received gifts too, though the least valuable of all the gifts given.

An advertisement Best and Company placed in 1894 illustrated the hierarchy. It suggested that "while busy buying 'things for Christmas'" for your own children, you might think of other children you know who are "less fortunate than your own." It advised that "a gift of serviceable clothing would be more than welcome." The company thoughtfully had supplied a special group of marked-down goods from which to choose. However, it concluded by noting that "For your own children we have the most desireable articles for Holiday Gifts. . . ." By making charity a personal offering that bound giver to recipient, Americans reinforced social unity as well as the status quo across a broad spectrum of income and back-ground.[48]

Still the economic system that created such poverty remained relatively unchallenged. The case was especially paradoxical in businesses where poorly paid Christmas help labored to supply large profits to clever owners and middlemen. Louis Prang, for example, thought women peculiarly suited to doing the delicate coloring his exquisite Christmas cards required and employed them in large numbers. Yet of all the women in the print industry, his received the lowest pay. When Macy's first began staying open in the evenings to serve the holiday trade, it had provided supper money for the workers. One employee remembered watching Abiel La-Forge, part owner of Macy's, escorting with obvious enjoyment a crowd of "cash girls" to a neighboring restaurant. But, during the 1870s at least, Macy's often required its clerks to work into the early morning hours during the hectic holiday rush. Some spent the remainder of short nights asleep on sales counters, using bolts of cloth for pillows.[49]

F. W. Woolworth maintained a consistent attention to his personal profit margin over the interests of employee, supplier, and consumer that exemplified business attitudes associated with the Gilded Age. While buying ornaments wholesale in Lauscha, Germany, Woolworth saw first hand the grim conditions of the trade but showed no signs that he was moved by them. "Tree ornaments," he wrote in a letter home, "are made by the very poorest class there is in Europe and we were obliged to go into their dirty hovels to see what we could use." In one place, he "found a man and a woman in one room with six small children, the youngest not over eight years old, and both man and woman hard at work." "It was the dirtiest and worst smelling place I was ever in," Woolworth continued. "We waded through mud ankle deep up hill and down in search of marbles and tree ornaments all day." For their labor, a typical family of six working six-day weeks to produce tree ornaments to sell to Woolworth earned the equivalent of $3 per week, about what a bricklayer in America made for a day's work.[50]

Woolworth also believed that wages should be kept low in his own stores. In 1892, just before the December rush, Woolworth made explicit his belief. "We pay out more than one third of our annual expenses for salaries," Woolworth announced in the annual letter of 1892. "We must have cheap help or we cannot sell cheap goods." He paid his "girls" $1.50 per week. That December the women employed in one of his stores went on strike for higher wages. Woolworth wrote his managers: "No doubt they take advantage now while we are so busy, and think we will pay the advance. All such girls you should remember when the dull season comes and give them the 'bounce.'"[51]

Nonetheless, employee demands cut into the company's profit margin, an ideal Woolworth set at 40 to 55 percent. By 1899, Woolworth, whose Christmas trade alone for 1899 totaled nearly half a million dollars, had worked out a system of bonuses in which he paid $5 for each year of service with a limit of $25. "Pay this present just before Christmas or the day after," Woolworth directed his managers. "Our object is to secure the services of our clerks at a time of the year when competitors are tempting them with higher wages."[52]

The culture's use of Christmas charity to balance symbolically the rapacious acquisitiveness of the age helped obscure these and other questionable or scandalous labor practices. The rich man was not condemnable if he recognized publicly that his riches meant little compared with his responsibility to humanity. That truth perceived and acted upon in highly public, seemingly generous fashion, he had made his peace. Thus, the age that inspired Thorstein Veblen to write of "conspicuous consumption" also produced a variety of philanthropy that might have been called "conspicuous charity."

The drama of wealth and charity, in many ways an American version of Dickens's story, could be found at its sentimental best in Thomas Nelson Page's *Santa Claus's Partner* (1899). On Christmas Eve, while figuring his accounts, one Berryman Livingstone (his name, no doubt, an observation on the contradiction that one so cold-hearted could actually be alive) discovered that he had become rich. The road had not been without sacrifice. He had forgone marriage to Catherine Trelane to pursue wealth. When he had finally proposed, she refused to marry him on the grounds that he brought her wealth but not himself.

That Christmas night Livingstone had a conversion experience that only the self-made man could have: He saw the hollowness of his life. Immediately Livingstone went to the home of Clark, his faithful clerk, who had a sick wife and eight children, and persuaded Clark's daughter to help him pick out toys. These he instructed her to deliver to a children's hospital in the guise of Santa's partner. More important, Livingstone, who had suddenly realized that he owed his wealth to Clark's advice and loyalty, paid off the rest of the mortgage on Clark's home (thereby indirectly helping Mrs. Clark recover), made Clark his business partner, and provided dinner and an abundance of toys for all Clark's family. "It is no use to deny it, Clark," he confessed, "—I have—I have!—I have been a brute for years and I have just awakened to the fact!" Later that day Livingstone saw Catherine Trelane, now widowed, and began again to hope he might marry her. [53]

Livingstone had been saved, his single-minded pursuit of riches rectified by a burst of generosity. This material means of salvation indicated a broader truth about Christmas and its gifts. In a world dominated by commerce, one important ritual of grace was spending money on others. [54]

CHAPTER 10

The American Santa Claus

S anta Claus, with his fur-trimmed red suit, sackful of toys, reindeer, sleigh, and home at the North Pole, became in the late nineteenth century as central to the American Christmas as gift-giving. His actions set into motion the excitement of Christmas Eve and morning. In Santa, a child could find solace and hope. Parents could depend on him to shape their children's attitude toward the world. He raised serious religious questions for some and represented simple Christmas charity to others. He helped merchants sell their wares. As a successful factory owner, philanthropist, and quasi-religious figure, Santa Claus bespoke the wistful yearnings of a nation that could neither fully embrace its wealth nor forsake its search for spiritual meaning. As a folk hero, he reflected the state of American society, providing a symbolic figure through which to experience, discuss, and criticize the effect and meaning of Christmas in the culture. A character who began as Clement Moore's exercise in family whimsy had been transformed by late in the century into a mediator between spiritual and material worlds for a culture torn by change. In short, Santa Claus became an American folk icon whose legend at once celebrated the myths of the Gilded Age and critiqued its realities. [1]

Clearly, Santa Claus had traveled a long way since the early nineteenth century, when representations of him had depended mainly upon associations with Belznickel, St. Nicholas, Father Christmas, and similar folk figures. Even Clement Moore's enormously popular "An Account of a

Visit from St. Nicholas" at first circulated only as a literary piece in a relatively narrow social setting. Yet by the Civil War, in part because of the new prominence of the Christmas holiday and new printing technology, a novel and uniform visual perception of Santa had begun to develop. He assumed an increasingly human dimension and, at the same time, his supernatural powers expanded. In a Protestant culture that traditionally looked upon visual representations of God, Jesus, and saints with great suspicion, this transition was significant.

The first pictures of Santa testified to the variety of ways in which Americans had once imagined the saint. A juvenile annual, *The Children's Friend, A New-Year's Present to the Little Ones from Five to Twelve* (1821), supplied one of the earliest images when it illustrated a lengthy poem about "the children's friend" with eight color lithographs. One of them pictured Santa in a red outfit that was neither quite like a suit of clothing an American might wear, nor like a flowing robe a bishop, such as Saint Nicholas, might wear. Neither did it resemble the old Dutch garb that St. Nicholas wore in descriptions written by Washington Irving and James K. Paulding.[2]

In 1837, nearly two decades after the first lithographs had been published, Robert Weir, who taught art at West Point, painted the first American portrait of Santa. He posed the saint just as he readied to ascend the chimney, the penultimate scene of Moore's poem. Perhaps inspired by his friend Gulian Verplanck, Moore's closest friend at the General Theological Seminary and an enthusiast of Irving's St. Nicholas, Weir depicted Santa as a short, beardless man, dressed in high boots, short coat, and stocking cap. He gave him a frightening sneer and a sack overflowing with toys for good children and switches for bad.

Weir's Santa reflected a number of influences. His dress and clay pipe suggested that American Dutch lore animated the rendering. Weir added a red cape edged in fur, reminiscent of traditional bishop's clothing, and daubed in what looked like a rosary. This melding of European, American Dutch, and perhaps even German imagery produced a figure of confused heritage. Apparently not even Weir was exactly certain of what he had created, for he titled his work "Santa Claus, or St. Nicholas."[3]

Other early versions of Santa reflected equally jumbled lineages. The "mysterious chimney-friend, 'Chriscringle,'" that Parkinson's Confectionery in Philadelphia displayed in 1841, mixed German tradition and American fancy. Dressed "in antique costume, with striped pants and stockings, and flying doublet; a tasselled cap on his head and a broad, benevolent grin on his face," and hands and pockets full of toys and candy, he was "reascending a chimney after having filled the stocking hung up by the faith of some young urchin, full of divers bagatelles," Isaac Mickle wrote. In 1859, a New York City woman described St. Nicholas as "a jolly, rosy-cheeked little old man, with a low-crowned hat, a pair of Flemish trunk-hose and a pipe of immense length. . . . " This Santa distinctly recalled New York's Dutch tradition, but this time he came from the cold north in a reindeer-drawn sleigh. The St. Nicholas Society of New York City distributed yet another vision of Santa. As it rededicated itself to civic purpose in midcentury, it circulated a woodcut of St. Nicholas, "good holy man," that it had commissioned Dr. Alexander Anderson to carve in 1810, over fifty years earlier.[4]

Over the years, *Godey's* presented a number of versions of a gift-bringer. Its December 1867 issue opened with an engraving of a bearded "Old Father Christmas" wearing a long tunic. He carried a staff in one hand and held out a doll toward a crowd of children with the other. In 1868, December's "Crafts" section carried instructions for making an "Old Father Christmas" from pine cones. This prickly Santa had a pack full of toys, apples, and nuts and carried a Christmas tree, "a nutcracker and a birch-rod." Flowing robes, long white hair and beard, and an odd, tall, peaked hat lent an aura of spirituality to the visitor in "Welcome, Kriss Kringle. Come In," the opening engraving in the 1878 Christmas edition. The same variety showed in the magazine's fiction. In "A Story About a Goose: A Christmas Story" (1862), Father Christmas brought the gifts; in "Journeying in the Cradle," a poem (1866), "old Santa Claus in his blue tiny sleigh" brought them.[5]

As Americans continued to experiment with his image, Santa's "live" appearance revealed an equally wonderful range of interpretation. When Santa finally got to Michigan (in 1864), one woman wrote to her brother that she had "often heard Santa Claus described, but never before saw the old fellow in person." He wore a buffalo coat with "presents fastened on his coat-tail . . . [and] a corn-popper on his back." However, when Santa visited a New York ball one Christmas Eve, he appeared clad in large buckskin boots, dark brown coat, fawn-colored pants with a blue stripe, and a red vest with big brass buttons that "encircled a truly aldermanic paunch." An "ample cloak of scarlet and gold" completed his attire, the *New York Herald* reported. "He was laden with toys—they hung from his arms, round his neck, his waist, and his back was heavily freighted." He distributed gifts to everyone as he chuckled "good humoredly" to himself.

When he visited 800 children at New York's Five Points Mission in 1884, he arrived "wrapped in a great coat of siberian wolf skins, over which his long beard hung down to his knees."[6]

Although Santa would continue to don an assortment of costumes, the nation grew most familiar with Clement Clark Moore's idea of Santa. Reprinted in magazines, newspapers, books, and copybooks, "An Account of a Visit from St. Nicholas" stimulated a common impression of Santa as a generous and genial American saint. At a quickening pace, innumerable artists, authors, editors, and doggerel poets elaborated on Moore's set-piece, reinforcing public opinion not only about how Santa acted but also about how he looked. Imagined in light of Moore's vivid word-pictures, Santa assumed a consistently cheerful and witty visage. Thus, when F. O. C. Darley illustrated Moore's poem in 1862, he drew a plump Santa, a pipe in his teeth, wearing a furry jacket and pointed hat. Indeed, by midcentury artists seldom portrayed Santa Claus except in association with "A Visit."[7]

Even Thomas Nast, the talented young cartoonist employed by *Harper's Weekly*, when he first illustrated an edition of "A Visit" in 1863 hewed closely to Moore's perception of St. Nick. His sketches of Santa changed little during the Civil War. Soon after, however, Nast began what would become a thirty-year project to create an entire world for Santa. "Santa Claus and His Works" (1866) was his first significant installment. At the center stood Mr. Claus himself, a figure so short that he needed a chair to reach the fireplace mantle. Around him, Nast composed a set of small drawings that revealed the environment in which Santa lived and the nature of his work—at home, in his ice palace, in his workshop, and looking through his telescope for "Good Children." Other scenes depicted him poring over a massive, waist-high "Record of Behavior" and resting his feet before an open fireplace during holiday week. Still another revealed the world that Santa represented to children—the toys, dollies, stockings, and Christmas tree. When Nast redrew these same images of Santa's life for a book of children's verse the following year, he gave Santa what was to become his characteristic dress, a bright red suit trimmed in white ermine.[8]

Another of Nast's contributions to the lore of Santa Claus was a drawing that has become something of an official portrait of Santa. It appeared in *Harper's Weekly* in 1881 and presented a round-cheeked, white-haired and bearded old fellow clad in a furry red coat. One hand cradled a long-stemmed pipe. The other rested lightly on his generously rotund middle, enabling him to hold a wooden horse, a doll, and other playthings in the crook of his arm. Nast trimmed Santa's hat with a sprig of holly and made him in other ways "traditional" in appearance. The strap, imprinted with "U S," that Nast draped over Santa's forearm and the prominent fan of toys beneath it reminded onlookers of the importance of nation and children.[9]

At the same time, others also had begun to describe a life for Santa outside the confines of the house in which "A Visit" took place. Some experimented boldly. Julia F. Snow, for example, called upon the romance of the American West when she described Santa's home as "a cave under Mount Hecla . . . supplied with water from a domesticated Geyser." His fireplace, she wrote, was "wide enough to give place to all the juvenile stockings of Brigham Young's family." Still, Nast provided the most compelling imagery, perhaps because he energetically and inventively engaged in the Christmas rituals of his own household. Together with his wife, he delighted in arranging the armloads of gifts that stores delivered to their home on Christmas Eve. On Christmas mornings, their children recalled, "there was always a multitude of paper dolls—marvelously big and elaborate paper dolls . . . arranged in processions and cavalcades, [and] gay pageants that marched in and about those larger presents along the studio mantel."[10]

In all, Nast's fanciful Christmas drawings illuminated a wide sphere of Santa's rule in the late nineteenth century. Moore had already supplied him with eight reindeer to pull his sleigh. Nast gave him more stockings to stuff, a workshop, ledgers to record children's conduct, and more children to please. He made him taller and dressed him in red. To this, Nast and others added a home at the North Pole, elves, a wife, and even, by some accounts, children. These amplifications drew upon conditions of the nation's material and spiritual life and imparted to Santa an ever more human and credible dimension.

Consider, for example, Santa's home at the North Pole. Exactly how it came to be is not clear. One historian suggested that after Santa adopted the sled as his mode of transportation, it was easy to move his homeland progressively northward to where the snow lasted year round. But he offered no evidence of earlier homelands. The beginning point of Santa's journeys had always been rather vague and often mysterious. John Pintard wrote that Santa Claus arrived from Spain, in a Dutch ship filled with toys, and docked each Christmas Eve in New York. A later version, from

New York City, said that he came "from the frozen regions of the North." More frequently, however, Santa seemed simply to appear and then to disappear after distributing his gifts. [11]

Perhaps the idea of an Arctic homeland reflected contemporary geographic and political concerns. The existence of a north pole had been known since ancient times and, according to Isaac Asimov, "there were many who held that beyond the snow and ice there was open sea and a pleasant environment." When John Franklin, an English navigator and naturalist, set out in the late 1840s to locate the Northwest Passage and failed to return, curiosity about the north swelled, becoming more intense in the early 1850s as two New York expeditions went to search for Franklin. Throughout the remainder of the century, articles on the North Pole sustained American interest in the geography of the Arctic. [12]

As Americans began to conceive of the existence and then geography of the North Pole, they also began referring to it as Santa's home. In 1859, one woman attended a church event where a mock post office had been set up. There she received a letter from one E. M. Morse, who claimed not only to have written from that place, but to have hoisted the stars and stripes on the pole itself. "Although this pole has been used for more than 6,000 years," he wrote her, "it is still as good as new." It was not long before the notion of such a frozen and unknown place gripped Nast's imagination: In 1866, as part of his drawing of "Santa Claus and His Works," Nast housed Santa in an ice palace. Eventually, he specified the North Pole as Santa's home, the "one entirely original touch," according to one historian, that Nast added to the Santa legend. Nast's grandson asserted that Nast chose the pole because it was equidistant from most countries in the Northern Hemisphere. It was also a place where Santa could work without interruption and one which no country could claim as its own. [13]

With his home at the Pole, Santa no longer needed to materialize out of winter skies. He could leave and then return at the end of his Christmas rounds to a warm hearth, just like any ideal Victorian head of house did after a long day of labor. But Santa did not reign over a typical household. Until 1899, when Katherine Lee Bates created a Mrs. Claus character in *Goody Santa Claus on a Sleigh Ride*, he had no wife. Nor did Santa have any children, at least in public lore. Indeed, Santa's work, the preparation and annual delivery of toys to children in other families, seemed much more important than home life. In this aspect, Santa also reflected the work-centered life of many Americans, although the circumstances of his work were inarguably unique.[14]

To meet the yearly demand for toys, Santa relied on helpful elves who worked long hours in their polar workshop. The idea for creating such a workplace apparently sprang from Nast's own imagination (perhaps as a nostalgic look at pre-factory production). Nast, however, did not invent the elves. A staple of Victorian literature, ghosts, elves, or fairies were a natural addition to a fairy tale such as that being spun about Santa Claus. Santa's elves had appeared as early as 1856, when Louisa May Alcott completed, but never published, a book titled "Christmas Elves." Elves had also been sighted in an engraving in *Godey's* from 1873, which showed them surrounding Santa at work. Edward Eggleston gave them additional recognition in 1876, with "The House of Santa Claus, a Christmas Fairy Show for Sunday Schools."[15]

A work force of skilled and reliable elf labor helped secure Santa's place in the pantheon of American financiers, manufacturers, and industrial moguls. These North Pole elves were not unlike immigrants working in the nation's sweatshops. Unassimilated, isolated from the rest of society, and undifferentiated by individual name or character, the best of them worked hard, long, and unselfishly. Their existence made manifest a maxim that hard work and a cheerful attitude benefited all.

Godey's drew an implicit parallel between Santa's workshop and elves and the foreign manufacture of toys. "The Workshop of Santa Claus," the frontispiece illustration for its 1873 Christmas issue, showed Santa encircled by toys and elves. The caption beneath it read: "Here we have an idea of the preparations that are made to supply the young folks with toys at Christmas time." The accompanying editorial addressed the realities of the situation; dolls, boats, tops, and toy soldiers were not fabricated in a magical workplace. Foreigners who were "very poor," not elves, made them. "Whole villages engage in the work, and the contractors every week in the year go round and gather together the six days' work and pay for it. They [i.e., the toys] are taken to their destination and packed for transportation," she wrote. "The cost of these toys is small; and yet there is a profit in them."[16]

The charming notion that Santa and his tiny helpers supplied all the Christmas toys encoded another highly romantic vision of American capitalism: Santa reigned without opposition over a vast empire, truly a captain of industry. Nearly everyone had whispered his name in awe at one time or another. From his fur coat to his full girth, he looked not unlike the portraits of the nation's Presidents or its well-fed financial moguls. The pocket watch he fingered, in Nast's 1870 portrait, suggested the clock by which the nation's economy kept time. It also symbolized Santa's dependability. Every year, his workshop turned out a seemingly limitless supply of quality goods. These Santa managed to distribute in an innovative, orderly, and timely fashion.[17]

Santa's credibility as a folk hero depended on his ability to exist in the world of practicality as a highly successful manufacturer and distributor of toys. Yet any analogies that might be drawn between his work and late nineteenth-century capitalism lay enmeshed in paradox, for, in significant ways, Santa Claus also represented values at odds with the system. Rather than acquire wealth, he shed it yearly. He was a robber baron in reverse. He never purchased gifts, but (with elf help) made his own to give away without regard for financial profit. Whereas industrialists prospered from the innocence and naïveté of the populace, Santa rewarded the most innocent and naïve of all—the children. With his quaintly antiquated sled-and-reindeer transportation, this old, secular saint recalled idyllic earlier times in which competition, progress, prosperity, and efficiency mattered little. Distant from the calumnies and banalities of everyday life, Santa Claus issued from a realm of dreams, hopes, wishes, and beliefs, not from the realities and compromises necessary to negotiate contemporary life.

Ultimately, the invention of Santa in all his many aspects, while perpetuated as a child's story, depended on adults to sustain and embellish it. Artists, poets, editors, and women "scribblers" helped to construct the myth and describe its minute details in the magazines for which they wrote and drew.[18]

Parents enumerated Santa's most essential and convincing traits, vouchsafing his authenticity for their children. This could be as simple and persuasive as a mention of Santa's omniscience to a recalcitrant child. For others, it might be as elaborate as it was ill-conceived. One devoted father, this one in Newcastle, Pennsylvania, decided to surprise his family by impersonating Santa on Christmas Eve in 1893. He safely scaled the chimney and began his downward slide. About halfway down, he got stuck. His muffled cries for help succeeded only in frightening his family into fleeing from their home. Neighbors eventually rescued him, but only after they had torn the chimney down to roof level so that they could lower a rope.[19]

Some parents penned letters to their children over Santa's forged signature. In at least one instance this became a rather elaborate and ongoing embroidery. On St. Nicholas's Eve, 1879, "Santa" wrote to two young sisters explaining that his reindeer had fallen through the ice on a prior trip to New London and that its replacement had been killed by a bear. The bear also "came near killing my youngest son, a little fellow only about 65 years old, but very bright and cunning and not at all afraid of bears." Santa wrote next on Christmas Eve, 1882, this time to the children's father. He promised that if he were unable to visit that night, he would send "one of my boys" in his place, that is if he could get another pair of deer. Bears had already killed two deer and "eaten them allmost up" before Santa could kill them. Besides, his 85-year-old "little boy" had a bad case of croup, forcing Santa "to send one of my other boys to you who had never been away Christmasing before wh[ich] was the reason for his cutting up as he did."[20]

Most fascinating in such stories as these is the degree to which adults became involved in vivifying the Santa myth. The phenomenon has led some scholars to concentrate on the meaning of Santa to adults rather than to children. One anthropologist, Wendell Oswalt, suggested that Santa personified "the idealistic world we have tried to create for small children." Santa brought whatever a child wanted, hardly what adults experienced in the world. "By supporting the myth of Santa," he argued, "we express our own misgivings about the psychological satisfactions derived from our materialistic cultural system." (One might also observe that, by distributing material gifts to children—the most innocent and therefore deserving recipients of bounty—Santa confirmed the prevailing nineteenth-century social and religious thought that equated wealth with goodness.) Warren O. Hagstrom speculated briefly on a Marxist interpretation of the Santa rituals, suggesting that they might be seen as a parental tool of control and oppression of children; or, conversely, that "belief in Santa is the sigh of the oppressed children. . . . It is the *opium* of childhood."[21]

At the time, many Americans began to worry that Santa would overshadow Christmas itself. This "Santa Claus folly has infected family life, literature, church services, everything almost, at this season," wrote "Germanicus" for the *Lutheran Observer* in 1883. He especially faulted Calvinists, "the denominations that have had no other holy-day but Sunday, and that have only recently adopted the Christmas," and charged them with embracing only the "outward and oftentimes most objectionable features" of the holiday.[22]

A number of writers, preachers, poets, and others who published their thoughts on the subject of Santa feared that children might compare Santa with God and that their belief in Santa might hinder or pervert faith. Some even worried that Santa had become a substitute and rival for Jesus. Centuries earlier, Puritans, concerned that saints might stand for God, had excluded them from their beliefs. Although the faith not only of Puritan Calvinists but of all Christians had modified over the intervening years, America's Protestant culture still looked upon an iconographic, human-like embodiment of Christmas with great suspicion. A letter to the Philadelphia *Lutheran* (December 22, 1881) came directly to the point when it cautioned, "do not substitute for the Babe of Bethlehem, the figure of a Santa Claus." One little girl, an evangelical magazine reported in 1906, was told that Santa did not exist. A few days later she refused to attend Sabbath school, reasoning, "Likely as not this Jesus Christ business will turn out just like Santa Claus."[23]

The simple equation of Jesus with Santa, however, did not illuminate the subtle ways in which a belief in Santa Claus had become entangled in the nuances of American Protestantism. As science increasingly collided with and overpowered faith, the existence of religious belief in many instances had become dependent upon reason and scientific proof. Santa, while not a religious figure per se, acted as a sometimes demonstrably palpable medium through which children and adults in late nineteenth-century America experienced and acted upon spiritual impulses.

A poem printed in *Demorest's Monthly* illustrated one way in which Santa acted as the catalyst through which a church's needs were met. In its few lines, a minister pondered the message of his Christmas sermon. He felt

> a wave of trouble [run] over his heart,
> because
> [his congregation] thought much less of Jesus Christ
> than they did of
> Santa Claus.

He had heard them eagerly whispering, one to another,

> "What will I get on Christmas? What will
> Santa Claus bring?"

In the end, the preacher dodged the implied challenge that believing in Santa posed to believing in Jesus. Rather than chastise his flock for their anticipation of Santa's gifts, he decided to give his lesson on the theme that it is "more blessed to give than to receive." The result, he discovered, was that his parishioners overwhelmed him with their generous spirit, and thereby justified the minister's strategy.[24]

More complicated were the ways in which the belief in Santa Claus had become a way in which Americans perceived the nature of religious belief. Commentary scattered throughout contemporary popular media indicated that even as they offered critiques on Santa, many were trying to assess the relationship of a child's belief in a generous secular saint to the condition of their own religious feelings.

Jacob Riis, famous for his work among the poorest of the nation, insisted that Santa would lead the believer to Jesus. "Because—don't you know, Santa Claus is the spirit of Christmas," he wrote in answer to his own question, "Is There a Santa Claus?" "[W]hen the dear little Baby was born after whom we call Christmas . . . that Spirit came into the world to soften the hearts of men and make them love one another. . . . Don't let anybody or anything rub it [Spirit] out," Riis pleaded. "Let them tear Santa's white beard off at the Sunday-school. . . . These are only his disguises. The steps of the real Santa Claus you can trace all through the world . . . , and when you stand in the last of his tracks you will find the Blessed Babe of Bethlehem smiling a welcome to you."[25]

The editor of *Open Court*, a Chicago publication, compared the literal belief in Santa to a naïve and undeveloped sense of spirituality. He also noted that this belief constituted a first step in religious faith. To argue the case, he drew an analogy between the reality of presents brought by Santa as a representation of parental love and the realities of life brought by the concept of God. "[T]he idea of Santa Claus," explained the author, "was simply an allegorical expression of the love of parents and grandparents who wished to give Christmas joy to good little children." He observed that "in the absence of the traditional characters which by the experience of centuries have become typical representations of certain spiritual realities of life," children tended to create their own inferior substitutes. This childish belief they would naturally outgrow. The editor also addressed the adult usage of Santa, albeit obliquely. "There are still many among us who believe that unless the letter of a myth be true there can be neither beauty nor truth in religion," he wrote. An adult's "belief in a God and Heaven is more like the children's belief in Santa Claus than a genuine faith in the grand realities that are symbolised in these names."[26]

Unquestionably, however, Frank Church, editor of the *New York Sun*, provided the most persuasive, and best-known, discourse on the spiritual meaning of Santa. A letter from one Virginia O'Hanlon, written in 1897, asked the plain question, "Is there a Santa Claus?" "Yes, Virginia, there is a Santa Claus," came the terse reply. Church's answer, though, was not a patent fib designed to placate a youngster. It proved an exposition on belief itself. "Virginia, your little friends are wrong," he wrote. "They have been affected by the skepticism of a skeptical age. They do not believe except they see." Drawing on the same imagery so authoritatively used by Jonathan Edwards to shame his Puritan congregation into humility before God, Church told Virginia that "In this great universe of ours man is a mere insect, an ant, in his intellect as compared with the boundless world about him, as measured by the intelligence capable of grasping the whole of truth and knowledge." Without Santa, he argued, "There would be no childlike faith then, no poetry, no romance to make tolerable this existence. . . . Nobody sees Santa Claus, but that is no sign that there is no Santa Claus." He concluded with an indirect but by no means weak assault on positivism and science. "The most real things in the world are those that neither children nor men can see. . . . Nobody can conceive or imagine all the wonders there are unseen and unseeable in the world."[27]

CHAPTER 11

A Frame of Mind: Christmas in the Twentieth Century

By the time Frank Church announced definitively that Santa did indeed exist, Americans had come to associate a distinct set of rituals, expectations, and attitudes with Christmas. These have endured and perhaps grown even stronger in the twentieth century. We still gather with family, trim the tree, send cards, wait for Santa, feast, sing, shop for and give gifts to excess, and respond to pleas for charity and social harmony. Changes in society and the economy have modified many of the particular ways in which we keep this "old-fashioned Christmas," but its larger themes retain a remarkable fidelity to those of the nineteenth century.

This has been especially true of the central conflict Americans experience in Christmas, the perceived war between material and spiritual satisfaction. We feel that mammon has overrun the "Christmas spirit," a vague and broadly inclusive term that covers almost any good deed or worshipful thought that does not directly involve money. More accurately, even as the materialistic features of the festival have flourished, its spiritual dimension has broadened. Nothing is more striking about Christmas in the twentieth century than, as secularization and an increased popular and legal recognition of religious pluralism have helped denude public life of a common religious experience, how Christmas has come to function as the last widely celebrated public recognition of the miraculous. Almost alone, the keeping of this holiday provides a communal and calendrical touchstone of the nation's faith, hope, and moral aspiration, a national moment of harmony and transcendence.

To understand how Christmas came to occupy this niche in our society, it is necessary to turn to the previous century. Throughout the nineteenth century, Americans celebrated Christmas primarily as a home and church festival, albeit one that frequently spilled into the public realm as vast numbers of strangers strolled side by side along crowded streets, reviewed Christmas-inspired store windows, and jostled one another in the aisles of great emporia. As the nineteenth turned into the twentieth century, Christmas became increasingly a public occasion in its own right, one more formal and, ironically, less commercial than earlier versions. Citizens of New York City erected a community Christmas tree in 1912, purported to be the first ever in the country. That same year, the cities of Hartford and Boston sponsored open-air music programs during Christmas week. Some 160 towns made preparations for similar events the next year. In these and other communities, Christmas came to be celebrated as a civic festival. By 1923, the vogue for public Christmases had even infected the White House as President Coolidge lit the first "National Christmas Tree" on his front lawn. Writing in *World Review*, Ruth Russell speculated in 1925 that "almost every village and large city in the country" would be planning a festival for its community. [1]

The emergence of this public form of Christmas coincided with the realization of other Progressive era reforms. Middle-class urbanites, many of whom feared the fraying of the slim last threads of community, joined Progressive battles against the decay, poverty, corruption, and disorder of city life. In creating a Christmas in the city center, they reasserted symbolically citizens' obligation to harmony, faith, family, and civic unity—the qualities believed necessary to keep the nation healthy and prosperous. Christmas became a community festival that, according to Russell, "fostered a sympathetic spirit of brotherhood, as all classes of citizens voice good will and loyalty to their common city and country." Thus, what had been seen as a domestic holiday with a relatively circumscribed public dimension now had a full civic and secular stage on which to be enacted. [2]

In its parts, this new public celebration mirrored the patterns of home and, especially, church celebration. It relied on the same carols, nativity scenes, evergreens, and gifts for children. As a complete exposition, though, it moved beyond private rituals. Town trees, plays, carolers, seasonal store displays, the bustle of shopping humanity, and all the other effects of the public festival brought people together and transformed the landscape and even the experience of public space. Decorated for Christmas, a city center became an environment quite different from what it was throughout the rest of the year, causing people who entered its ambience to feel and act differently than they did at other times. It became an arena for exchanges of goodwill, cheerful greetings, and benign purpose.[3]

To be sure, the appearance of diverse groups enjoying Christmas together fulfilled an expectation that in Christmas lay a key to social peace, a goal grown more important as immigration rates rose higher and higher in the late nineteenth and early decades of the twentieth century. Martha J. Lamb suggested as much in 1883: "The close resemblance of the [Christmas] ceremonials in different climes, and among nations speaking different languages . . . may form an element in the solution of many a troublesome problem." Jacob Riis saw similar potential in the holiday. "The banners of United Italy, of modern Hellas, of France and Germany and England, hang side by side with the Chinese dragon and the starry flag—signs of the cosmopolitan character of the congregation," he wrote of a well-attended Christmas festival held in an English-speaking Sunday school in the Bowery. "Greek and Roman Catholics, Jews and jossworshipers, go there; few Protestants, and no Baptists." And Daniel De Leon, writing for the *Daily People* in 1900, observed that "The latent goodness in the human heart is shown at this season when thousands of people, buffeted, spurned, wronged, and abused by the world, make an attempt to be merry, and to give a message and a greeting of good cheer to their fellow men."[4]

Nor was it only the underclass or recent immigrants who found in Christmas a respite from everyday life. A "Contributor" to the *Atlantic* reported in 1930 that she and her family had "for years gone on Christmas Eve to midnight Mass. To be among hundreds of people of all colors and races, of all walks of life, who are drawn together by a common emotion, a common faith, is to be at once in harmony with the Christmas mood," Dorothy W. Nelson wrote. She likened her experience to "that of a foreigner visiting a strange land," one "with which my own land has never been at war, toward which I have inherited no bitterness, no fear, no strong emotions of any kind." For her, beginning Christmas in a church had a way of dissolving what Walter Lippman called the "acids of modernity" that had broken life into an array of inharmonious elements.[5]

For American Jews, however, the celebration of Christmas posed a serious dilemma. Besides acknowledging American cultural harmony, keeping Christmas recognized Christian belief as well. When their numbers were few and their presence was considered a curiosity, at least some

Jews were noticed participating in Christmas. The Philadelphia *Times*, for example, reported in 1877 that "the Hebrew brethren did not keep aloof" from Christmas. By the turn of the century, the Jewish population had increased enough to assert forthrightly its identity and to question participation in the Christian holiday.[6]

The public discussion about Jews keeping Christmas, which had begun at least as early as 1903, exposed two prevalent viewpoints. Rabbi Judah L. Magnes expressed a common attitude that Jews should neither fear nor reject the holiday. Christmas might even help them strengthen their own beliefs, he argued. He supported his point by noting that while many Jews protested, others "silently bring in the trees and the lights" into their homes. A Rabbi Schulman took an opposing view. He objected particularly to the Christmas entertainment in public schools and to the Christology that was part of it.[7]

Schulman's perspective had become especially pertinent because in December 1905, New York school principal F. F. Harding had exhorted his mostly Jewish audience to be more Christlike. The Jewish community responded decisively, persuading the Committee on Elementary Schools of New York City's Board of Education to warn Harding against sectarian teaching in the schools. When the problem remained unsettled the next Christmas, Jews in synagogues throughout New York City met, according to the *Tribune*, to discuss "Christmas and Christmas festivities in their relation to Jewish thought, and especially as applied to Jewish children attending public schools." As a result, Jewish parents and their children boycotted the school's closing holiday exercises.

As Christmas became more entrenched in the general culture and as the first generations of American-born Jews of the great turn-of-the-century migrations faced choices concerning acculturation, the central question of celebrating Christmas remained unsolved. In a 1939 airing of the issue in *Christian Century*, Rabbi Louis Witt asserted that Jews should keep Christmas, arguing that Christians had become more liberal and now emphasized the "universal humanness" of Jesus' teaching rather than a particular spiritual belief. "If Christmas were only Christian, the Jew would be only Jewish," Witt declared. "A theological, ecclesiastical Christmas finds and leaves the Jew the same 'infidel' he has ever been."[8]

However, Witt found more in Christmas than Christianity. Claiming that his children had felt deprived of the joys of the holiday in their youth, he thought that the "friendliness and good will" of Christmas made it nearly irresistible to anyone, including Jews. "After all," he pointed out, "the Jew is only human." Celebrating the holiday did not ordain that he was "thereby drawn by even the breadth of a hair nearer to the worship of an ecclesiastical Christ." A Jew keeping Christmas meant only that he met Christians on common ground, a strategy that protected him and other American Jews from being ostracized from a culture that had befriended them.[9]

The *Century's* Christian editor sided with Witt's "effort to release the spirit of Jewry from bondage to a tradition which denies it the right to participate in a free and gladsome celebration of the birthday of Jesus," but he focused on keeping Christmas as a sign of being an American, not on its Christian meaning. Americans, Jew and Christian, living in "a world of tolerance, of political liberalism, of democracy," the editor thought, should naturally acknowledge Jesus' Jewishness and share "this common historical ground. . . . [I]n the environment of American tolerance . . . it is not fair to democracy to cherish a religious faith which provides a sanction for racial or cultural or any other form of separatism."[10]

The *Century* exchange rested on an assumption that Christmas existed in a fairly definable, dual field of community and religion, that it had something to do with concepts of allegiance and belonging, perhaps even participation. In an eagerness to obtain consensus on Christian terms, though, Witt and the *Century's* editors failed to examine some implications of their arguments. Rabbi Edward Israel did not let the matter pass unnoticed. Calling Witt's opinions an "affront to my devout Christian friends," he asserted that "the truly devout Christian . . . has far more respect for the Jew who, conscientious in his own religious loyalties, does not observe Christmas, than for the Witt type of Jew who tries to crawl into Christmas observance, salving what remains of his Jewish conscience by endeavoring to water down and compromise with Christian doctrine." The "only one honest way for the Jew to celebrate Christmas," he concluded, "is as Christ's birthday." However, Rabbi Israel had neither Christmas's own history nor trends in American society on his side. More and more, Christmas emerged as a secular, community celebration, one replete with public pageants, a long and well-planned shopping season, and common but only faintly Christian trappings of which even Jews, should they wish, might partake.[11]

It was not the pluralism of a publicly celebrated Christmas alone that altered the character of Christmas, but the exigencies of market-driven economies. One of the most important and noticeable attributes of the holiday was fast becoming its commercial aspect, a description that still holds popular sway. According to one study, American families allocate an average of 4 percent of their incomes for Christmas gifts. This means that a family with an income of $30,000 per year might spend $1200 on presents. Another survey estimated that the "average American planned to spend upward of $750 on Christmas" in 1991. Totaled, expenditures reached $37 billion, or more than Ireland's gross national product.[12]

Many industries, especially those associated with the production and sale of luxury goods, and the consumer economy in general rely on Christmas sales to carry them through the year. Department stores sell over 40 percent of their toys, and more than 25 percent of their candy, cosmetics, toiletries, stationery, greeting cards, books, and art each December. Every year, large portions of advertising allowances go toward generating these sales. Seiko spends 60 percent of its annual budget in the last quarter of the year, as do companies that sell health and beauty products. Polaroid uses 50 percent of its media money at Christmas time. Newspapers, magazines, radio, and, not least of all, television thrive on December revenues, even as they dizzy consumers with seemingly unlimited gift choices to be made.[13]

Thinking that money has overdetermined the meaning of Christmas, many premise their critiques of the holiday on the notion that its sacred meaning and its secular celebration form two separate spheres, and that profane (which is commercialization) has edged aside sacred (which has to do with the spirit). Russell Baker assessed the holiday wholly on the basis of his commercial experience. Christmas "nowadays persists like an onset of shingles," he wrote in 1976. "You spend a month getting ready for it and two weeks getting over it. . . . If Scrooge . . . had started dreaming on November 25 and spent the next four weeks being subjected to desperate sales clerks and electronically amplified 'Jingle Bells,' he would probably have stopped at the Cratchits' on that fateful evening only long enough to smash Tiny Tim's little crutch." Margaret Perry had already made essentially the same observation in 1921, complaining in the *Atlantic* that "Christmas has been even more thoroughly commercialized and desecrated [than Easter], the better to fill moneybags that are already bursting open." She thought it "high time we remembered that the Christmas spirit has nothing in common with the gains of profiteers or with crowded shops and overworked saleswomen; still less with the giving of perfunctory and awkward thanks for perfunctory and undesired 'remembrances.'"[14]

In fact, it is a "paradoxical ambiguity," as F. E. Manning calls it, between spiritual and what is usually regarded as profane—the "gains of profiteers" and "electronically amplified 'Jingle Bells'" in this case—that animates America's Christmas, engaging us in a tension of opposites: reaffirmation and subversion, ritual and play. Arguably, commerce has aggrandized a unique role that encroaches on a significant portion of both sides. As a result, we have become increasingly suspicious that the market has reoriented, even corrupted, our sense of what is properly Christmas. The historian Daniel Boorstin has commented on this phenomenon in terms of "our notion of time and the seasons," which he claims the marketplace has "blurred as never before. . . . In *Publisher's Weekly*, Santa Claus arrives with his Christmas picture book gift items on the Fourth of July. We anticipate ourselves so that manufacturers and merchandisers always live in several seasons at once."[15]

Still, we cannot overlook our own collusion in what has become generally known as the commercialization of Christmas. Commerce has devised, but customers have responded approvingly to strategies that fuse the spheres of sacred and profane into a compelling certainty. At Christmas, merchants traditionally have transformed display windows, aisles, and atria into wonderlands and sanctuaries that veil a mercenary purpose. In the 1870s, one historian has observed, department stores "often outdid the churches in religious adornment and symbolism, with pipe organs, choirs, religious paintings and banners, statues of saints and angels. . . . " In this way, he argued, stores bathed "consumption in the reflected glory of Christianity."[16]

Although in time they abandoned their churchly guises, stores nevertheless continued to undergo marvelous alteration at holiday time, becoming strikingly "other" places. During the 1940s, Chicago's Marshall Field & Company, competing for the attention of holiday crowds grown used to being entertained as they shopped, changed its huge department store into "a glittering fairyland . . . [with] the world's most gorgeous Christmas tree, [and] a brilliant pageantry." Every year it developed a secret new theme for its Christmas decorations, each requiring an additional 4000 workers.[17]

Besides creating a spatial sense of Christmas that set the season visually apart from the remainder of the year, commerce also exploited the flimsy partition between sacred and profane time at Christmas, beginning its quest for holiday profits in late November or still earlier at Halloween and before. One highly successful tactic made Thanksgiving a springboard for Christmas sales (although this holiday already informally marked a turn toward the winter). In 1920, Ellis Gimbel, partner in the fabled department store, organized fifteen cars and fifty people into the first Thanksgiving Day parade. The high point, though, was the fireman he recruited to dress as Santa Claus. In 1924, Hudson's, a Detroit store, inaugurated its "Santa's Thanksgiving Day Parade." That same year, Macy's organized its first parade, drawing 10,000 potential customers into the streets of New York City. The final float carried Santa Claus himself, attended by "elves, toy soldiers and more!" to signal the beginning of the commercial Christmas season. Thus, on a holiday once devoted mainly to giving thanks with friends and family, at home and in church, Santa Claus made his own first claim each season. [18]

So vital did Thanksgiving prove in inaugurating the Christmas season that commercial interest conspired in resetting its date. During the Great Depression of the 1930s, profits for Ohio's Federated Department Stores declined. In 1939, earnings promised to be especially spare because Thanksgiving fell on the last day of the month. Fred Lazarus, Jr., who was to become the next president of Federated, noted that by advancing the date of Thanksgiving one week, six additional days for Christmas shopping could be added to sales calendars. Persuaded by his logic, President Franklin Roosevelt moved the feast from the 30th to the 23rd of November, and in 1941, Congress set the annual date of Thanksgiving at the fourth (rather than the last) Thursday in November. As such, it could fall no later than the 28th (nor earlier than the 22nd) and thereby ensured a four-week shopping season each year. [19]

As merchants successfully tinkered with Christmas space and time, they also manipulated Christmas folklore to enhance profit. In one instance, Marshall Field's boldly modeled a rival to Santa Claus himself. Discovering that other stores had copied its "Night Before Christmas" theme in 1948, Field's invented Uncle Mistletoe. Described as "a black-browed, winged sprite, wearing a cape and top hat" (and resembling "a benign and smiling John L. Lewis"), he lived with his wife Aunt Holly on the eighth floor of the department store, in Cloud Cottage. Crowds from all over America, a quarter of a million daily during the season's peak, clamored not only to see the spectacle of the Christmased Field's, but to visit with Uncle. "By Heaven!" snorted one adversary, "you fellows have stolen Christmas!" [20]

While Uncle Mistletoe enjoyed a brief success, it was probably inevitable that business remained fixed on the "real" Santa Claus to turn a profit for them. Merchants had learned much earlier that Santa's endorsement could be particularly useful in promoting sales. Before the Civil War, stores had at times used him to attract customers, but these folk representations were largely curiosities employed with little calculation. By the first decades of the twentieth century, charities were enlisting the old saint to solicit funds. In 1914, charity leader John D. Gluck chose Santa as the most appropriate figure to deliver contributions of food and clothing to the poor.[21]

Santa demonstrated himself to be equally valuable in the marketplace. In the beginning of the century, printed advertisements occasionally used his image. This escalated dramatically as a significant increase in spendable income, a multiplying number of products, and the sophistication that the advertising industry lent the task of selling came to bear on the Christmas market. Santa soon pitched for a host of products, from socks to typewriters to Coca-Cola. Between 1936 and 1938, 20 percent of the Christmas gift advertisements in the *Ladies' Home Journal* and *Saturday Evening Post* contained illustrations of St. Nick. By 1940, Santa Claus had so completely infiltrated the business of selling that one magazine credited him with yearly sales of $500,000,000 (this included the curious note that he accounted for the sale of 51 percent of all men's bathrobes). It claimed flatly that Santa had "gone completely commercial," and editorialized, "he extracts this fabulous sum from a sentimental American public through the exploitation of a great deal of whimsical pap which has ceased to have any ethical, religious, or moral significance."[22]

Santa Claus's success in print advertising encouraged a demand for his appearance in the flesh. It seemed only logical to Charles W. Howard, himself a career Santa, to open a Santa Claus School in 1937. Students paid $150 each for a week-long course in showmanship, salesmanship, child psychology, the economics of the toy industry, and Santa history. Within two years, Howard moved the school to Santa Claus, Indiana, a town incorporated under that name in 1928, where he drew applicants from the ranks of reporters, teachers, and similarly reputable professions. Graduates of the school anticipated earning a minimum of $75 weekly, but soon found their new career brought with it the same worries as other callings. Round-figured impostors lowered standards and took away work. Donald Duck and Mickey Mouse, first unveiled in stores' Christmas display windows in 1938, also threatened their livelihood, pressing trained Santas to join the newly formed National Association of Professional Santas. So, as commerce continued to pervade Christmas, it had reshaped yet one more sign of the holiday: Santa, once an ethereally elusive saint, became a common worker, as corporeal as he was corpulent.[23]

Meanwhile, a potent combination of commerce and new communication media had enabled the festival to permeate nearly all levels of American life. In addition to print advertising, radio, movies, books, songs, and television molded its salient images and language into a Christmas more uniform and secular than any preceding it, and found a following for it in every corner of the nation. Under media influence, millions of listeners and viewers experienced the same modern Christmas lore simultaneously, the annual rewindings and rerunnings of Christmas programs themselves becoming a nostalgic ritual for many Americans.

In its reach for bigger audiences, media recreated Christmas in the language of the twentieth century. It introduced new stories based on old themes and simplified further the complex issues of Christmas materialism and Christmas spirit. This tendency toward reductionism skirted hard questions about keeping Christmas even as it reinforced cultural truisms formulated in the last century. Thus, the cliché of Christmas's rampant materialism threaded its way unexamined through nearly every story line, and cultural dilemmas such as those raised by Rabbis Witt and Israel in the *Christian Century* debate lay buried in the avalanche of a media-manufactured Christmas. However, media did no more than the culture that it spoke to allowed. Its portrayals of Christmas in the twentieth century sketched a familiar outline of modern life that sharpened the dialectic between the spiritual and the material, and ultimately located in the holiday a commentary on American life. It is in this light that *Rudolph the Red-Nosed Reindeer*, *Miracle on 34th Street*, *Amahl and the Night Visitors*, *The Nightmare Before Christmas* and other twentieth-century attempts to invoke Christmas must be seen.

The first significant index of the modern character of Christmas in the twentieth century can be found, appropriately enough, in an advertising gimmick. In 1939, the same year that President Roosevelt fixed the date of Thanksgiving, the Montgomery Ward department store distributed copies of *Rudolph the Red-Nosed Reindeer* to the children of its customers. Written by an employee named Robert L. May, the story-poem had a rhyme pattern nearly indistinguishable from Moore's "A Visit from St. Nicholas." It told about a young reindeer taunted and shunned by all the other deer, one whose nose was "red as a beet!" but twice as big and bright. Rudolph knew they were right. However, he always behaved well and obeyed his parents, comforting himself with the knowledge that on judgment day, which after all is what Christmas was in this case, Santa would bring him as many gifts as the "happier, handsomer reindeer who teased him."[24]

As it turned out, Christmas Eve was very foggy and dark. Santa, worried about his upcoming rounds, urged Dasher, Dancer, Prancer, Vixen,

Comet, Cupid, Donder, and Blitzen to hurry. Repeatedly they got tangled in tree tops and one barely missed hitting a plane. The fog thickened and Santa found it increasingly difficult to see. Sometime past midnight he stopped at Rudolph's home and upon entering the deer's bedroom, found it a relief to have his way lit by the dim glow of the sleeping deer's nose.

It was then that Santa had "the greatest idea in all history!" He awakened Rudolph and, referring tactfully to Rudolph's "wonderful forehead" instead of his "big, shiny nose," asked him to lead the way. Of course Rudolph agreed, and when he returned from his travels he found that the other reindeer envied him. Whereas before they did "nothing but tease him," now they would do "*anything* . . . only to please him!"

As a story of an outcast youngster and written during the Great Depression, Rudolph's adventure ratified the American dream in terms of merit and acceptance rather than money. Rudolph saved Christmas and earned the esteem of his own reindeer community. The message: A worthy soul, given the opening, can turn a liability into an asset. Success will surely follow.

And succeed *Rudolph* did. Ward handed out nearly two and a half million copies of *Rudolph* the year May wrote it, then abandoned the booklet until 1946, when it distributed over three and a half million copies to another generation. That year Sewell Avery, chair of Montgomery Ward, transferred the *Rudolph* copyright to May, who had six children to put through college and a sick wife. May immediately sold the rights to a children's book publisher, who in 1947 brought out an edition that sold 100,000 copies in two years. In 1949 Johnny Marks, a friend of May, wrote a 113-word song based on the Rudolph story. Gene Autry recorded it, and two million copies sold during the first Christmas season. In subsequent years, 500 licensed Rudolph products appeared, from cookie cutters to cuckoo clocks. The story has been translated into 25 languages, and since 1964, network television has aired an animated version of it.[25]

While *Rudolph*'s good fortune indicates the trajectory of Christmas in the twentieth century toward mass marketing and an increasing emphasis on children, movies have more closely depicted the role of Christmas in our culture. The film industry streamlined, consolidated, and revised the holiday to match modern American life. In the first of these movies, *Holiday Inn* (1942), a romantic triangle acted out its diverting plot line at a hotel open only on holidays. More notable was its music, a folio of songs written by Irving Berlin, a Russian-born American Jew. The best of them, "White Christmas," sung by Bing Crosby, won an Oscar in 1942.

Appealingly sentimental, "White Christmas" endures as the holiday's quintessential expression. It has no dark side. War is forgotten. It bears no hint of commerce, not even a gift, but only describes perfection. Its verse begins with an image of a perfect day, of green grass and swaying orange and palm trees in Beverly Hills, California. However, the singer longs for a different, more nostalgically fulfilling moment. On this December 24 he is "dreaming of a White Christmas" just like those he "used to know." Crosby's rendition of this winter-clear vision, with its glistening treetops and children listening for "sleigh bells in the snow," engaged American imaginations; the commercial popularity of the movie song exceeded even *Rudolph.* Since 1942, over 30 million copies have sold, making it the worldwide best-selling song in history.[26]

Holiday Inn's "White Christmas" marked only the beginning of Hollywood's influence on the way in which Americans envisioned Christmas. Two movies in particular have become part of any movie buff's Christmas lexicon. The first, Frank Capra's *It's a Wonderful Life* (1946), raises some of the same issues as Dickens's *A Christmas Carol,* but from a wholly opposite perspective. It examines the life of a small-town man who, although he always worked hard, believes that he has failed. On Christmas Eve, he turns away from his family and attempts to end his life. Saved by his guardian angel, who reveals to him what would have happened if, as he wished, he had never been born, the hero returns home to find that the whole town has come to his aid.[27]

In many ways, Valentine Davies's *Miracle on 34th Street* (1947), the second important holiday movie to be made, only recirculated messages from Christmas pieces of the nineteenth century; Kris Kringle's line in the movie, "Christmas isn't just a day. It's a frame of mind," could have easily come straight out of William Gilmore Simms's southern story "Maize in Milk," written in the 1840s. However, the movie does not restrict its viewer to a regional or bygone Christmas, but delves into the essence of the modern Santa Claus and along the way comments on nearly all the holiday's clichés. It set a "real" Santa amid the commerce and competition of New York City and confirmed the relevance of faith, imagination, cooperation, and traditional family structure in a modern age of rationality.[28]

Davies's novella, on which the film was based, begins disarmingly simple and turns more sentimentally complex. Officials at Maplewood Home for the Aged evict Kris Kringle because he persists in claiming himself to be

Santa Claus. Soon after, as Kringle stands watching preparations for Macy's Thanksgiving Parade, the Santa Claus that Macy's had hired topples off a float in his drunkenness. Desperate, Doris Walker, Macy's personnel director, conscripts Kringle to ride in the parade, and the next day she hires him to be the store's official Santa.[29]

Macy's new Santa proves himself to be a marvelous success. Convinced that Christmas has degenerated into "pure commercialism," he hopes to answer positively his own question, "Is there no true Christmas spirit left in the world?" He promises a child a fire engine that Macy's does not carry, then informs the mother exactly where she can find it. He sends another to arch-rival Gimbel's for skates. Indeed, in the dog-eat-dog world of American business, only Santa can persuade the owners of Macy's and Gimbel's that by referring customers to their competitors they enhance their own image and not incidentally reap greater financial profit.[30]

Walker, though, feels uneasy about Kringle, who continues to say he is really Santa. She and Susan, "a rather serious child of six," live alone in a "small and sternly modern apartment." As a single mother, she has raised Susan to hold a hard-nosed belief in "utter realism and truth." (To Kringle, mother and daughter "were but unhappy products of their times.") She is particularly troubled to find that when Fred Gayley, an attorney and warm family "uncle," introduces the unblinking little Susan to Santa, a warm friendship develops. Yet others besides Walker feel apprehensive about Kris Kringle. Finally, an employee plot led by Albert Sawyer, Macy's psychologist, lands Kringle in a Bellevue mental ward.[31]

Kringle's success in getting the municipal court to confirm his sanity seems bleak, until Gayley, who offered to be Santa's attorney, drags a bulky mail sack into the courtroom and empties its hundreds of letters addressed to Santa. The United States Post Office would never collude in promoting a fraud, Gayley argues, and therefore, by intending to deliver these letters, it confirms the existence of Santa Claus. Faced with such irrefutable logic, the judge finds Kris Kringle quite sane. In the end, Santa's presence has changed Doris and Susan Walker's lives dramatically. Walker, taking a cue from her daughter, warms to Santa Claus and consequently gives up her career at Macy's to marry Fred (after some matchmaking on Kringle's part).[32]

Through Kris Kringle, *Miracle on 34th Street* rejected modern notions of rationality and female independence. It validated instead what it treated as their opposites: sentiment, love, family, and faith. However, a closer look at Kris Kringle in this film reveals a Santa Claus less powerful than any of his forebears. As an aging man with few friends, Santa's power in a world of changed social and economic realities had weakened. In the nineteenth century, he would have swept in from some uncharted region in the north to shower toys on children. In this century he counted little more than thirty dollars in his pocket, which forced him to ask the zookeeper in Central Park for a temporary home. He needed the job at Macy's even though it depended on his ability to generate business. He could not fulfill gift wishes, only tell mothers where to shop for them. Before long, the logic of psychoanalytic theory sent him in an asylum. It took a lawyer to get him released.

At every turn, Kringle's actions and dilemma revised the Santa legend. Repeatedly, with the Walkers and at work, he resorted to charm and cunning to get the results he wanted. Understandably, Kringle did not promote a belief in Santa per se, but preached the values of imagination and belief in and of themselves. When Susan Walker had confided in Kringle that her Christmas wish was for a real home and, implicitly, a real mother, a real father, and a real house, not an apartment, Kringle helped set the stage for the realization of Susan's dream, but he lacked the magic to insure a happy outcome.[33]

Even as *Miracle on 34th Street* pictured a Santa humanized and in decline, the movie also portrayed a child possessed of a guileless potency, one who protected adults and transformed their world. Susan Walker rescued her mother from the work world and gave her renewed domestic purpose. Fred Gayley, who certainly had ample motivation, could not accomplish this task by himself. Nor could Kris Kringle. Indeed, the very existence of Santa depended on a child's hope for authentication. The situation had been quite different when Virginia O'Hanlon had raised the question of Santa's reality some forty years earlier. Frank Church, a big-city news editor, an adult, had vouched for Santa's truth: "Yes, Virginia, there is a Santa Claus."[34]

That a child should exercise this type and degree of power was a new theme of Christmas. Christmas stories throughout the nineteenth century portrayed adults as the mediators of happiness and faith. In "An Account of a Visit from St. Nicholas," a father watched over Santa's gift deliveries while his children stayed "sleeping all snug in their beds." In *A Christmas Carol*, despite the strong image of crippled Tiny Tim, Bob Cratchit and Scrooge, the men of the story, controlled the tale. Later in the century, women, particularly mothers, played central roles in Christmas dramas. In

Willa Cather's "The Burglar's Christmas" (1896), for instance, the mother welcomed home her prodigal son on the holiday.[35]

In the twentieth century, the role of catalyst devolved to children and other relatively vulnerable figures. Susan Walker's part in *Miracle on 34th Street* is but one example. In *Rudolph the Red-Nosed Reindeer*, Santa lacks the necessary skills to negotiate the foggy Christmas sky. A youngster and social outcast comes to his rescue. *Amahl and the Night Visitors*, an opera composed by Gian-Carlo Menotti especially for NBC television in 1951, illustrates again the child's ascendant role in modern Christmas visions. When the three wise men stop to rest on their way to Bethlehem, they catch Amahl's mother stealing their gold. Amahl, a poor and badly crippled shepherd boy, leaps to his mother's rescue, forcefully pleading her goodness. The wise men, disarmed by his fervor, forgive her. Besides showing himself to be a gallant protector, Amahl displays an innocent and open-handed generosity. When he learns that the wise men intend their gifts for Baby Jesus, he asks that his own crutch be added to the wealth. Instantly his disability vanishes, permitting him to leave his mother (and his infirmity) behind to travel with men, a fate quite different from Tiny Tim's, who at the close of *A Christmas Carol* remains perched upon his father's shoulder, still protected by him.[36]

Not surprisingly, the culture's reliance on children as exemplars of Christmas spirit found one of its strongest statements in a children's book by Dr. Seuss (Theodore Geisel), *How the Grinch Stole Christmas* (1957). Totally imaginary, it did not fuss with traditional humanitarian themes, expositions of miracles, or even the more conventional debates over the holiday's commercialism and materialism. It suggested instead that even the tangible, secular components of Christmas (the Whos' Christmas has no Christian symbols)—trees, wreaths, mistletoe, bells, lights, gifts, roast beast, and ornaments—were not necessary to the holiday. Thus, this vastly popular twentieth-century Christmas fable constructed a version of the modern Christmas in which the essence of the holiday lay wholly in its "spirit" and sense of community, and not in any of its material trappings.[37]

The story itself gives a twist to Scrooge in *A Christmas Carol* and a nod to the narrative style of "An Account of a Visit from St. Nicholas." The old and crotchety Grinch who lives just north of Who-ville so hates Christmas that he conceives the "wonderful, awful idea!" of stealing Christmas from the residents of the town. Dressed as Santa (and his dog Max outfitted with antlers), he slides down the chimney of the first Who house and systematically stuffs all the holiday presents—

> Pop guns! And bicycles! Roller skates! Drums!
> Checkerboards! Tricycles! Popcorn! And plums!

—"up the chimbley!" then takes all their food, "quick as a flash." As he reaches for the Christmas tree, he notices "little Cindy-Lou Who, who was not more than two" quietly watching him. The Grinch claims he is there to repair the lights. So satisfied, the innocent child returns to her bed. The Grinch continues on his way, looting every other Who's house of Christmas. On Christmas morning, he anticipates how quiet and unhappy the Whos will be, but hears instead "every Who down in Who-ville . . . singing! Without any presents at all!" The Grinch "HADN'T stopped Christmas from coming! IT CAME!" This puzzles him, until he comprehends that

> "Maybe Christmas," he thought, "*doesn't* come from a store."
> "Maybe Christmas . . . perhaps . . . means a little bit more!"

Upon this discovery, the Grinch's heart triples in size. He returns all the Christmas things to Who-ville and sits at the head of the feast table, carving the roast beast and savoring the joyous, true Christmas feeling of a community celebrating together.[38]

While this final scene focuses on the Grinch's epiphany, the story's more profound message is that the Whos have understood the real meaning of Christmas all along, a truth grasped when one reads the Who-ville drama through the eyes of Cindy-Lou. As with Amahl, Rudolph, and other small heroes of Christmas tales, her untainted faith and true-hearted goodness enable her to trust that, in the end, there will be a Christmas.[39]

By encapsulating this information in this way, Dr. Seuss distilled a complex of facts, sentiments, beliefs, and moral imperatives into actions and thoughts made more persuasive because they are those of a defenseless or mere child. This strategy has not been restricted to a handful of memorable stories. Television, novels, short stories, and even computer networks have with increasing frequency made the youngster's ingenuous conviction the culture's received view of the holiday. When openly considering America's Christmas, each has tended to leave unquestioned as well the perceived tension between material and spiritual, vilifying materialism and championing "truth" as if exclusively opposite.

Movies especially have engaged in this simplification. When Christmas is not the central theme nor even a minor one in a film's story line, directors, screenwriters, and others have further codified the fragmented reminders of the holiday into highly telegraphic renditions. A quarter, and perhaps even a majority of top-grossing motion pictures released in recent years at least mention Christmas or have a scene with a Christmas icon – a fleeting cameo of a Christmas tree, or the trailing melody of an oft-hummed carol – regardless of the movie's actual theme. These further circumscribe Christmas in order to convey a potent, highly condensed expression of American faith and values. The holiday establishes the essential "other" that summarizes almost instantaneously Susan Walker, Rudolph, Amahl, and a redeemed Grinch. In the Christmas celebration reside all goodness, kindness, hope, and tranquility. It stands as the all-purpose point against which the greed, violence, selfishness, and dishonesty of the late twentieth century are gauged.[40]

Directors rely on these cinematic flashcards to convey to the audience a contrasting and naïve optimism, confident that the audience knows, at least intuitively, how to read the scene. Gene Hackman, for example, dresses in a Santa costume to make a drug bust in *The French Connection* (1971). Movies like *Silent Night, Bloody Night* (1973), *Black Christmas* (1975), and *Silent Night, Deadly Night III – Better Watch Out!* (1989) invert Christmas, making it a day of horror. Christmas illuminates the seaminess of the settings and scenes in *Brazil* (1985), *Havana* (1990), and *Goodfellas* (1990), and provides the colorful backdrop against which a wily youngster battles robbers in *Home Alone* (1990). In two "action" movies, *Die Hard* (1988) and *Die Hard 2* (1990), it provides an implicit comparison of brutish male outlawry with a quiet world in which wives and families exist. A lone, decorated Christmas tree is the only evidence of Christmas in *Other People's Money* (1992); when the money-hungry protagonist declares his love and proposes marriage to the attorney for his arch rival, the camera briefly takes in a view of a glittery evergreen. *Deep Cover* (1992) opens with a snowy Christmas scene in which a black child's father is shot robbing a liquor store. It is also the scene in which the father warns his child away from a life of crime and, in his dying breath, tells his son that he loves him. Christmas brackets the entirety of *Batman Returns* (1993), where Batman triumphs over the Penguin and all his bad retinue.[41]

In 1993, Tim Burton enlarged these truncated media representations of Christmas into a full-length animated film, *The Nightmare Before Christmas*. In an otherworld of holidays, Jack the Pumpkin King discovers the pathway to Santa Claus's duchy of Christmas. Inspired by the liveliness and good humor of its citizens, he plans to replicate their community in his gloomy night world of Halloween. He busies his fellow haunters with making toys, constructs a sleigh from a coffin, and orders the fabrication of reindeer. He sends several small pranksters to kidnap Santa Claus himself in order to give the old man a much-needed vacation. Of course, the entire scheme fails miserably. Jack makes no one happy. The toys he takes to the waiting children scare them and alarm the entire Christmas town. Santa's Christmas, Jack learns when he and his sleigh are gunned from the sky, is not a permeable world. Bad, even when donated with good intentions, cannot succeed there. However, the mission does result in some good. Contact with Christmas revitalizes the kingdom of Halloween keepers and Jack finds in his own domain a girl to love.

As has the media, we have developed our own still pictures of Christmas and made it a place to visit. In Christmas we sustain the expectation of renewing our connection with seasonal time and ritual, of recalling some past and more perfect moment of faith and transcendence. Yet, in this late moment of the twentieth century, the quest seems increasingly difficult. As a metaphor for a more perfect world, our national Christmas provides a contrast to, not a celebration of, our own. At the same time, profanation, secularization, commercialization, and prevalence throughout American life have delustered it.

Still, we do not give it up. Christmas remains the most important holiday on our nation's calendar, even though questions of proper celebration perplex us as they did Governor Bradford, the "newcomers" to Plymouth Colony, and other Americans over the nation's centuries. The holiday continues as always to cross the fluid boundaries between the realms of the sacred, secular, and profane. Sooner or later, on television or in church, its arrival brings individuals and culture into direct confrontation with ideals. It causes us to examine relationships with our families, our community, and our faith. At Christmastide, we must, directly or even by omission, set our priorities, establish our tolerances, and square our hopes with reality.

Notes

Foreword

1. James Barnett pioneered the study of this holiday in *American Christmas: A Study in National Culture* (New York: Macmillan, 1954). Of the recent work on Christmas see, for example, Stephen Nissenbaum, "Revisiting 'A Visit from St. Nicholas': the Battle for Christmas in Early Nineteenth-Century America," in *The Mythmaking Frame of Mind: Social Imagination and American Culture*, James Gilbert et al., eds. (Belmont, Calif.: Watson Publishing, 1992), 25–70; Leigh Eric Schmidt, "Joy to [Some of] the World. Christianity in the Marketplace: Christmas and the Consumer Culture," *Cross Currents* 42 (Fall 1992): 350–51; William B. Waits, *The Modern Christmas in America. A Cultural History of Gift Giving* (New York: New York Univ. Press, 1993); and J. M. Golby and A. W. Purdue, *The Making of the Modern Christmas* (London: B. T. Batsford, 1986).

2. Eric Hobsbawm and Terence Ranger, eds., *The Invention of Tradition* (Cambridge: Cambridge Univ. Press, 1983). See especially Hobsbawm, "Introduction: Inventing Traditions," in ibid., 1–14.

Chapter 1. European Inheritances

1. Philadelphia *Democratic Press*, Dec. 18, 1810, quoted in Don Yoder, "Introduction," in Alfred L. Shoemaker, *Christmas in Pennsylvania: A Folk-Cultural Study* (Kutztown: Pennsylvania Folklife Society, 1959), 5.

2. "Editor's Easy Chair," *Harper's New Monthly Magazine*, Dec. 1857, p. 23 (hereafter, *Harper's Monthly*); Alan Dundes, "Christmas as a Reflection of American Culture," *California Monthly* (San Francisco: privately printed by A. R. Tommasini, 1970; orig. *California Monthly* 78 (Dec. 1967):9–15), 4; George William Douglas, *The American Book of Days*, rev. by Helen Douglas Compton (New York: H. W. Wilson, 1948), 658. On the date of Jesus' birth, see John Gunstone, *Christmas and Epiphany* (London: Faith Press, 1967), 9;

and John Ashton, *A Righte Merrie Christmasse!!!: The Story of Christ-tide* (n.p., n.d.; rpt., New York: Benjamin Blom, 1968), 1–5.

3. A. Allan McArthur, *Evolution of the Christian Year* (London: SCM Press, 1953), 36, 47; Dom Bernard Botte, *Les Origines de la Noel et de l'Epiphanie*, 1932, cited in ibid., 36; Cheslyn Jones, Geoffry Wainwright, and Edward Yarnold, eds., *The Study of Liturgy* (New York: Oxford Univ. Press, 1978), 414.

4. William Auld, *Christmas Traditions* (New York: Macmillan, 1932), 28–30; Dundes, "Christmas as a Reflection of American Culture," 5; Ashton, *A Righte Merrie Christmasse!!!*, 5; Miles, *Christmas in Ritual and Tradition*, 23–24; Gunstone, *Christmas and Epiphany*, 14; McArthur, *Evolution*, 46.

5. Miles, *Christmas in Ritual and Tradition*, 20, 23; Gunstone, *Christmas and Epiphany*, 24; Jones, Wainwright, and Yarnold, eds., *Study of Liturgy*, 414.

6. William Sandys, *Christmastide: Its History, Festivals and Carols* (London: John Russell Smith, n.d.), x–xi; R. Chambers, ed., *The Book of Days: A Miscellany of Popular Antiquities*, 2 vols. (London: Edinburgh: W. R. Chambers, 1864), 2:745; Gregory Dix, *The Shape of the Liturgy* (1945), cited in McArthur, *Evolution*, 37.

7. Miles, *Christmas in Ritual and Tradition*, 25–26; Gregory of Nazianzen, quoted in Golby and Purdue, *Modern Christmas*, 24; Earl W. Count, *4000 Years of Christmas* (New York: Schuman, 1948), 28.

8. Jones, Wainwright, and Yarnold, eds., *Study of Liturgy*, 414–15; Gunstone, *Christmas and Epiphany*, 15, 18, 22, 26; quote on 18. McArthur, *Evolution*, 46, 47. See Gunstone, *Christmas and Epiphany*, 25–36, for discussion of various times Christmas and Epiphany became established throughout Gaul, Jerusalem, Alexandria, and surrounding areas.

9. McArthur, *Evolution*, 46; Ashton, *A Righte Merrie Christmasse!!!*, 4; George Buday, *History of the Christmas Card* (London: Spring Books, 1964), 20n; Philip Reed Rulon, *Keeping Christmas: The Celebration of an American Holiday* (Hamden, Conn.: Archon Books, 1990), 3; Katherine L. Richards, *How Christmas Came to the Sunday-Schools: The Observance of Christmas in the Protestant Church Schools of the United States* (New York: Dodd, Mead, 1934), 17; Samuel L. Macey, *Patriarchs of Time: Dualism in Saturn-Cronus, Father Time, the Watchmaker God, and Father Christmas* (Athens: Univ. of Georgia Press, 1987), 115. John Ashton writes that Anglo-Saxons and early English referred to the season as Yule, a term derived from the old Norse *jøl*, which means feasting and revelry (*A Righte Merrie Christmasse!!!*, 6). Although the *Oxford English Dictionary* informs us that the abbreviation "Xmas" did not come into use before 1551, Tom Burnam states that the Old English word for Christmas begins with an "X" and can be found in the Anglo-Saxon Chronicle, written near the beginning of the 12th century. It is not known, however, whether this "X" stood for the cross or for the Greek word for Christ, which begins with the Greek letter chi or "x" (*Dictionary of Misinformation* (New York: Ballantine Books, 1975), 329).

10. Tristram Potter Coffin, *The Book of Christmas Folklore* (New York: Seabury Press, 1973), 7.

11. For this and following paragraph, see Golby and Purdue, *Modern Christmas*, 29–30; Sandys, *Christmastide*, 105; Miles, *Christmas in Ritual and Tradition*, 184. Ashton, *A Righte Merrie Christmasse!!!*, 21, 24–25; Michael Harrison, *The Story of Christmas* (London: Odhams Press, n.d.), 126. See William F. Dawson, *Christmas: Its Origins and Associations* (London: Elliott Stock, 1902; rpt., Gale Research, 1968), 122–96, for Christmas court activities during the reigns of Edward VI, Mary, Elizabeth, and James I.

12. Richards, *How Christmas Came to the Sunday-Schools*, 37, 45.

13. Stubbes, quoted in Walter Tittle, comp., *Colonial Holidays, Being a Collection of Contemporary Accounts of Holiday Celebrations in Colonial Times* (New York: Doubleday,

Page, 1910), n.p.; Prynne, quoted in Warner, "Christmas Past," 16, and in Tittle, comp., *Colonial Holidays*, n.p.

14. Golby and Purdue, *Modern Christmas*, 31; Hester Dorsey Richardson, *Sidelights on Maryland History* (Baltimore: Williams & Wilkins, 1913), 26; Harrison, *Story of Christmas*, 126.

15. For this and the following paragraph, see: Sandys, *Christmastide*, 118–19, 127–28; Miles, *Christmas in Ritual and Tradition*, 184–85; Ashton, *A Righte Merrie Christmasse!!!*, 35–36; Golby and Purdue, *Modern Christmas*, 33; Dorothy A. Neuhoff, "Christmas in Colonial America," *Social Studies* 40 (Dec. 1949):340. The June 3, 1647, law that "strongly prohibited" the keeping of Christmas also banned Easter, Whitsuntide, and other holy days, since the Bible made no provision for them. Sandys, *Christmastide*, 118–19.

16. Ashton, citing Whitelock, *Memorials*, 1682, p. 666, remarks that "Cromwell himself seems to have been somewhat ashamed of these persecutions and severities. . . ." Ashton, *A Righte Merrie Christmasse!!!*, 40.

17. John Smith, *The Generall Historie of Virginia, New-England, and the Summer Isles*, March of America Facsimile Series, no. 18 (Ann Arbor: University Microfilms, 1966), 74; *Ark* diary, quoted in Richardson, *Sidelights on Maryland History*, 25.

18. William T. Davis, ed., *Bradford's History of Plymouth Plantation, 1606–1646* (1908; New York: Barnes & Noble, 1959), 126–27, 195. The *Mayflower*'s crew and, perhaps, some of Bradford's people celebrated on Christmas night, 1620, with "Beere" and "diverse times." For accounts of this incident, some with commentary suggesting that Pilgrims participated in a Christmas celebration, see ibid., 105; *Chronicles of the Pilgrims*, quoted in Hezekiah Butterworth, *Wonderful Christmases of Old* (Boston: Lothrop, 1885), n.p.; Ashton, *A Righte Merrie Christmasse!!!*, 21; Tittle, *Colonial Holidays*, 1; and George Willison, *The Pilgrim Reader: The Story of the Pilgrims as Told by Themselves and Their Contemporaries, Friendly and Unfriendly* (Garden City, N.Y.: Doubleday, 1953), 118. See also John Winthrop's journal entries for Dec. 24 and 26 (there is none for Dec. 25), 1630, James Kendall Hosmer, ed., *Winthrop's Journal "History of New England" 1630–1649*, 2 vols. (New York: Barnes and Noble, 1908, rpt., 1959), 1:55.

19. Douglas, *American Book of Days*, 661. Henri Joutel, *Journal of la Salle's Last Voyage, 1684–71*, Henry Reed Stiles, ed. (1906), 116, quoted in Walter Prescott Webb, "Christmas and New Year in Texas," *Southwestern Hist. Quart.* 44 (Jan. 1941):357. Emphasis in original.

20. Charles Fenno Hoffman, "The Pioneers of New York." Address delivered to the Saint Nicholas Society of Manhattan, Dec. 6, 1847 (New York, 1848), quoted in Charles W. Jones, *Saint Nicholas of Myra, Bari, and Manhattan: Biography of a Legend* (Chicago: Univ. of Chicago Press, 1978), 331. The demographic statistic is for 1643.

21. H. D. Biddle, ed., *Extracts from the Journal of Elizabeth Drinker, 1759–1807* (Philadelphia: J. B. Lippincott, 1889), Dec. 25, 1797, quoted in Yoder, "Introduction" to Shoemaker, *Christmas in Pennsylvania*, 8. In addition to those mentioned, other Christian sects throughout the colonies, such as German Reformed, Welsh Baptists, Scots-Irish Presbyterians, and Lutherans, as well as Roman Catholics, also kept Christmas. Quakers, Puritans, Separatists, and Baptists generally shunned it.

22. John A. Fulton, Cambridge, Massachusetts, quoted in William W. Newell, "Christmas Maskings in Boston," *Journal of American Folk-lore* 9 (1896):178; Douglas, *American Book of Days*, 5–6.

23. Chambers, ed., *Book of Days*, 2:739.

24. William S. Walsh, *Curiosities of Popular Customs*, (Philadelphia: J. B. Lippincott, 1898), 297–98, 729; Miles, *Christmas in Ritual and Tradition*, 301.

25. Miles, *Christmas in Ritual and Tradition*, 299; Douglas, *American Book of Days*, 6.

26. Douglas, *American Book of Days*, 5–6. H. E. Scudder, ed., *Recollections of Samuel Breck with Passages from His Note-Books (1771–1862)* (Philadelphia, 1877), 35–36, quoted in Shoemaker, *Christmas in Pennsylvania*, 23.

27. J. Thomas Scharf and Thompson Westcott, *History of Philadelphia*, 3 vols. (Philadelphia: L. H. Everts, 1884), 2:935.

28. "Holidays," *United States Review* 3 (July 1854):64; Gabriel Furman, "Winter Amusements," *New-York Hist. Quart. Bull.* 23 (Jan. 1939):11. This article was "written about 1830."

29. Thad W. Tate, "The Seventeenth-Century Chesapeake and Its Modern Historians," in *The Chesapeake in the Seventeenth Century*, Thad W. Tate and David L. Ammerman, eds. (New York: W. W. Norton, 1979), 26, 35, 37; Philip Alexander Bruce, *Social Life of Virginia in the Seventeenth Century*, 2nd ed. (Lynchburg, Va.: J. P. Bell, 1927), 137, 144–49, 182, 187, 195.

30. Julian P. Boyd, *Christmas at Monticello* (New York: Oxford Univ. Press, 1964), 10, 14; Bruce, *Social Life of Virginia in the Seventeenth Century*, v. Traveler quoted in Harnett T. Kane, *The Southern Christmas Book* (New York: David McKay, 1958), 15, and in Boyd, *Christmas at Monticello*, 19. Waits were members of groups of public musicians in England who serenaded for gratuities, usually at Christmas.

31. *London Magazine*, quoted in Kane, *Southern Christmas*, 14.

32. For this and next paragraph: Hunter Dickinson Farish, ed., *Journal and Letters of Philip Vickers Fithian, 1773–74* (Richmond, Va.: Williamsburg Restoration Historical Studies, 1943), vii, x; Dec. 18, 1773, pp. 44–45; Dec. 25, 1773, pp. 53–54; Dec. 26, 1773, p. 55. Emphasis in original.

33. The term "Christmas-boxes" was first used by priests "who ordered masses at times to be made to the saints for the sins of the people. The mass was called Christ mass, and the boxes in which the money was collected to pay for it were called Christmas-boxes." People were permitted to collect the money by "chanting the nightly carols." In time, "'Christmas-box' came to mean any gift to a dependent or poor person. . . . In consequence of the multiplicity of business on Christmas-day, the giving of the Christmas-boxes was eventually delayed until the 26th, St. Stephen's Day, which became the established Boxing-day." Warner, "Christmas Past," 8–9.

34. Louis B. Wright and Marion Tinling, eds., *The Great American Gentleman: William Byrd of Westover, His Secret Diary for the Years 1709–1712* (New York: G. P. Putnam's Sons, 1963), 56, 202. Boyd, *Christmas at Monticello*, 14. Olive [Drinkwine] Bailey, *Christmas with the Washingtons: Being a Special Account of Tradition Rites Observed in Virginia and Historic Yuletides of One First Family, the Washingtons of Mount Vernon*, 2nd ed. (Richmond, Va.: Dietz Press, 1952), 22–23.

35. Boyd, *Christmas at Monticello*, 14. *Virginia Gazette*, Dec. 1739, quoted in Rulon, *Keeping Christmas*, 11–12. Emphasis in original.

36. Ivor Debenham Spencer, "Christmas, the Upstart," *New England Quart.* 8 (Dec. 1935):501; *Records of . . . Massachusetts*, vol. 4, part 1, pp. 366–67, quoted in ibid., George E. Ellis, *Puritan Age and Rule in the Colony of the Massachusetts Bay* (Boston: Houghton Mifflin, 1888), 258.

37. Neuhoff, "Christmas in Colonial America," 340; Prince, "An Examination of Peters's 'Blue Laws,'" 155n; Rulon, *Keeping Christmas*, 14; Milton Halsey Thomas, ed., *Diary of Samuel Sewall, 1674–1749*, 2 vols. (New York: Farrar, Straus and Giroux, 1973), Dec. 20, 21, 22, 24, and 25, 1686, 1:127–28.

38. Annie Russell Marble, "Christmas Carols, Ancient and Modern," *Bookman*, Dec. 1901, p. 360; Samuel A. Green, ed., *Diary of Increase Mather* (Cambridge, Mass.: 1900), 54, quoted in Jones, *Saint Nicholas of Myra*, 332; Increase Mather, *A Testimony Against*

Several Profane and Superstitious Customs Now Practiced by Some in New England (London, 1687), quoted in Rulon, *Keeping Christmas*, 14–15.

39. Cotton Mather, *A Brand Pluckt Out of the Burning*, in George Lincoln Burr, ed., *Narratives of the Witchcraft Cases, 1648–1706* (New York: Charles Scribner's Sons, 1914), 274; *Diary of Cotton Mather, 1709–1724* (Boston: Massachusetts Hist. Soc., 1912), Dec. 30, 1711, p. 146.

40. Cotton Mather quoted in Abraham English Brown, "The Ups and Downs of Christmas in New England," *New England Magazine*, Dec. 1903, n.s., p. 483.

41. Richards, *How Christmas Came to the Sunday-Schools*, 50; Thomas, ed., *Diary of Samuel Sewall*, Dec. 25, 1685, 1:90; and Dec. 19, 20, 21, 22, 1722, 2:1000–1001. Sewall's Dec. 25 entries run from 1685 to 1727. Entries for 1697, 1705, 1706, 1714, 1716, 1722, 1724, and 1725 remark that the shops had remained open on Christmas Day. Ibid., Dec. 25, vols. 1 and 2.

42. Nelson Rollin Burr, *The Story of the Diocese of Connecticut: A New Branch of the Vine* (Hartford: Church Missions Publishing, 1962), 74; Thomas, ed., *Diary of Samuel Sewall*, Dec. 25, 1727, 2:1057–58n; Sewall quoted in Brown, "Ups and Downs of Christmas," 482; Minister quoted in Burr, *Story of the Diocese*, 74.

Chapter 2. Red-Letter Days

1. Frances Ann Butler [Kemble], *Fanny Kemble in America, or the Journal of an Actress Reviewed with Remarks on the State of Society in America and England*, 2 vols. (Philadelphia: Carey, Lea & Blanchard, 1835), Dec. 25, 1832, 2:47–48; Elizabeth Cady Stanton, *Eighty Years and More: Reminiscences 1815–1897* (New York: Shocken Books, 1971), 14; Samuel G. Goodrich, *Recollections of a Lifetime or Men and Things I Have Seen*, 2 vols. (New York: Miller, Orton and Mulligan, 1857), 2:86; Charles Haswell, *Reminiscences of an Octogenarian, 1816–1860* (New York: Harper and Bros., n.d.), 98.

2. Hugh Cunningham, *Leisure in the Industrial Revolution, c. 1780–c. 1880* (London: Croom Helm, 1980), 57.

3. Jones, *Saint Nicholas of Myra*, 292–93.

4. Emile Durkheim, *The Elementary Forms of Religious Life* (New York: Free Press, 1965), 347, quoted in Eviatar Zerubavel, *The Seven Day Circle: The History and Meaning of the Week* (New York: Free Press, 1985), 116; E. R. Leach, "Two Essays Concerning the Symbolic Representation of Time," in *Rethinking Anthropology* (1961; London: Athlone Press; New York: Humanities Press, 1968), 132; Clifford Geertz, "Person, Time, and Conduct in Bali," in *The Interpretation of Cultures* (New York: Basic Books, 1973), 391, quoted in Eviatar Zerubavel, *Hidden Rhythms: Schedules and Calendars in Social Life* (Chicago: Univ. of Chicago Press, 1981), 101.

5. Hawke, *Everyday Life*, 88; Jones, *Saint Nicholas of Myra*, 337.

6. Carl Horton Pierce, *New Harlem: Past and Present* (New York: New Harlem Publishing, 1903), 70; W. DeLoss Love, *Fast and Thanksgiving Days of New England* (Boston and New York: Houghton, Mifflin, 1895), 163; Washington Irving, *A History of New York*, Michael L. Black and Nancy B. Black, eds., (1809; rpt., Boston: Twayne, 1984), 251.

7. Hawke, *Everyday Life*, 89; Burr, *Story of the Diocese*, 74.

8. David Hackett Fischer, *Albion's Seed: Four British Folkways in America* (New York: Oxford Univ. Press, 1989), 370. Hock Tuesday falls on the second Tuesday after Easter. "Holidays," *United States Review*, 60.

9. Miles, *Christmas in Ritual and Tradition*, 337–38, 349; Maude H. Woodfin, ed., *Another Secret Diary of William Byrd of Westover, 1739–1741* (Richmond, Va.: Dietz Press,

1942), 28; Jack P. Greene, ed., *The Diary of Colonel Landon Carter of Sabine Hall, 1752–1778*, 2 vols. (Charlottesville: Univ. Press of Virginia, 1965), 2:334; Bailey, *Christmas with the Washingtons*, 17.

10. Hawke, *Everyday Life*, 94–95; Fischer, *Albion's Seed*, 164–65; Louis B. Wright, *Life in Colonial America* (New York: Capricorn, 1971), 208; Thomas, ed., *Diary of Samuel Sewall*, Feb. 15, 1686/87, 1:133.

11. Wright, *Life in Colonial America*, 206–8; Minister, quoted in ibid., 207; anonymous, quoted in ibid., 206–7; Fischer, *Albion's Seed*, 164–65. On Thanksgiving: Thomas, ed., *Diary of Samuel Sewall*, Nov. 24, 1709, 2:268.

12. Hawke, *Everyday Life*, 90–91, 100; Timothy Breen, *Tobacco Culture: The Mentality of the Great Tidewater Planters on the Eve of the Revolution* (Princeton, N.J.: Princeton Univ. Press, 1985), 55; Custom House Calendar, *American Register* (New York, 1775), cited in Jones, *Saint Nicholas of Myra*, 334–35.

13. Hawke, *Everyday Life*, 90–91, 100.

14. Zerubavel, *Seven Day Circle*, 83. See also Leach, "Two Essays Concerning the Symbolic Representation of Time," 129.

15. [Hezekiah Prince], *Journals of Hezekiah Prince, Jr., 1822–1828*, intro. by Walter Muir Whitehill and foreword by Robert G. Albion (New York: Crown, 1965), 307–8.

16. John Goodell, ed., *Diary of William Sewall* (Springfield, Ill.: Hartford Printing, 1930), 78.

17. "The Origin of Thanksgiving Day," *Magazine of American History*, Nov. 1882, p. 759; Love, *Fast and Thanksgiving Days*, 73; Goelet, quoted in Tittle, comp., *Colonial Holidays*, 9.

18. Thomas, ed., *Diary of Samuel Sewall*, Nov. 28, 1717, 2:870; Whittier to William James Allinson, Nov. 19, 1842, in John B. Pickard, ed., *The Letters of John Greenleaf Whittier*, 3 vols. (Cambridge, Mass.: Harvard Univ. Press, 1975), 1:582 (emphasis in original); *Diary of Charles Francis Adams*, vol. 3: *Sept. 1829–Feb. 1831*, Marc Friedlaender and L. H. Butterfield, eds., (Cambridge, Mass.: Belknap Press, 1968), Dec. 26, 1830, p. 374.

19. "Holidays," *United States Review*, 62–63; "A Glimpse of an Old Dutch Town," 525; Furman, "Winter Amusements in the Early 19th Century," 11; Douglas, *American Book of Days*, 3–4.

20. Gayle Thornbrough, ed., *The Diary of Calvin Fletcher, Vol. I, 1817–1838: Including Letters of Calvin Fletcher and Diaries and Letters of His Wife Sarah Hill Fletcher* (Indianapolis: Indiana Hist. Soc., 1972), Jan. 1, 1822, pp. 86–87; J. P. Bryan, ed., *Mary Austin Holley: The Texas Diary, 1835–1838* (Austin: Univ. of Texas Press, 1965), Dec. 30, 1835, p. 43.

21. Philadelphia *Democratic Press*, Dec. 18, 1810, quoted in Yoder, "Introduction" to Shoemaker, *Christmas in Pennsylvania*, 5. The newspaper also noted that Pennsylvanians, "for the greater part," did not observe Easter, Whitsuntide, or Hallow-eve either. *West Chester* (Pennsylvania) *American Republic*, Dec. 29, 1812, quoted in ibid., 8 (emphasis in original); Diary of Nathaniel Wright, Dec. 21, 1816, Dartmouth College Library, Hanover, New Hampshire (hereafter DCL).

22. *Journal of Rev. Francis Asbury*, 3 vols. (New York: Eaton & Mains; Cincinnati: Jennings & Pye, n.d.), 3:212.

23. Clark, quoted in John E. Baur, *Christmas on the American Frontier, 1800–1900* (Caldwell, Idaho: Caxton Printers, 1961), 78; see also Elliott Coues, ed., *The History of the Lewis and Clark Expedition, by Meriwether Lewis and William Clark*, 3 vols. (1893; rpt., New York: Dover, n.d.), Dec. 25, 1805, 2:738; Cox, quoted in Baur, *Christmas on the American Frontier*, 92–93; Annie H. Abel, ed., *Chardon's Journal at Fort Clark, 1834–1839* (Pierre, S. Dak.: n.p., 1932), Dec. 25, 1836, p. 92.

24. Richmond *Enquirer*, Dec. 25, 1804, Dec. 25, 1833; *Salisbury* (North Carolina) *Western Carolinian*, Dec. 25, 1821; *Providence* (Rhode Island) *Gazette*, Dec. 24, 1823.

25. On Samuel Rodman, see, for example, entries for Dec. 24 or 25, 1821, 1823, 1834, and 1837, in Pease, ed., *Diary of Samuel Rodman*, 12, 25, 138, 177; [Prince], *Journals of Hezekiah Prince, Jr.*, 106–7; Diary of Edwin Stone, 1823–31, microfilm, Minnesota Historical Society; Benjamin T. Hill, ed., *Diary of Isaiah Thomas*, 2 vols. (Worcester, Mass.: American Antiquarian Society, 1909), Dec. 25, 1819, 2:39; Goodell, ed., *Diary of William Sewall*, 32. These instances consider primarily the activities of educated, working, male city-dwellers on December 25, and reflect the general tone and content of each diarist's entries on that date for other years as well (if any entry was made at all). For examples of how other urban groups celebrated the holiday, see Chapters 3 through 5, in which women and the persistence of traditional forms of celebration in the city environment are discussed.

26. Thornbaugh, ed., *Diary of Calvin Fletcher*, 1:46, 84–85, 212, 214; Nathaniel Paine, ed., *Diary of Christopher Columbus Baldwin, Librarian of the American Antiquarian Society, 1829–1835* (Worcester, Mass.: American Antiquarian Society, 1901; rpt., Johnson Reprint, 1971), Dec. 25, 1829, p. 45; Hill, ed., *Diary of Isaiah Thomas*, 1:337; Jacob Morris to Abraham M. Walton, Nov. 25, 1806, William L. Clements Library, University of Michigan, Ann Arbor (hereafter WLCL).

27. *Diary of Charles Francis Adams*, vol. 2: *July 1825–September 1829*, Aida DiPace Donald and David Donald, eds. (Cambridge, Mass.: Harvard Univ. Press, 1964), 326–27; Arthur H. Cole, ed., *Charleston Goes to Harvard: The Diary of a Harvard Student of 1831* (Cambridge, Mass.: Harvard Univ. Press, 1940), July 4, 1831, p. 52; see also Julia A. Wilbur to Mrs. Barnes, Dec. 27, 1863, WLCL; "The Origin of Thanksgiving Day," *Magazine of American History*, Nov. 1882, p. 762; Breen, *Tobacco Culture*, 50.

28. James Iredell, Jr., to Ebenezer Pettigrew, Jan. 11, 1805, and Pettigrew to Iredell, Jr., March 20, 1805, in Sarah McCulloh Lemmon, ed., *The Pettigrew Papers, 1685–1818* (Raleigh, N.C.: State Dept. of Archives and History, 1971), 357.

29. "E.F." to sister, Dec. 27, 1819, WLCL. Emphasis in original.

30. John Pintard to Eliza Noel Pintard Davidson, May 24, 1823, entry for May 27, in Dorothy C. Barck, ed., *Letters from John Pintard to His Daughter Eliza Noel Pintard Davidson, 1816–1833*, 4 vols. (New York: New-York Historical Society, 1940–41), 2: 137–38.

31. Irving, *History of New York*, 288. Washington Irving, "Christmas," in *Old Christmas and Bracebridge Hall* (Boston and New York: Houghton Mifflin, 1919), 7.

32. Washington Irving, "The Vindication of Christmas, Pages from the Notebook of Washington Irving," sent as a Christmas greeting from Cornelia and Walker Barrett, 1961, Humanities Resource Center, University of Texas, Austin (hereafter HRC).

33. Washington Irving, "Christmas Eve," in *The Sketchbook of Geoffrey Crayon, Gent.*, in Richard Dilworth Rust, gen. ed., *The Complete Works of Washington Irving* (Boston: Twayne, 1978), 164; Irving "The Christmas Dinner," in ibid., 183.

34. Quotations in this and the following two paragraphs are in ibid., 162, 175–83, passim. The "fiery persecution of poor Mince pie" (p. 176) refers to Cromwell's ban on Christmas in England during the Puritan Directory (see Chapter 1).

Chapter 3. The Beginnings of a Modern Christmas

1. Franklin B. Dexter, ed., *The Literary Diary of Ezra Stiles*, 3 vols. (New York: C. Scribner's Sons, 1901), Dec. 25, 1769, 1:29, and Dec. 25, 1770, 1:267.

2. Edmund Morgan, *Gentle Puritan: A Life of Ezra Stiles* (New Haven: Yale Univ. Press, 1962), 112, 117.

3. Dexter, ed., *Literary Diary*, Dec. 25, 1772, 1:324–25, emphasis in original. It should be noted, as Stiles did, that Kelly "scarcely mentioned the Birth of Christ . . . preached on Regeneration John iii, 3, except a man be born &C. . . . "

4. Ibid., Dec. 25, 1776, 2:103; Dec. 25, 1782, 3:50.

5. [William Bentley], *Diary of William Bentley, D.D.*, 4 vols. (Salem, Mass.: Essex Institute, 1914), Dec. 25, 1808, 3:405; Dec. 25, 1812, 4:141; diary entries for Dec. 25, 1839, 1845, 1847–49, 1851, 1852, in Increase N. Tarbox, ed., *The Diary of Thomas Robbins, D.D.*, 2 vols. (Boston: Beacon Press, 1886, 1887), 2:553, 807, 888, 924, 960, 1030, 1058; Pease, ed., *Diary of Samuel Rodman*, 170; Alexander, quoted in Phillip Snyder, *December 25th, The Joys of Christmas Past* (New York: Dodd, Mead, 1985), 268.

6. *Pittsburgh Gazette*, Dec. 26, 1874, in Yoder, "Introduction" to Shoemaker, *Christmas in Pennsylvania*, 5. Milton Rugoff, *The Beechers* (New York: Harper & Row, 1981), 115–16.

7. William Parker Cutler and Julia Perkins Cutler, eds., *Life Journals and Correspondence of Rev. Manasseh Cutler, LL.D.*, 2 vols. (Cincinnati: Robert Clarke, 1888), Dec. 25, 1802, 2:114; Diary of Sally Knowles, Christmas 1848, Historical Society of Pennsylvania, Philadelphia (emphasis in original); Allan Nevins and Milton H. Thomas, eds., *The Diary of George Templeton Strong*, vol. 1: *Young Man in New York* (New York: Macmillan, 1952), xxi; Strong, Private Journal, Dec. 25, 1841, 1:523, microfilm, New-York Historical Society, New York (hereafter, Strong, Private Journal, NYHS).

8. Alexis de Tocqueville, *Democracy in America*, J. P. Mayer, ed., George Lawrence, trans. (Garden City, N.Y.: Doubleday Anchor, 1969), 449. Excerpts from Robbins's diary in this and the next paragraph in Tarbox, ed., *Diary of Thomas Robbins, D.D.*, 1:244, 343, 381, 880, 880n, 949.

9. Furman, "Winter Amusements in the Early 19th Century," 10–11; Scott poem in *Daily National Intelligencer*, cited in Jones, *Saint Nicholas of Myra*, 350.

10. "Stranger's Account," in Horatio Smith, *Festivals, Games and Amusements* (New York, 1831), quoted in Snyder, *December 25th*, xx.

11. *Diary of Charles Francis Adams*, Jan. 1, 1834, 3:239; Philip English Mackey, ed., *A Gentleman of Much Promise: The Diary of Isaac Mickle, 1837–1845*, 2 vols. (Philadelphia: Univ. of Pennsylvania Press, 1977), Dec. 26, 1842, 1:344.

12. On the point of forming new communities, see Stuart M. Blumin, *Urban Threshold, Growth and Change in a Nineteenth-Century American Community* (Chicago: Univ. of Chicago Press, 1976), esp. 150–65.

13. *Boston Centinel*, Dec. 25, 1833, p. 2, cited in *Diary of Charles Francis Adams*, vol. 5: *Jan. 1833–Oct. 1834*, Marc Friedlander and L. H. Butterfield, eds. (Cambridge, Mass.: Harvard Univ. Press, 1974), 234; Strong, Private Journal, Dec. 25, 1840, 1:447; Dec. 25, 1841, 1:523–24. Emphasis in original.

14. Kate Sullivan, "The Christmas Party," *Godey's Lady's Magazine*, Dec. 1849, p. 421. *Godey's Lady's Book* was published under a number of similar titles from 1830–92. In this and all subsequent references I use the shortened title *Godey's* to refer to any edition of the magazine.

15. Horace Bushnell, *Christian Nurture* (New Haven: Yale Univ. Press, 1967; orig. pub. as "Discourses on Christian Nurture," 1847, rewritten and enlarged in 1861), 294.

16. Throughout this chapter, the terms "mumming" or "masking" refer generally to what I have come to see as a widespread and loosely related set of eighteenth- and nineteenth-century practices that included shooting, disguising, and ritual begging during the Christmas season. See Herbert Halpert, "A Typology of Mumming," in *Christmas*

Mumming in Newfoundland: Essays in Anthropology, Folklore, and History, H. Halpert and G. M. Story, eds. (Toronto: Univ. of Toronto Press, 1969), 34–61, for a useful descriptive framework of the variety of mumming behaviors. For other examples of mumming-type rituals in the colonial era and among American slaves, see Chapters 1 and 6.

17. *Columbia* diary, quoted in Baur, *Christmas on the American Frontier,* 74 (emphasis in original); Ordway quoted on 92–93. Juanita Brooks, ed., *On the Mormon Frontier: The Diary of Hosea Stout, 1844–1861,* 2. vols. (Salt Lake City: Univ. of Utah Press, 1964), Dec. 25, 1852, 2:466.

18. Snyder, *December 25th,* 46; Whipple, quoted in Baur, *Christmas on the American Frontier,* 83.

19. John Hyde Braley, *Memory Pictures, an Autobiography* (Los Angeles: Neumer, 1912), 37; James S. Lamar, *Recollections of Pioneer Days in Georgia* (n.p.: n.d.), 35.

20. James Flint, "Jeffersonville, (Indiana), May 19, 1819," entry for Jan. 1, 1819, letter in *Flint's Letters to America, 1818–1820* (Chicago: Arthur H. Clark, 1904; orig. *Letters from America,* (1822), 151; J. C. A. Hamilton to mother, "Christmas Morning," Hamilton-Schuyler Papers, undated and unlocated, Miscellaneous Bound Collection, WLCL. Julia A. Wilbur to Mrs. Barnes, Dec. 27, 1863, WLCL.

21. Frederic Law Olmsted, *Journey Through Texas: A Saddle-Trip on the Southwestern Frontier,* James Howard, ed. (Austin, Tex.: Von Boeckmann-Jones, 1962), Dec. 25, 1856, p. 20.

22. George Sample, quoted in Snyder, *December 25th,* 186; Max Freund, trans. and ed., *Gustav Dresel's Houston Journal* (Austin: Univ. of Texas Press, 1954), xiii, 90; Brooks, ed., *On the Mormon Frontier,* Dec. 25, 1858, 2:672; Cleland and Brooks, eds., *Mormon Chronicle,* Dec. 27, 1866, 2:40.

23. Margaret Robertson, "The Symbolism of Christmas Mummering in Newfoundland," *Folklore* 93 (Feb. 1982):178–79; A. P. Rossiter, *English Drama from Early Times to the Elizabethans: Its Background, Origins and Developments* (New York: Hutchinson's University Library, 1950), 33–34. Roger D. Abrahams and Richard Bauman, "Ranges of Festival Behavior," in *The Reversible World: Symbolic Inversion in Art and Society,* Barbara A. Babcock, ed. (Ithaca: Cornell Univ. Press, 1978), 195.

24. Flint, "Cincinnati, Ohio, 30th December, 1818," entry for Dec. 25, *Flint's Letters to America, 1818–1820,* 147; Bert Göbel, *Langer als ein Menschenleben in Missouri* (St. Louis; (1877)), 80–81, quoted in Robbins, "Christmas Shooting Rounds in America," 48. Göbel refers to the 1830s.

25. J. Thomas Scharf and Thompson Wescott, *History of Philadelphia,* 3 vols. (Philadelphia: L. H. Everts, 1884), 1:157.

26. Ibid., 32–33; "Holidays," *United States Review,* 64; Eliza Cope Harrison, ed., *Philadelphia Merchant: The Diary of Thomas P. Cope, 1800–1851* (South Bend, Ind.: Gateway Editions, 1978), Jan. 1, 1844, p. 419; Mackey, ed., *A Gentleman of Much Promise,* Dec. 31, 1841, 1:248.

27. Furman, "Winter Amusements in the Early 19th Century," 15; Susan G. Davis, "'Making Night Hideous': Christmas Revelry and Public Order in Nineteenth-Century Philadelphia," *American Quart.* 34 (Feb. 1982):188; *Philadelphia Daily Chronicle,* Dec. 26, 1833, quoted in Shoemaker, *Christmas in Pennsylvania,* 86; *Pittsburgh Daily Commercial Journal,* Dec. 27, 1848, quoted in ibid., 113. I found Davis's insights into the issues surrounding Philadelphia mumming, and particularly those concerning a redefinition of public and private spheres in that city during the nineteenth-century, to have been extremely valuable. See Davis, "'Making Night Hideous,'" 185–99.

28. For a broader look at violence in antebellum America, see, for example, Leonard L. Richards, *Gentlemen of Property and Standing: Anti-abolition Mobs in Jacksonian America*

(New York: Oxford Univ. Press, 1970), and Michael Feldberg, *The Turbulent Era: Riot and Disorder in Jacksonian America* (New York: Oxford Univ. Press, 1980). However, neither of these studies looks specifically at holiday mayhem other than that of election days. There is no evidence that families of maskers were not also gathering at the hearth at Christmastide. Rather, masking had probably lingered as an additional part of the holiday.

29. Davis, "'Making Night Hideous,'" 188–89. *Easton* (Pennsylvania) *Sentinel*, Jan. 10, 1834, quoted in Charles E. Welch, *Ob! Dem Golden Slippers* (New York and Camden: Thomas Nelson, 1970), 30. On the point of the development of working-class consciousness in the antebellum period, see, for example, Paul Johnson, *A Shopkeeper's Millennium: Society and Revivals in Rochester, New York, 1815–1837* (New York: Hill and Wang, 1978), and Anthony F. C. Wallace, *Rockdale: The Growth of an American Village in the Early Industrial Revolution* (New York: Knopf, 1978).

30. Gayle Thornbrough, ed., *The Diary of Calvin Fletcher, Vol. I, 1817–1838: Including Letters of Calvin Fletcher and Diaries and Letters of His Wife Sarah Hill Fletcher* (Indianapolis: Indiana Historical Society, 1972), 166; John Pintard to Eliza Pintard Davidson, Jan. 2, 1828, in Barck, ed., *Letters from John Pintard*, 3:1. Although I concentrate on the contrast between public mumming and the private Christmas, the ethnic conflicts between groups of mummers should not be ignored. See, especially, Davis, "'Making Night Hideous,'" 185–99. For a discussion similar to Davis's, but about the Christmas season in New York, see Nissenbaum, "Revisiting 'A Visit from St. Nicholas,'" 25–70.

31. *Friends Intelligencer*, "The Season," Jan. 3, 1846, quoted in Yoder, "Introduction" to *Christmas in Pennsylvania*, 9.

32. Brooks, ed., *Mormon Chronicle*, Dec. 25, 1867, 2:94.

Chapter 4. Home for Christmas I

1. "Letters from New York, Lydia Maria Child," in Gail Parker, ed., *The Oven Birds: American Women on Womanhood, 1820–1920* (Garden City, N.Y.: Anchor Books, 1972), Dec. 8, 1842, p. 87.

2. John Mather Austin, *A Voice to the Married* (Utica, 1841), 38, quoted in Mary P. Ryan, *Cradle of the Middle Class* (Cambridge, Mass.: Cambridge Univ. Press, 1981), 147; Horace Bushnell, *Christian Nurture*, (New Haven: Yale Univ. Press, 1967; orig. pub. as "Discourses on Christian Nurture," 1847), 295.

3. Barbara Welter, "The Feminization of American Religion," in *Dimity Convictions: The American Woman in the Nineteenth Century* (Athens: Ohio Univ. Press, 1976), 83–102.

4. Ibid., 88; Bronson Alcott to Anna, Louisa, and Elizabeth, Dec. 25, 1841, in Richard L. Herrnstadt, ed., *The Letters of A. Bronson Alcott* (Ames: Iowa State Univ. Press, 1969), 58.

5. Beriah Green, "The Savior's Arms Open to Little Children: A Discourse" (Utica, 1836), 12, quoted in Ryan, *Cradle of the Middle Class*, 99. Bushnell, *Christian Nurture*, 291 (emphasis in original).

6. McDannell, *Christian Home in Victorian America*, 99, 104.

7. Martin Ebon, *Saint Nicholas: Life and Legend* (New York: Harper & Row, 1975), 9. For a detailed version of the St. Nicholas story, see Jones, *Saint Nicholas of Myra*, 54–57.

8. Ebon, *Saint Nicholas*, 52, 54, 70–71, 87.

9. Rivington's *Gazateer* quoted in Charles W. Jones, "Knickerbocker Santa Claus," *New-York His. Soc. Quart.* 38 (1954):363; Jones, *Saint Nicholas of Myra*, 330, 332–33.

10. Brian McGinty, "Santa Claus," *Early American Life* 10 (Dec. 1979):52–53.

11. Jones, *Saint Nicholas of Myra*, 340, 342, 345–47; McGinty, "Santa Claus," 33. On

John Pintard, see Barck, ed., *Letters from John Pintard*, 1:x. Samuel White Patterson, *The Poet of Christmas Eve: A Life of Clement Clark Moore, 1779–1863* (New York: Morehouse-Gorham, 1956), 17; Robert W. G. Vail, *Knickerbocker Birthday: A Sesqui-centennial History of the New York Historical Society 1804–1954* (New York: New-York Historical Society, 1954), 370 (emphasis in original); Jones, *Saint Nicholas of Myra*, 340–43; McGinty, "Santa Claus," 53.

12. John Pintard to Eliza Noel Pintard Davidson, Jan. 19, 1819, in Barck, ed., *Letters from John Pintard*, 1:164; Pintard to Davidson, Dec. 22, 1832, entry for Dec. 26, in ibid., 4:116.

13. Irving, *A History of New York*, 58–59.

14. Jones, *Saint Nicholas of Myra*, 345–347; James K. Paulding, quoted in ibid., 352.

15. Henry Litchfield West, "Who Wrote 'Twas the Night Before Christmas'?," *Bookman* 52 (Dec. 1920):301; Martin Gardner, ed., *The Annotated Night Before Christmas* (New York: Summit Books, 1991), 22; Clement Clarke Moore, "A Visit from St. Nicholas," illus. by F. O. C. Darley (New York: James D. Gregory, c. 1962), reproduced in *Yankee Doodle's Literary Sampler of Prose, Poetry, and Pictures*, intro. by Virginia Haviland and Margaret N. Coughlan (New York: Thomas Y. Crowell, 1974), 169–75. Martin Gardner notes that the original printing of the poem ended with "Happy Christmas to all. . . ." It was printed as "Merry Christmas to all," probably for the first time, in *A Visit from Saint Nicholas*, illus. by F. O. C. Darley (New York: Hurd and Houghton, 1862, and Cambridge: Riverside Press, 1862) (Gardner, *Annotated Night*, 42). Well into the middle 1840s, there existed two opening lines to "A Visit from St. Nicholas." One began "'Twas the night before New Year's" (Jones, *Saint Nicholas of Myra*, 350).

16. Moore, interviewed at age 83, quoted from 1862 interview for the New-York Historical Society, in West, "Who Wrote 'Twas the Night Before Christmas'?," 302. There is a largely ignored controversy over whether Moore actually penned "A Visit from St. Nicholas." Henry West sets the premise of the argument, suggesting that Moore, owing to his professional and religious connections, tended to be too "distinctly sober and grave" to have been its author. The issue has been most fervently pursued by William S. Thomas, who claims that his great-grandfather Henry Livingston, Jr. (1748–1828), wrote "A Visit" (West, "Who Wrote 'Twas the Night Before Christmas'?," 301, 305). Tristram Coffin argues for Livingston's authorship, noting that he "was a whimsical chap who once switched the lyrics in his music book from 'God Save the King' to 'God Save Congress' and who produced a steady stream of light, occasional verse, much of it in the same meter as 'The Night Before . . .'" (Coffin, *Book of Christmas Folklore*, 90).

17. Irving, *History of New York*, 93, 94.

18. Ibid., 76–77.

19. *The Children's Friend, a New-Year's Present to the Little Ones from Five to Twelve* contains eight hand-colored lithographs and the poem excerpted here. It is generally supposed to have been the first book produced by lithography and the first about St. Nicholas published in America (Brian McGinty, "Santa Claus," 103). See this chapter, note 35, for full text of this poem and a note about its authorship.

20. Woodward, "Moore's St. Nick: Model and Motif," 253; Michael Wigglesworth, "The Day of Doom," in Perry Miller, ed., *The American Puritans: Their Prose and Poetry* (Garden City, N.Y.: Anchor Books, 1956), 282–94; Moore, "A Visit," in *Yankee Doodle's Literary Sampler*, 169–75.

21. Ibid. Stephen Nissenbaum interprets Moore's poem as statement of the uneasiness that the conservative upper class, which included Moore, Washington Irving, John Pintard and others, felt with democracy and the rowdy element empowered by it (Nissenbaum, "Revisiting 'A Visit from St. Nicholas,'" 44–60, passim).

22. West, "Who Wrote 'Twas the Night Before Christmas'?," 300; Douglas, *American Book of Days*, 662; Gardner, *Annotated Night Before Christmas*, 22.

23. Snyder, *December 25th*, 217; Shoemaker, *Christmas in Pennsylvania*, 327.

24. Anon. to Mashell C. Ewing, Dec. 24, 1821, WLCL.

25. Shoemaker, *Christmas in Pennsylvania*, 45–46, 50; "Holidays," *United States Review*, 62.

26. "St. Iclaus" and "St. Aclaus," in Pease, ed., *Diary of Samuel Rodman*, 187, 214; "Santus Klaas," in "Holidays," *United States Review*, 62; "Old Santaclaw," in *False Stories Corrected* (Samuel Wood, 1812), in Jones, *Saint Nicholas of Myra*, 345, and in McGinty, "Santa Claus," 103; "St Claas," in John Pintard to Eliza Noel Pintard Davidson, Jan. 19, 1819, in Barck, ed., *Letters from John Pintard*, 1:164; St. a Claus, in Rivington's *Gazateer*; Jones, "Knickerbocker Santa Claus," 363; "Sancte Claus, goed heylig man!," Official minutes of Society meeting, *Commercial Advertiser*, Dec. 11, 1810, quoted in Vail, *Knickerbocker Birthday*, 369. According to Charles W. Jones, the variant spelling continued up to the Civil War (Jones, *Saint Nicholas of Myra*, 339).

27. Mrs. Schuyler Van Rensselaer, *History of the City of New York in the Seventeenth Century*, 2 vols. (New York: Macmillan, 1909), 2:152. Stanton, *Eighty Years and More*, 15. Susan D. Smedes, *A Southern Planter*, 4th ed. (New York: James Pott, 1890), 161. Charlotte Gilman, *Recollections of a Southern Matron and a New England Bride*, rev. ed. (Philadelphia: John E. Potter, 1867), 114. On Hertha, see Douglas, *American Book of Days*, 661.

28. Robert Blair Risk, "Observed and Noted," *Lancaster Daily Examiner*, Dec. 21, 1912, quoted by Yoder, "Introduction" to Shoemaker, *Christmas in Pennsylvania*, 12; Thomas Nelson Page, *Social Life in Old Virginia Before the War* (New York: Charles Scribner's Sons, 1898), 94; Cuyler, quoted in Snyder, *December 25th*, 228; Theodore C. Pease and James G. Randall, eds., *The Diary of Orville Hickman Browning*, vol. 1, *1850–1864* (Springfield: Trustees of the Illinois State Historical Library, 1925), Dec. 25, 1859, p. 387.

29. Stanton, *Eighty Years and More*, 15–16; Smedes, *A Southern Planter*, 161; Ella Benton to Carrie Grant, Jan. 16, 1876, Connecticut Historical Society, Hartford (hereafter CHS).

30. John Shlien, "Santa Claus: The Myth in America," *Etc.: A Review of General Semantics* 16 (Summer, 1959):398 (emphasis in original). Late in the nineteenth century, concerned writers began to address the problem of defining the relationship between Jesus and Santa. The substance of their ideas is discussed in Chapter 10.

31. Ibid., 389–94. According to Shlien, heroes can be judged according to ten traits. Of them, the three "epic" characteristics are "(1) a distinguished or divine origin, (2) mysterious portents at birth, and (3) perils menacing his infancy." The remaining seven are "ritualistic" and include "initiation or revelation, . . . a quest, . . . a magical contest, . . . a trial or persecution, . . . a last scene, . . . a violent or mysterious death, and . . . a resurrection or ascension" (ibid., 390).

32. Dundes, *Christmas as a Reflection of American Culture*, 6, 17.

33. *Godey's*, Dec. 1847, p. 7; Francis J. Grund, "Christmas and New Year in France and Germany," ibid., Jan. 1848, p. 6; Hogg, quoted in Baur, *Christmas on the American Frontier*, 143; Cuyler, quoted in Snyder, *December 25th*, 228.

34. The full text of the poem as it appeared in *The Children's Friend*:

> Old Santeclaus with much delight
> His reindeer drives this frosty night
> O'er chimney-tops, and tracks of snow,
> to bring his yearly gifts to you,

The steady friend of virtuous youth,
The friend of duty, and of truth,
Each Christmas eve he joys to come
Where love and peace have made their home.

Through many houses he has been,
And various beds and stockings seen,
Some, white as snow, and neatly mended,
Others, that seem for pigs intended.

Where e'er I found good girls or boys,
That hated quarrels, strife and noise,
I left an apple, or a tart,
Or wooden gun or painted cart;

To some I gave a pretty doll,
To some a peg-top, or a ball;
No crackers, cannons, squibs, or rockets,
To blow their eyes up, or their pockets.

No drums to stun their Mother's ear,
Nor swords to make their sisters fear;
But pretty books to store their mind
With knowledge of each various kind.

But where I found the children naughty,
In manners rude, in tempers haughty,
Thankless to parents, liars, swearers,
Boxers, or cheats, or base tale-bearers,

I left a long, black, birchen rod,
Such as the dread command of God
Directs a parent's hand to use
When virtue's path his sons refuse.

The Santa Book, 12–13. This source, from which the full text of this poem has been reprinted, attributes the poem's authorship to James K. Paulding. Martin Gardner, however, attributes its writing and illustration to one Arthur J. Stansbury, a Presbyterian minister (*Annotated Night Before Christmas*, 30).

35. Edward Wagenknecht, ed., *Mrs. Longfellow: Selected Letters and Journals of Fanny Appleton Longfellow (1817–1861)* (New York: Longmans, Green, 1956), 196–98; Cuyler, quoted in Snyder, *December 25th*, 228.

36. Risk, quoted in Yoder, "Introduction" to Shoemaker, *Christmas in Pennsylvania*, 12; Stanton, *Eighty Years and More*, 4, 15–16.

37. Marion Harland, "A Christmas Talk with Mothers," *Godey's*, Dec. 1865, p. 401; [Anonymous] article attributed to the *Baltimore Minerva and Emerald*, reprinted in *Philadelphia Daily Chronicle*, Feb. 5, 1830, quoted in Shoemaker, *Christmas in Pennsylvania*, 50.

38. *Kriss Kringle's Book for all Good Boys and Girls*, (Philadelphia: C. G. Henderson, 1852), 5–6, quoted in Shoemaker, *Christmas in Pennsylvania*, 50–51.

39. *Philadelphia Saturday Courier*, Dec. 23, 1848, quoted in ibid., 50.

40. Wendell H. Oswalt, *Understanding Our Culture: An Anthropological View* (New York: Holt, Rinehart and Winston, 1970), 10.

41. See *Reading* (Pennsylvania) *Gazette*, quoted in Shoemaker, *Christmas in Pennsylvania*, 46.

Chapter 5. Home for Christmas II

1. Miles, *Christmas in Ritual and Tradition*, 271–72.

2. Walsh, *Curiosities of Popular Customs*, 241–43.

3. Clement A. Miles, *Christmas in Ritual and Tradition, Christian and Pagan*, 2nd ed. (London: T. Fisher Unwin, 1913), 264; diary quoted in ibid., 265; Walsh, *Curiosities of Popular Customs*, 243–44. St. Francis introduced the creche in the beginning of the thirteenth century (Harrison, *The Story of Christmas*, 214–15).

4. O. M. Spencer, "Christmas Throughout Christendom," *Harper's Monthly*, Jan. 1873, pp. 251–52; "Grenville's memoirs of Dec. 29, 1829," quoted in Walsh, *Curiosities of Popular Customs*, 244; Miles, *Christmas in Ritual and Tradition*, 266–67.

5. Zahm, quoted in Shoemaker, *Christmas in Pennsylvania*, 52. One Captain John Whistler made an earlier, but unverified, claim, in 1804, to a Christmas tree in Fort Dearborn (Chicago) (William I. Schreiber, "First Christmas Trees in America," *Journal of German-American Studies* 15 (1980):25). Collectors of Christmas tree facts record the drama of its introduction with a string of "firsts." For examples, including descriptions of early Moravian tree forms, see ibid.; Shoemaker, *Christmas in Pennsylvania*, 104; Dr. William N. Schwarze, trans., "Transcription of Items from the Bethlehem Diary Relating to Early Celebrations of Christmas in Bethlehem, Pennsylvania," *Proceedings of the Pennsylvania German Folklore Soc.*, 6:14, quoted in ibid.; Snyder, *December 25th*, 130; "New World Cradle of Christmas Tree" *Austin* (Texas) *American*, Dec. 1, 1954, n.p.; and Gary Walther, "A Christmas Heritage: The German Tree in America," *American History Illustrated* 17 (1982):15–17.

6. Phillip V. Snyder, *The Christmas Tree Book* (New York: Viking, 1976), 28. Simon Snyder Rathvon, *Lancaster* (Pennsylvania) *Intelligencer*, Dec. 24, 1881, quoted in ibid., 61–62; *Pennsylvania Gazette*, Dec. 23, 1823, quoted in ibid., 52. Krimmel made at least two sketches of trimmed trees around 1819 or 1820, which are among the oldest American pictorial accounts (Snyder, *Christmas Tree Book*, 53). Another Pennsylvanian, Lewis Miller, also left a sketch, which Alfred Shoemaker claims to be the earliest (Shoemaker, *Christmas in Pennsylvania*, 53).

7. Haswell, *Reminiscences of an Octogenarian*, 330; Catherine Sedgwick, "New Year's Day," *Token and Atlantic Souvenir*, 1836, quoted in ibid., 54.

8. Schreiber, "First Christmas Trees," 25, and Kane, *Southern Christmas Book*, 24–25; Martineau, *Retrospect of Western Travel*, 2 vols. (London: Saunder and Otley; New York: Harper and Brothers, 1838), 2:179; Schreiber, "First Christmas Trees in America," 25.

9. Thomas J. McCormack, ed., *Memoirs of Gustave Koerner 1809–1896* (Cedar Rapids, Iowa: 1909), 1:330, quoted in Dorothy J. Caldwell, "Christmas in Early Missouri" *Missouri Hist. Rev.* 65 (Jan. 1971):127, and in Schreiber "First Christmas Trees," 25; Rutherford Hayes to S. Birchard, Dec. 25, 1858, in Charles Richard Williams, ed., *Diary and Letters of Rutherford B. Hayes: Nineteenth President of the United States*, 5 vols. (Columbus: Ohio State Archeological and Historical Society, 1922), 1:538.

10. Anna Ticknor, *The Travel Journals of George and Anna Ticknor In the Years 1815–1819 and 1835–1838* (Ann Arbor, Mich.: Xerox University Micro., in collaboration with DCL), Dec. 24, 1835, pp. 590–92.

11. George S. Hillard, ed., *Life, Letters, and Journals of George Ticknor*, 6th ed., 2 vols. (Boston: James R. Osgood, 1877), Dec. 24, 1835, 1:460–61.

12. Mrs. Longfellow to Mary Longfellow Greenleaf, Dec. 26, 1843. Mrs. Longfellow

had at least known about Christmas trees by then, though. She had been in Europe from 1835–37, and had described a German Christmas tree in a letter to Emmeline Austin in 1841. See Edward Wagenknecht, ed., *Mrs. Longfellow: Selected Letters and Journals of Fanny Appleton Longfellow (1817–1861)* (New York: Longmans, Green, 1956), 22, 78, 98–99.

13. William Wetmore Story, diary entry, Dec. 24, 1849, Story Family Papers, HRC.

14. Robert Blair Risk, "Observed and Noted," *Lancaster Daily Examiner*, Dec. 21, 1912, quoted in Shoemaker, *Christmas in Pennsylvania*, 12; Lydia Maria Child to Lucy Osgood, Jan. 23, 1845, in Patricia G. Holland and Milton Meltzer, eds., *The Collected Correspondence of Lydia Maria Child, 1817–1880* (Millwood, N.Y.: Kraus Microfilm: 1980).

15. Snyder, *December 25th*, 132–33. This was probably in 1850, when Hattie was fourteen. According to Milton Rugoff, Stowe had first allowed a Christmas tree in the house before 1854 (Rugoff, *The Beechers: An American Family in the Nineteenth Century* (New York: Harper & Row, 1981), 337).

16. Martineau, *Retrospect of Western Travel*, 2:179. On the point of the tree as metaphor, see E. Douglas Branch, *The Sentimental Years, 1836–1860* (1934; New York: Hill and Wang, 1965), 145, 148.

17. Richards, *How Christmas Came to the Sunday-Schools*, 70, 77–78; Caroline Cowles Richards, *Diary of Caroline Cowles Richards, 1852–1872* (Canandaigua, N.Y.: n.p., 1908), 65; [Abraham Joseph Warner], *The Private Journal of Abraham Joseph Warner*, extracted by Herbert B. Enderton (San Diego, Calif.: n.p., 1973), 96.

18. Schreiber, "First Christmas Trees," 25; Snyder, *Christmas Tree Book*, 31.

19. Snyder, *December 25th*, 117, 133, 167; Schreiber, "First Christmas Trees," 25; "Christmas Green," *New York Tribune*, Dec. 25, 1878, p. 2; *Gleason's Pictorial*, Dec. 25, 1852, quoted in Shoemaker, *Christmas in Pennsylvania*, 59.

20. Diary of Mahala Eggleston, Christmas 1851, in Katherine M. Jones, *Plantation South* (Indianapolis and New York: Bobbs-Merrill, 1957), 304.

21. [Illus.], *Godey's*, Dec. 1850, n.p.

22. "The Christmas Tree" [illus.], *Godey's*, Dec. 1855, pp. 489, 528.

23. Snyder, *Christmas Tree Book*, 36; *Godey's*, Dec. 1860, pp. 505–6 (emphasis in original).

24. *Godey's*, Dec. 1860, pp. 505–6; Lee to Miss Nellie Whitely, Dec. 11, 1860, in Francis R. Adams, Jr., "An Annotated Edition of the Personal Letters of Robert E. Lee, part 1" (Ph.D. diss., University of Maryland, 1955), 706; Mrs. Charles William Woolsey to daughters, Dec. 24, 1861, in *Letters of a Family During the War for the Union, 1861–1865*, 2 vols. (n.p.: privately printed, 1899), 1:231–32; Abby Howland Woolsey to Georgeanna Muirson Woolsey & Eliza Woolsey Howland, Dec. 26 [1861], in ibid., 1:234.

25. Mrs. Charles William Woolsey to daughters, Dec. 24, 1861, in *Letters of a Family*, 1:231–32; Macey, *Patriarchs of Time*, 128–29.

26. Miles, *Christmas in Ritual and Tradition*, 168; L. D. Ettlinger and R. G. Holloway, *Compliments of the Season* (London: Penguin Books, 1947), 14.

27. Miles, *Christmas in Ritual and Tradition*, 276–77; Douglas, *American Book of Days*, 2; Sandys, *Christmastide*, 99–102; Macey, *Patriarchs of Time*, 133–34.

28. Diary quoted in Snyder, *December 25th*, 61; Martha J. Lamb, "Christmas Season in Dutch New York," *Magazine of American History*, Dec. 1883, p. 473; Snyder, *December 25th*, 58–59; Kane, *Southern Christmas Book*, 17.

29. Thomas, ed., *Diary of Samuel Sewall*, 2:937; Anna Winslow, *Diary of Anna Green Winslow: A Boston School Girl of 1771*, Alice Morse Earle, ed. (Boston and New York: Houghton Mifflin, 1894), iii–iv; Dec. 27, 1771, p. 11; Jan. 1, 1772, p. 13.

30. Elliott Coues, ed., *The History of the Lewis and Clark Expedition, by Meriwether Lewis and William Clark*, 3 vols. (1893; New York: Dover, n.d.), Dec. 25, 1805, 2:738 n24.

31. Caldwell, "Christmas in Early Missouri," 128–29; Furman, "Winter Amusements in the Early 19th Century," 10–11.

32. Furman, "Winter Amusements in the Early 19th Century," 15; "Holidays," *United States Review*, 63; Harrison, ed., *Philadelphia Merchant*, Jan. 1, 1801, p. 56.

33. On this point, see Cheal's discussion of what he labels the "theory of contradictory consciousness," in David Cheal, *Gift Economy* (London and New York: Routledge, 1988), 6.

34. Pintard to Eliza Davidson, Dec. 16, 1830, entry for Dec. 24, in Barck, ed., *Letters from John Pintard*, 3:206; Mrs. Lee to Mrs. Thomas Tracy [Ann Bromfield], Dec. 1842, in Henry and Mary Lee, *Letters and Journals, with Other Family Letters, 1802–1860*, prep. by Frances R. Morse (Boston: Thomas Todd, 1926), 275, 278; Mary Austin Holley to Harriette, Dec. 23, 1845, Papers of Mary Austin Holley, Barker Texas History Center, University of Texas, Austin (hereafter Holley Papers, BTHC).

35. "Stranger's account," in [Anon.], *Festivals, Games and Amusements* (1831), quoted in Snyder, *December 25th*, xx; Allan Nevins and Milton Halsey Thomas, eds., *Diary of George Templeton Strong*, vol. 2: *The Turbulent Years, 1850–1859* (New York: Macmillan, 1952), Dec. 24, 1858, pp. 427–28; diary of Edward S. Johnson, Dec. 24, 1855, New York State Library, Albany (hereafter NYSL); William Paisley to Emma Butler Paisley, Dec. 17, 1879, in Elizabeth Paisley Huckaby and Ethel C. Simpson, eds., *Tulip Evermore: Emma Butler and William Paisley, Their Lives in Letters, 1857–1887* (Fayetteville: Univ. of Arkansas Press, 1985), 352.

36. *Augusta (Georgia) Daily Chronicle & Sentinel*, Jan. 3, 1843. See, for example, December issues of *New York Times* for 1851. See also "For the Holidays," *New York Daily Times*, Dec. 25, 1852.

37. Mary Holley to Harriette, Jan. 1, 1830, Holley Papers, BTHC; Pease, ed., *Diary of Samuel Rodman*, Jan. 1, 1837, p. 170; Lydia Maria Child to Francis George Shaw, in Holland and Meltzer, eds., *Collected Correspondence*, Jan. 15, 1843; Lydia Maria Child to Anna Loring, ibid., Dec. 20, 1840. See also diary of Edward S. Johnson, NYSL.

38. Bayard Tuckerman, ed., *Diary of Philip Hone, 1828–1851*, 2 vols. (New York: Dodd, Mead, 1889), Jan. 2, 1847, 2:291; Increase N. Tarbox, ed., *Diary of Thomas Robbins, D.D.*, 2 vols. (Boston: Beacon Press, 1887), 2:851.

39. JBH [Julia B. Hammond] to Katherine Hammond Billings, Dec. 1897, quoted in Carol Bleser, ed., *The Hammonds of Redcliffe* (New York: Oxford Univ. Press, 1981), 232–33; Robert Blair Risk, "Observed and Noted," *Lancaster Daily Examiner*, Dec. 21, 1912, in Shoemaker, *Christmas in Pennsylvania*, 12.

40. *New York Herald* quoted in Snyder, *December 25th*, 60; James G. Randall, ed., *The Diary of Orville Hickman Browning*, vol. 2 (Springfield: Trustees of the Illinois State Historical Library, 1933), Dec. 25, 1868, p. 232.

41. Richards, *Diary of Caroline Cowles Richards*, 58.

42. Theodore Caplow, "Christmas Gifts and Kin Networks," *American Sociological Rev.* 47 (June 1982):391; Cheal, *Gift Economy*, 14–15, 18; Lewis Hyde, *The Gift: Imagination and the Erotic Life of Property* (New York: Vintage, 1983), xiv; Cheal, *Gift Economy*, 5, 14–15. For a discussion of these points as they relate to late twentieth-century gift practices, see ibid., 5, 12, 14–15, 104–5, passim. Marcel Mauss, *The Gift: Forms and Functions of Exchange in Archaic Societies*, Ian Cunnison, trans. (London: Cohen & West, 1966), 11. In this chapter I have attempted to restrict the discussion of the social implications of gift-giving to the antebellum period and to familial interaction. See Chapter 9 for a discussion of the implications of these theories as they pertain to broader social issues.

43. Mauss, *The Gift*, 4. However, Anthony Heath argues that status in American

society is determined by birth or occupation and there is no room for competitive gift-giving to change that role, as may have happened among Indians (Caplow, "Christmas Gifts and Kin Networks," 390).

44. Richard Sterba has suggested that the labor of these duties particularly suited the woman; shopping, wrapping, and secret-keeping symbolize aspects of pregnancy, and once the gifts are opened, there follows an exhaustion similar to that after childbirth (Sterba, "On Christmas," *Psychoanalytic Quart.* 13 (1944):80–81.

45. Ella Benton to Carrie Grant, Jan. 16, 1876, CHS; Nevins and Thomas, eds., *Diary of George Templeton Strong*, Dec. 25, 1859, 2:481; Strong, Private Journal, Dec. 23, 1869, p. 266, NYHS. The trends of exchange remained basically static throughout the nineteenth and continue in the twentieth century. Recent studies have sought to differentiate patterns, showing that different expectations arise out of different personal relationships. See, for example, Cheal, *Gift Economy*, 6, 12, 181; Mihaly Csikszentmihalyi and Eugene Rochberg-Halton, *The Meaning of Things: Domestic Symbols and the Self* (Cambridge, Eng.: Cambridge Univ. Press, 1981), 86; Michael Schudson, *Advertising, the Uneasy Persuasion: Its Dubious Impact on American Society* (New York: Basic Books, 1984), 139–40; Caplow, "Christmas Gifts and Kin Networks," *American Sociological Review* 47 (June 1982):383–89, passim.

46. Editorial note, *Godey's*, Dec. 1864, p. 546; editorial note, ibid., Dec. 1866, p. 538.

47. Hillard, ed., *Life, Letters, and Journals of George Ticknor*, Dec. 24, 1835, 1:460–61.

48. *Mothers' Monthly Journal*, April 1836, p. 30; quoted in Ryan, *Cradle of the Middle Class*, 161.

49. Horace Bushnell, *Christian Nurture* (New Haven: Yale Univ. Press, 1967; orig. pub. as "Discourses on Christian Nurture," 1847), 292, 294–95; Snyder, *December 25th*, 239–40.

50. Dundes, *Christmas as a Reflection of American Culture*, 29–30; quote in Snyder, *December 25th*, 95. Also see Pintard to Davidson, in Barck, ed., *Letters from John Pintard*, Dec. 31, 1819, 1:256–57.

51. "Old Annuals," in "Contributor's Club," *Atlantic*, Jan. 1893, p. 139; Branch, *The Sentimental Years*, 114. See, for example, *The Gift: a Christmas and New Year's Present* (1843) or *The Christian Souvenir: an Offering for Christmas and the New Year*. In 1851 Daniel Press issued *Christmas: A Vigil* by C[harles] J[ames] C[ruttwell], which is believed to be the first gift book designed expressly for Christmas giving (Walter Klinefelter, ed., *A Bibliographical Check-list of Christmas Books* (Portland, Me.: Southworth-Anthoesen Press, 1937), v–vi).

52. Branch, *Sentimental Years*, 127. Two annuals reviewed were *The Saint Nicholas Annual. A Christmas and New Year's Gift: made expressly under the direction of Saint Nicholas, for all good boys and girls* and *Kris Kringle's Book*. "Editor's Book Table," *Godey's*, Dec. 1842, p. 307.

53. Rev. Thomas P. Hunt, *The Book of Wealth* (1836), quoted in *The Sentimental Years*, 35. Douglas Branch notes that Dewey's sermons "might well have been entitled 'The Divine Existence, as Illustrated and Exemplified by Our Commerce, Society, and Politics.'" Ibid.

Chapter 6. Christmas in the Slave South

1. Simms to Richard Henry Wilde, May 1, 1844, in intro. to William Gilmore Simms, *Castle Dismal, or The Bachelor's Christmas* (New York: Burgess, Stringer, 1845), n.p., 9, 10, 32.

2. Ibid., 32–33.

3. See Farish, ed., *Journal and Letters of Philip Vickers Fithian*, Dec. 18, 1773, pp. 44–45; Dec. 25, 1773, pp. 53–54; Dec. 26, 1773, p. 55. An account of Fithian's Virginia

Christmas is related in Chapter 1. Fischer, *Albion's Seed*, 370, 395. On the point of plantation work time versus social time, but in the context of the eighteenth-century Caribbean, see Robert Dirks, *The Black Saturnalia: Conflict and Its Ritual Expression on British West Indian Slave Plantations* (Gainesville: Univ. of Florida Press, 1987), 186, 189. English custom had made December 25 one of the four days each year in which reckoning of financial accounts was undertaken (Chambers, ed., *The Book of Days*, 2:736).

4. Kane, *The Southern Christmas Book*, 63, 66–69; Page, *Social Life in Old Virginia*, 80–81; Catherine Clinton, *The Plantation Mistress: Woman's World in the Old South* (New York: Pantheon, 1982), 177–78; Dairy of Nathaniel Wright, Dec. 21, 1816, DCL. Songaree is a wine concoction; sack posset is made of sherry, ale, eggs, and milk; and syllabub is a brew of white wine and whipped cream (Clinton, *Plantation Mistress*, 177). Booker T. Washington remembered that slaves on the Virginia plantation where he lived would choose the biggest, greenest log at Christmas, soak it in water until the next Christmas and then light it. The Christmas holiday lasted until the soggy log burned into two pieces (Louis R. Harlan and John Blassingame, eds., *The Booker T. Washington Papers*, vol. 1: *The Autobiographical Writing* (Urbana: Univ. of Chicago Press, 1972), 397).

5. See William Gilmore Simms, "Maize in Milk: A Christmas Story of the South," in *Stories and Tales*, intros. and notes by John Caldwell Guilds (Columbia: Univ. of South Carolina Press, 1974), esp. 315–23 for quotations; narrator quoted in ibid., 314–15. The story was first published serially in *Godey's*, Feb. 1847, pp. 657–62; March 1847, pp. 146–52; April 1847, pp. 199–204; and May 1847, pp. 249–58.

6. Simms, "Maize in Milk," 332–35.

7. Ibid., 345–48. The children had hung stockings and clothing with pockets at the chimney, each with a sprig of greenery, which Father Christmas took as he left an appropriate gift. Simms explained that "Santa Claus visits us in the south, too, but under no such Dutch appellation. . . . With us, the good genius of the nativity, in a merely social point of view, is good old Father Christmas himself" (ibid., 345).

8. Ibid., 349–50.

9. Ibid., 353–55.

10. Ibid., 355–56 (emphasis in original).

11. Edith Wharton Sinkler, Dec. 29, 1842, in Katherine M. Jones, *Plantation South* (Indianapolis and New York: Bobbs-Merrill, 1957), 151 (emphasis in original); Salmon to William Fay, Dec. 22, 1849, WLCL; Eliza Ripley, *Social Life in Old New Orleans, Being Recollections of My Girlhood* (New York: D. Appleton, 1912), 260–61.

12. Smedes, *A Southern Planter*, 162; Henry Benjamin Whipple, quoted in Jones, *Plantation South*, 156. For other examples, see Miss Mary Sharpe Jones to Miss Laura E. Maxwell, Dec. 25, 1854, quoted in Robert Manson Myers, ed., *Children of Pride* (New Haven: Yale Univ. Press, 1972), 115; and Patience Pennington, *A Woman Rice Planter* (New York: Macmillan, 1913), 273–74. Page, *Social Life in Old Virginia*, 80, 84–100, passim.

13. Guion Griffis Johnson, *Ante-bellum North Carolina, a Social History* (Chapel Hill: Univ. of North Carolina Press, 1937), 550; Charles Joyner, *Down by the Riverside* (Urbana and Chicago: Univ.of Illinois Press, 1984), 127; Eugene Genovese, *Roll, Jordan, Roll: The World the Slaves Made* (New York: Pantheon, 1974), 566–69; George Caulton, Caroline Ates, and Arthur Carlson, in Jan Hillegas and Ken Lawrence, eds., *Georgia Narratives* III (1), part 1, in George P. Rawick, gen. ed., *The American Slave: A Composite Autobiography* (Westport, Conn.: Greenwood Press, 1977), 3:25, 170, 219 (hereafter, only individual volumes of *The American Slave* will be cited); Jones, in George P. Rawick, ed., *Texas Narratives* VI (2), part 5, p. 2104 (Easter and Good Friday were noted by Joseph James, ibid., 1931); James Mellon, ed. and intro., *Bullwhip Days: The Slaves Remember* (New

York: Weidenfeld and Nicolson, 1988), 143. For a general discussion of slave holidays, "de big times," see Genovese, *Roll, Jordan, Roll*, 566–84.

14. Sara Crocker, in Hillegas and Lawrence, eds., *Georgia Narratives*, III (1), part 1, pp. 224–25; Nancy Wilson, in Charles L. Perdue, Jr., Thomas E. Barden, and Robert K. Phillips, eds., *Weevils in the Wheat: Interviews with Virginia Ex-Slaves* (Charlottesville: Univ. Press of Virginia, 1976), 318–19.

15. Mrs. Fannie Berry, in Perdue, Barden, and Phillips, eds., *Weevils in the Wheat*, 49; George Fleming, in Rawick, ed., *North Carolina and South Carolina Narratives* XI (1), p. 135; Aunt Cicely Cawthon, in Hillegas and Lawrence, eds., *Georgia Narratives* III (1), part 1, p. 189; Johnson, quoted in Genovese, *Roll, Jordan, Roll*, 576.

16. George Fleming, South Carolina, in George P. Rawick, ed., *North Carolina and South Carolina Narratives* XI (1), p. 135; Johnson, *Ante-bellum North Carolina*, 552; Hillegas and Lawrence, eds., *Georgia Narratives* III (1), part 1, pp. 171, 219. The number varied by plantation, but three days seemed most usual. See, for example, Jones, *Plantation South*, 151, 163; Caroline Gilman, *Recollections of a Southern Matron and a New England Bride*, rev. ed. (Philadelphia: John E. Potter, 1867), 116; and Joyner, *Down by the Riverside*, 101.

17. Gilman, *Recollections*, 116; Eliza Ripley, *Social Life in Old New Orleans*, 258. Only rarely do records reveal that such gifts were reciprocated. In one instance a new mistress accepted offerings of chicken eggs, totaling about 100, from her servants (Sinkler, Dec. 29, 1842, in Jones, *Plantation South*, 151–52.

18. Pollard, in Perdue, Barden, and Phillips, eds., *Weevils in the Wheat*, 229; Pringle, *Chronicles of Chicora Wood*, 151–53. See also Plantation Journal of John W. Milliken, Mulberry Plantation, Dec. 25, 1854, quoted in Taylor, *Antebellum South Carolina*, 54; and Mrs. Holley, Dec. 20, 1829, entry for Dec. 26, Holley Papers, BTHC.

19. Ates, quoted in Hillegas and Lawrence, eds., *Georgia Narratives* III (1) part 1, p. 25; "Twelve Years a Slave: Narrative of Solomon Northrup," in Gilbert Osofsky, ed., *Puttin' on Ole Massa* (New York and Evanston: Harper and Row, 1969), 343.

20. Berry, in Perdue, Barden and Phillips, eds., *Weevils in the Wheat*, 49. Mary Austin Holley, Dec. 20, 1829, Holley Papers, BTHC; Gilman, *Recollections*, 116; Fleming, in Rawick, ed., *North Carolina and South Carolina Narratives* XI (1), p. 135; Hurt, in Rawick, ed., *Texas Narratives* V (2), part 4, p. 1839; Frederick Douglass, *The Life and Times of Frederick Douglass* (1898; New York: Collier, 1962), 146. On the point of slaves and alcohol, see also Booker T. Washington, *Up from Slavery: An Autobiography* (New York: Doubleday, Page, 1901), 133, and Harris, "Something about 'Sandy Claus,'" in *On The Plantation*, 104–121.

21. Boyd, *Christmas at Monticello*, 33–34; Jack P. Greene, ed., *The Diary of Colonel Landon Carter of Sabine Hall, 1752–1778*, 2 vols. Virginia Historical Society Documents (Charlottesville: Univ. Press of Virginia, 1965), 2:909.

22. Perdue, Barden, and Phillips, eds., *Weevils in the Wheat*, 82. Mattie Gilmore, in Rawick, ed., *Texas Narratives* V (2), part 4, pp. 1494–95; Edwin Adams Davis, *Plantation Life in the Florida Parishes of Louisiana, 1836–1846, as Reflected in the Dairy of Bennet H. Barrow* (New York: Columbia Univ. Press, 1943), Dec. 26, 1836, p. 85; Dec. 24, 1839, p. 175. However, on Dec. 23, 1841, Barrow "Gave the negros . . . $700. all went to Town to day" (ibid., Dec. 24, 1841, p. 218).

23. Barrow quoted in Davis, *Plantation Life in the Florida Parishes of Louisiana*, 380; Farm Journal of David Golightly Harris, Spartanburg District, Dec. 28, 1856, quoted in Rosser H. Taylor, *Antebellum South Carolina: A Social and Cultural History* (Chapel Hill: Univ. of North Carolina Press, 1942), 54; "The Journal of Thomas B. Chaplin (1822–1890)," in Theodore Rosengarten, *Tombee: Portrait of a Cotton Planter* (New York: William

Morrow, 1986), Dec. 28, 1857, p. 704; Calhoun correspondence, quoted in Taylor, *Antebellum South Carolina*, 54.

24. Henry Gray Klugh, South Carolina, in Rawick, ed., *North Carolina and South Carolina Narratives* XI (1), p. 233; Ferdinand Roemer, *Texas*, 48, quoted in Webb, "Christmas and New Year in Texas," 371. Roemer did not note whether these were free blacks. Gilman, *Recollections*, p. 116.

25. Whipple, Dec. 25, 1843, in Jones, *Plantation South*, 156; Gilman, *Recollections*, 116; Salmon to William Fay, Dec. 22, 1849, WLCL.

26. This custom was known as "John Canoeing" in Edenton, North Carolina, and "John Kunering" in Wilmington (Johnson, *Ante-bellum North Carolina*, 553). Other variations include John Canoe, Who-Who's, and jocooner, names used throughout eastern North Carolina. West Indians used John Canoe, John Kooner, John Coony, Junkanoes, John Kuner, and Jonkanoo. "Another source," Reid claims, "refers to a *John Crow*, a *Koo-Koo* and *John Crayfish* in the West Indies." Or, John Canoe may have been a corruption of "gens inconnu," which means "unknown folk," or a "twisted form of 'jongleur,'" French minstrels of the Middle Ages. Ira De A. Reid, "The John Canoe Festival: A New World Africanism," *Phylon* 3 (Fourth Quarter, 1942):358 (emphasis in original). On the Guinea Coast of Africa, the name seems to have been John Connu or John Conny (ibid., 357).

27. Diary of Rev. Moses Ashley Curtis, Dec. 25, 1830, quoted in Bertram Wyatt-Brown, *Southern Honor: Ethics and Behavior in the Old South* (New York: Oxford Univ. Press, 1982), 444. The "John Canoe festival," although confined generally to the Yule season, was also seen on the Fourth of July and at Halloween (Reid, "John Canoe Festival," 351).

28. Description in this and succeeding paragraph in Edward Warren, *A Doctor's Experiences in Three Continents* (Baltimore: Cushings & Bailey, 1855), 201–2. For other accounts of "Koonering" see Capt. Gregory Seaworthy [George Higby Throop], *Bertie: or, Life in the Old Field* (Philadelphia, 1851), 217–19, and "Christmas at Buchoi, a North Carolina Rice Plantation," *North Carolina Booklet* 13 (July 1913):3–9.

29. Coffin, *Book of Christmas Folklore*, 150; William Bosman, *A New and Accurate Description of the Coast of Guinea* (London, 1705), quoted in Reid, "The John Canoe Festival," 356–57. see Reid, "John Canoe Festival," 352–53, 356, for various interpretations of the origins of Koonering.

30. Sinkler, Dec. 29, 1842, in Jones, *Plantation South*, 151–52; Whipple, Dec. 27, 1843, in ibid., 162–63. Scholars of Koonering have suggested that "Koonering" exhibitions took place only in North Carolina, or at least only along the eastern seaboard, and on a few Caribbean islands. See "His Worship the John Kuner," 161, and Reid, "John Canoe Festival," 350–51. Where it occurred elsewhere I have not found it to be referred to as Koonering, but certain aspects of it, such as described in the text, bear, at the least, a close relationship.

31. Mary Austin Holley to Harriette, Dec. 20, 1829, entry for Dec. 26, Holley Papers, BTHC.

32. Reid's remarks as well on the similarity between Koonering and mumming, comparing Koonering with an eighteenth-century Boston account. However, he rejects any Old World connections (Reid, "John Canoe Festival," 351, 354–58).

33. Dr. James Norcom, Legislative Papers, June 18, 1825, quoted in Johnson, *Antebellum North Carolina*, 552–53; Foby, "Management of Servants," (1853), quoted in Genovese, *Roll, Jordan, Roll*, 579 (emphasis in original).

34. Sir James George Frazer, *Golden Bough: A Study in Magic and Religion*, 3rd ed. (1913, New York: St. Martin's Press, 1955), 9:307–8. See also Macey, *Patriarchs of Time*, 117–18.

35. Frederick Douglass, "New Relations and Duties," in *Christmas Gif*, Charlemae Rollins, comp. (Chicago: Follett, 1963), 54; Reid, "John Canoe Festival," 362.

36. Williams, in Purdue, Barden, and Phillips, eds., *Weevils in the Wheat*, 318.

37. Whipple, Dec. 27, 1843, in Jones, *Plantation South*, 162–63; Helm, quoted in Baur, *Christmas on the American Frontier*, 41.

38. For this and the succeeding paragraph, see Dirks, *Black Saturnalia*, ix, xi, 184–90, passim.

39. Joyner, *Down by the Riverside*, 127–28 (emphasis in original). On the point of asserting claims to free time, see also Genovese, *Roll, Jordan, Roll*, 571, 575, and Douglass, *Life and Times*, 145.

40. Genovese argues that the totality of slave life and slave-master relations contributed to the establishment of white hegemony in the plantation culture, one in which blacks accepted their place and whites asserted dominion (Genovese, *Roll, Jordan, Roll*, 580–84).

41. Jones, in Rawick, ed., *Texas Narratives* VI (2), part 5, pp. 2104–5, for this and preceding paragraph.

42. Mary Holley to Harriette, Dec. 20, Jan. 1, 1830, Holley Papers, BTHC; Wyatt-Brown, *Southern Honor*, 444–45; Kane, *Southern Christmas Book*, 163; Gilman, *Recollections*, 116.

43. Quattelbaum, in Rawick, ed., *South Carolina Narratives* III (3), pp. 285–86; Griffen, in Rawick, ed., *Texas Narratives* V (2) part 4, pp. 1609–10; Hadnot, in ibid., 1627.

44. William Kauffman Scarborough, ed., *Diary of Edmund Ruffin* (Baton Rouge: Louisiana State Univ. Press, 1972), Dec. 25, 1859, p. 385; Jones, in Rawick, ed., *Texas Narratives* VI (2), part 5, p. 2132; Johnson, Yazoo, Mississippi, quoted in Norman R. Yetman, ed., *Life Under the "Peculiar Institution": Selections from the Slave Narrative Collection* (New York: Holt, Rinehart and Winston, 1970), 190; Ripley, *Social Life in Old New Orleans*, 259.

Chapter 7. A Holiday for the Nation

1. "Holidays," *United States Review*, 56; "Editor's Easy Chair," *Harper's Monthly*, Feb. 1856, p. 415; *Washington National Intelligencer*, Dec. 25, 1857; "Editor's Easy Chair," *Harper's Monthly*, July 1854, p. 261; April 1855, p. 694.

2. "Holidays," *United States Review*, 56 (emphasis in original); "Editor's Easy Chair," *Harper's Monthly*, Aug. 1855, p. 414; Randall, ed., *Diary of Orville Hickman Browning*, vol. 1, Dec. 22, 1852, p. 86.

3. [T. Lewis], "Editor's Table," *Harper's Monthly*, July 1852, p. 265.

4. *Diary of Charles Francis Adams*, 3:374; Tucker quoted in Greninger, "Thanksgiving: An American Holiday," *Social Science* 54 (Winter 1979):4. See W. DeLoss Love, *Fast and Thanksgiving Days of New England* (Boston: Houghton Mifflin, 1895), for a detailed history of the holiday, and a chart (pp. 465–514) of all documented Thanksgiving and fast days. Edwin T. Greninger offers a shorter version in "Thanksgiving," 3–15.

5. "The Origin of 'Thanksgiving Day,'" *Magazine of American History*, Nov. 1882, p. 763. Yoder, "Introduction" to Shoemaker, *Christmas in Pennsylvania*, 14; Greninger, "Thanksgiving," 5–6; Garrison to George W. Benson, Nov. 27, 1835, in Walter M. Merrill, ed., *I Will Be Heard: Letters of William Lloyd Garrison* (Cambridge, Mass.: Harvard Univ. Press, 1971), 561. According to Charles Norton, southern opposition to Thanksgiving was rooted, at least in part, in political antipathies dating to the early Republic and before, and not just in pre-Civil War tensions (Norton, "Thanksgiving Day," 560).

6. *Diary of Charles Francis Adams*, vol. 4: March 1831–Dec. 1832, Marc Friedlaender and L. H. Butterfield, eds. (Cambridge, Mass.: Harvard Univ. Press, 1968), Dec. 1, 1831, pp. 188–89; Garrison to George W. Benson, Nov. 27, 1835; Elizabeth Hayward and Roscoe Ellis Scott, eds., *To Thee This Temple: The Life, Diary and Friends of Jacob Richardson Scott* (Chester, Pa.: American Baptist Historical Society, 1955), Nov. 29, 1832, p. 103.

7. Diary of Charles Francis Adams, Dec. 25, 1857, Massachusetts Historical Society, Boston (hereafter MHS); Journal of Samuel C. Gale, Dec. 5, 1854, p. 27, microfilm, Minnesota Historical Society, Minneapolis; Greninger, "Thanksgiving," 5, 6. See App: "The Years in Which the States Made Thanksgiving a Legal Holiday and Set It at the Fourth Thursday in November," for a complete accounting (ibid., 13–15).

8. "National Thanksgiving," in "Editor's Table," *Godey's*, Nov. 1857, p. 466. See also David Freeman Hawke, *Everyday Life in Early America* (New York: Harper & Row, 1988), 90–91.

9. Douglas, *American Book of Days*, 614; "Thanksgiving Day," in "Editor's Tale," *Godey's*, Sept. 1856, p. 274; ibid., Nov. 1854, p. 461.

10. *Godey's*, Dec. 1858, p. 462; "National Thanksgiving," ibid., Nov. 1857, p. 466.

11. Strong, Private Journal, Dec. 25, 1841, 1:523, NYHS; Longfellow, quoted in Richards, *How Christmas Came to the Sunday-Schools*, 103; *Reading* (Pennsylvania) *Berks and Schuylkill Journal*, Dec. 28, 1861, quoted in Yoder, "Introduction" to Shoemaker, *Christmas in Pennsylvania*, 11; *The [Sunday School] Times*, Dec. 31, 1864, quoted in Richards, *How Christmas Came to the Sunday-Schools*, 115.

12. "An act to regulate the damages on protested Bills of Exchange," Acts passed at the First Session of the Thirteenth Legislature of the State of Louisiana, 1837, no. 52; "An Act concerning days of grace on commercial paper, in certain cases," passed Dec. 16, 1838, Arkansas Legislature; Diary of Charles Francis Adams, Dec. 25, 1857, MHS. See "Table I: Dates of First Legal Recognition of Christmas Day by States and Territories (1836–1890)," in Barnett, *American Christmas*, 20. Note, however, that in some cases, archival research yields different information. For example, the first reference to Christmas in Alabama legislative records is in 1852, not in 1836 as stated in Barnett's book. See "Paper due on Christmas, fourth of July, and first of January, to be paid the day previous," 1852 *Code of Alabama*, Sec. 1528. Except in the case of Good Friday, which is a movable holiday, and the traditionally observed day of rest, Sunday, many of the reserved days were named as dates, not as holidays. Nearly all holiday declarations were, in fact, banking laws.

13. According to current legal definition, "a holiday has only the sanctity attached to it by statute, . . . a day on which "any business may be transacted except that which is positively forbidden" (*American Jurisprudence*, 2nd ed. (San Francisco: Bancroft-Whitney, 1974), 73:782–83, secs. 1 and 2).

14. "The Approach of Christmas," *Harper's Monthly*, Aug. 1850, p. 454; Sarah Josepha Hale, "Christmas Hymn," music composed by G. Kinglsey, *Godey's*, Feb. 1841, pp. 90–91; William Gilmore Simms, "Maize in Milk: A Christmas Story of the South," ibid., Jan. 1841, pp. 62–66; March 1841, pp. 146–152; April 1841, 199–204; May 1841, pp. 249–58. Christmas was not the only holiday to have an indistinct place on the publishing calendar. See, for example, the Halloween story published in the December 1843 issue of *Godey's*, p. 279. At least in part, publishing schedules might explain this quirk. However, the increasing tendency to print articles according to their season probably reflected as much the formalizing of the American calendar. By the 1860s, the inconsistency had largely ended.

15. Kate Sullivan, "The Christmas Party," *Godey's*, Dec. 1849, pp. 421–24; Mrs. J. C. Neal, "The Christmas Gathering," ibid., Dec. 1849, p. 40; G. W. Haskins, "The Ingle Nook: A Simple Story for Christmas," ibid., Dec. 1850, pp. 328–31. For other examples, see F. A. Druivage, "The Old Family Mansion: A Sketch from Domestic History," ibid.,

Dec. 1842, pp. 276–79, and Francis J. Grund, "Christmas and New Year in France and Germany," ibid., Jan. 1848, p. 6. For Christmas recipes, see, for example, ibid., Dec. 1857, pp. 553–54; Dec. 1861, p. 529; Dec. 1862, pp. 601–3; Dec. 1863, pp. 579–81; and Dec. 1864, p. 541.

16. Grund, "Christmas and New Year in France and Germany," ibid., Dec. 1848, p. 7 (emphasis in original). For other examples, see Mrs. John K. Laskey's poem, "Christmas Night," ibid., Dec. 1844, p. 243, and "A Christmas Eve" (fiction), ibid., Dec. 1858, pp. 528–32.

17. "A Christmas in Hamburg," *Harper's Monthly*, Feb. 1859, pp. 359–61, 364–65.

18. Diary of Charles Francis Adams, Dec. 25, 1857, MHS.

19. Nevins and Thomas, eds., *Diary of George Templeton Strong*, Dec. 25, 1859, 2:481 (emphasis in original); Lizzie McIntyre, "The Christmas Tree," *Godey's*, Dec. 1860, pp. 505–6.

20. Allan Nevins and Milton Halsey Thomas, eds., *The Diary of George Templeton Strong*, vol. 3: *The Civil War, 1860–65* (New York: Macmillan, 1952), Dec. 24, 1862, 3: 282.

21. J. B. Jones, *A Rebel Clerk's Diary*, 2 vols., Howard Swiggett, ed. (New York: Old Hickory Bookshop, 1935), 1:224; 2:119; Georgeanna Muirson Woolsey, Philadelphia, Dec. 1860, *Letters of a Family*, 1:23–24; William Nicholson to sister, Jan. 18, 1863, Barker Texas Historical Center, University of Texas, Austin; C. Vann Woodward, ed., *Mary Chesnut's Civil War* (New Haven and London: Yale Univ. Press, 1981), 270.

22. T. H. Pearce, ed., *Diary of Captain Henry A. Chambers* (Wendell, N.C.: Broadfoot's Bookmark, 1983), 78; Kate Cumming, *Kate: The Journal of a Confederate Nurse*, Richard Barksdale Harwell, ed. (Baton Rouge: Louisiana State Univ. Press, 1959), Dec. 25, 1865, p. 246; [Wilder Dwight], *Life and Letters of Wilder Dwight* (Boston: Ticknor and Fields, 1868), Dec. 25, 1861, p. 180 (emphasis in original); Dwight to [unknown], Dec. 29, 1861, in ibid., 178; Leon Basile, ed., *The Civil War Diary of Amos E. Stearns, a Prisoner at Andersonville* (Rutherford, Madison, and Teaneck: Fairleigh Dickinson Univ. Press, 1981), Dec. 25, 1864, p. 101; John L. Ransom, *Andersonville Diary* (Auburn, N.Y.: privately pub., 1881), Dec. 24, 1863, p. 21.

23. Daniel B. Weber, ed., *The Diary of Ira Gillaspie of the Eleventh Michigan Infantry* (Mount Pleasant: Central Michigan Univ. Press, 1965), Dec. 25, 1861, p. 14; Francis Bacon to Georgeanna Muirson Woolsey, Dec. 24, 1861, in *Letters of a Family*, 1:226; George M. Neese, *Three Years in the Confederate Horse Artillery* (New York and Washington: Neale Publishing, 1911), Dec. 25, 1862, p. 141. The tables turned before long. "The Yankees celebrated Christmas by bombarding the city [Charleston] furiously . . . ," wrote Emma Holmes in 1864 (John F. Marszalek, ed., *The Diary of Miss Emma Holmes, 1861– 1866* (Baton Rouge: Louisiana State Univ. Press, 1979), Jan. 30, 1864, p. 335).

24. Williams, ed., *Diary and Letters of Rutherford B. Hayes*, Dec. 25, 1861, 2:168; Ransom, *Andersonville Diary*, Dec. 24, 1863, p. 21; Basile, ed., *Civil War Diary of Amos E. Stearns*, Dec. 25, 1864, p. 28; Neese, *Three Years in the Confederate Horse Artillery*, Dec. 25, 1863, p. 247; journal entry of Eliza Woolsey Howland, Dec. 25, 1861, in *Letters of a Family*, 1:232; Jones, *A Rebel Clerk's Diary*, Dec. 25, 1863, 2:119.

25. "A Christmas Pastime: The Gypsies," in *"Godey's* Arm-Chair," "Juvenile Department," *Godey's*, Dec. 1865, p. 545.

26. "Ella Moore's Letters from the City," in *"Godey's* Arm-Chair," *Godey's*, Dec. 1861, pp. 539–41; Douglas, *American Book of Days*, 614.

27. The titles of Nast's holiday drawings that appeared in *Harper's Weekly* are: "Thanksgiving Day, November 26, 1863," Dec. 5, 1865; "New Year's Day," which contrasts the conviviality of the holiday with death, Jan. 2, 1864; "Our Flag," July 16, 1864;

"Thanksgiving-Day November 24, 1864," Dec. 3, 1864; "The Union Christmas Dinner," Dec. 31, 1864; and "Palm Sunday," May 20, 1865 (Morton Keller, *The Art and Politics of Thomas Nast* (New York: Oxford Univ. Press, 1968), plates 5-9).

28. Jones, *Saint Nicholas of Myra*, 355; "Santa Claus in Camp" (illus.), *Harper's Weekly*, Jan. 3, 1863; "A Christmas Furlough" *Harper's Weekly*, Dec. 26, 1863. Louis Prang brought out the edition of "A Visit" in 1863. *Godey's* published its own "Christmas in Camp" in the Dec. 1864 issue, a drawing of a black man in a military camp, holding a Christmas fowl as he jumped and waved his hat in apparent elation ("Christmas in Camp" (illus.), *Godey's*, Dec. 1864, p. 477).

29. "Christmas Is Coming" (illus.), *Godey's*, Dec. 1863, n.p., and "Editor's Table," ibid., Dec. 1863, p. 582.

30. Ruth E. Finley, *The Lady of Godey's, Sarah Josepha Hale* (Philadelphia: J. B. Lippincott, 1931), 202; "Thanksgiving," *New York Times*, Nov. 25, 1864, p. 1.

31. "American National Thanksgiving," in "Editor's Table," *Godey's*, Nov. 1865, p. 441.

32. "Christmas Is Coming" in "Editor's Table," ibid., Dec. 1865, p. 538.

33. Ibid.

34. "Godey's Arm-Chair," ibid., Dec. 1866, p. 541; George C. McWhorter, "The Holidays," *Harper's Monthly*, Jan. 1866, p. 168.

35. "The Last Thursday of November," in "Editor's Table," *Godey's*, Nov. 1867, p. 447; "Christmas Is Coming," Dec. 1865, p. 543 (emphasis in original).

36. "An Act making the first Day of January, the twenty-fifth Day of December, the fourth Day of July, and Thanksgiving Day, Holidays, within the District of Columbia," Ch. 167, June 28, 1870. The law applied only the District of Columbia and had no binding effect on states.

Chapter 8. A Traditional American Christmas

1. Charles Dudley Warner, "Christmas Past," *Harper's Monthly*, Dec. 1884, p. 17.

2. T. J. Jackson Lears, *No Place of Grace: Antimodernism and the Transformation of American Culture, 1880-1920* (New York: Pantheon, 1980), esp. chs. 1, 5, 6, and Introduction. Lears links this indulgence in what he calls "evasive banality" to cultural change, a tie in which emphasis shifted from producer to consumer and from self-denial to more therapeutic and immediate gratification. Yet to apply Lear's perceptions to Christmas without qualification renders the holiday meaningless except as a tool of cultural hegemony and an indicator of a loss or misuse of its spiritual meaning.

3. See Robert Crunden, *Ministers of Reform: The Progressives' Achievements in American Civilization, 1889-1920* (New York: Basic Books, 1982), 90, for the apt term "innovative nostalgia." Crunden applies it to Progressive artists working at the turn of the century, but as a concept it fits nicely with what I see as a more general trait in the popular culture of Christmas.

4. *Lancaster Intelligencer*, Dec. 26, 1866, quoted in Yoder, "Introduction" to Shoemaker, *Christmas in Pennsylvania*, 11; "Editor's Easy Chair," *Harper's Monthly*, Jan. 1862, p. 410. The editor attributed the ready acceptance of the German Christmas tree, in part, to its "pure domesticity." (ibid.); George C. McWhorter, "The Holidays," ibid., Jan. 1866, p. 168; "Christmas Presents," *Nation*, Dec. 20, 1883, p. 257.

5. George C. McWhorter, "The Holidays," *Harper's Monthly*, Feb. 1866, p. 365; "Merry Christmas," *Catholic World*, Jan. 1871, p. 469; George William Curtis, "Christmas," *Harper's Monthly*, Dec. 1883, pp. 6, 13. The incidence of not celebrating Christmas remained notable well past Puritan days. *Catholic World* reported that "Indeed, there are

some people from that section of the country [New England] who even now do not know what Christmas means" (*Catholic World*, Jan. 1871, p. 469).

6. "Editor's Easy Chair," *Harper's Monthly*, Jan. 1876, pp. 290–91.

7. McWhorter, "The Holidays," Jan. 1866, p. 168. Curtis, "Christmas," 3–4, 6, 13, 15. Articles such as "The First Christmas Under the Puritan Directory," published in 1884 (*Saturday Review* 58 (1884):813–14), added to Puritan culpability.

8. Coffin, *The Book of Christmas Folklore*, 98, 105; Marble, "Christmas Carols, Ancient and Modern," 358.

9. William Hone, *Ancient Mysteries Described* (1822), in Macey, *Patriarchs of Time*, 157; Marble, "Christmas Carols, Ancient and Modern," 358, 360; Paul Davis, *The Lives and Times of Ebenezer Scrooge* (New Haven: Yale Univ. Press, 1990), 19. Waits were members of groups of public musicians in England, who serenaded for gratuities, usually at Christmas.

10. Reginald Nettle, *Christmas and Its Carols* (London: Faith Press, 1960), 119. England produced its best carols in the fifteenth century (ibid., 114–15, 188); Snyder, *December 25th*, 176; Thomas Nast St. Hill, *Thomas Nast's Christmas Drawings for the Human Race* (New York: Harper & Row, 1971), 123; Snyder, *December 25th*, 176–77; Foley, *Christmas in the Good Old Days*, 114.

11. Snyder, *December 25th*, 177; "Our Musical Column," in "Godey's Arm-Chair," *Godey's*, Dec. 1863, p. 588.

12. Snyder, *December 25th*, 168–69; Coffin, *Book of Christmas Folklore*, 109; Nettle, *Christmas and Its Carols*, 118; Richards, *How Christmas Came to the Sunday-Schools*, 175.

13. Richards, *How Christmas Came to the Sunday-Schools*, 174; Benjamin A. Botkin, ed., *Treasury of New England Folklore*, rev. ed. (New York: Crown, 1965), 422; Snyder, *December 25th*, 174, 176.

14. Dec. 30 (year unknown), diary of unknown woman, WLCL; Patience Price, "'As I Was a Saying': A Christmas Sketch," *Godey's*, Dec. 1866, p. 521.

15. "Evergreens for the Holidays," *New York Tribune*, Dec. 23, 1881; Snyder, *Christmas Tree Book*, 40.

16. Ripley, *Social Life in Old New Orleans*, 259; John E. Baur, *Christmas on the American Frontier, 1800–1900* (Caldwell, Idaho: Caxton Printers, 1961), 117–18; Caldwell, "Christmas in Early Missouri," 128; Snyder, *Christmas Tree Book*, 40.

17. *Harrisburg* (Pennsylvania) *Daily State Journal*, Dec. 24, 1872, quoted in Shoemaker, *Christmas in Pennsylvania*, 61; Simon Snyder Rathvon, *Lancaster* (Pennsylvania) *Intelligencer*, Dec. 24, 1881, quoted in ibid., p. 61; "Work Department," *Godey's*, Dec. 1874, pp. 556–57; *Philadelphia Record*, Dec. 21, 1890, quoted in Shoemaker, *Christmas in Pennsylvania*, 64.

18. Maggie Rogers, with Judith Hawkins, *The Glass Christmas Ornament: Old and New* (Forest Grove, Ore.: Timber Press, 1977), 6, 7. During this time, American glass-maker William A. DeMuth was also making silvered balls and chains of bead ornaments.

19. Snyder, *Christmas Tree Book*, 36–37, 55–56; Snyder, *December 25th*, 140; Rogers, *Glass Christmas Ornament*, 7. There have been only a few attempts to chronicle the history of Christmas ornaments. In particular, see Snyder, *Christmas Tree Book*, 55–100, and Rogers, *Glass Christmas Ornament*.

20. Snyder, *Christmas Tree Book*, 104, 108–9.

21. See descriptions in Mrs. Charles William Woolsey to daughters, Dec. 24, 1861, *Letters of a Family*, 1:231–21, and Snyder, *Christmas Tree Book*, 103. See ibid., 101–11 passim, for additional details on other candleholders and tree-lighting inventions.

22. Snyder, *Christmas Tree Book*, 108–9.

23. *Reading* (Pennsylvania) *Weekly Eagle*, Jan. 2, 1886, quoted in Shoemaker, *Christmas in Pennsylvania*, 64; Snyder, *Christmas Tree Book*, 113–16.

24. Snyder, *Christmas Tree Book*, 19, 37; Shoemaker, *Christmas in Pennsylvania*, 63.

25. *Lancaster* (Pennsylvania) *Daily New Era*, Dec. 31, 1877, quoted in Shoemaker, *Christmas in Pennsylvania*, 61; Snyder, *Christmas Tree Book*, 153. It should be noted that the Pennsylvania Dutch brought with them the custom of enclosing a tree with a fence and adding a surrounding scene, but the original vision kept to a much smaller scale than these late nineteenth-century creations.

26. John Lewis, quoted in Snyder, *December 25th*, 136–27.

27. Ibid.; *Lancaster* (Pennsylvania) *Daily New Era*, Dec. 31, 1877, quoted in Shoemaker, *Christmas in Pennsylvania*, 61.

28. *Philadelphia Times*, Dec. 26, 1877, quoted in ibid., 59; Snyder, *December 25th*, 295.

29. *New York Times*, quoted in ibid., 142.

30. *New York Times*, quoted in ibid., 99; *Reading* (Pennsylvania) *Berks and Schuylkill Journal*, Dec. 26, 1874, quoted in Shoemaker, *Christmas in Pennsylvania*, 51; *Easton* (Pennsylvania) *Daily Express*, Dec. 24, 1879, quoted in ibid.; anonymous woman, quoted in Snyder, *December 25th*, 99.

31. Ella Benton to Carrie Grant, Jan. 16, 1876, CHS.

32. "Christmas Presents," *Nation*, Dec. 20, 1883, p. 502.

33. Buday, *History of the Christmas Card*, 16, 198; Daniel J. Boorstin, *The Americans: The National Experience* (New York: Random House, 1965), 130–35; William J. Peterson, "Postcard Holiday Greetings," *Palimpsest* 48 (Dec. 1967):580.

34. Mary Margaret Sittig, "L. Prang & Company, Fine Art Publishers," (M.A. Thesis, George Washington University, 1970), pp. 27–29, 37; Buday, *History of the Christmas Card*, 75; David A. Holtz, "Red Crayon American: A Study of Louis Prang" (M.A. Thesis, Wichita State University, 1965), p. 35. Prang designed the oversized cards c. 1864. Three of them measured 11″ × 27,″ and a smaller one 11″ × 14.″

35. Sittig, "L. Prang & Company," 46, 48; Chase, *Romance of Greeting Cards*, 26; Peter C. Marzio, *The Democratic Art: Pictures for a 19th Century America: Chromolithography, 1840–1900* (Boston: David R. Godine, 1979), 99; Buday, *History of the Christmas Card*, 75.

36. Sittig, "L. Prang & Company," 152–54; [Graydon LaVerne] Larry Freeman, *Louis Prang: Color Lithographer Giant of a Man* (Watkins Glen, N.Y.: Century House, 1971), 92, 94, 96, 99; Louis Prang, "Autobiography," in Sittig, "L. Prang & Company," appendix I. Sittig suggests that Prang wrote this short recollection in 1875, but internal evidence suggests a later date.

37. L. D. Ettlinger and R. G. Holloway, *Compliments of the Season* (London: Penguin, 1947), 15–16.

38. George Buday, *The Story of the Christmas Card* (London: Odhams Press, n.d.), 14; Ettlinger and Holloway, *Compliments of the Season*, 12; Freeman, *Louis Prang*, 92; Chase, *Romance of the Greeting Card*, 16; Buday, *History of the Christmas Card*, 6, 16. Sixteen-year-old William Maw Egley drew another of the early cards, but its date is unclear. Chase sets it at 1842, but Ettlinger and Holloway write of Egley's card as an 1848 successor to Horsely's card (Ernest Chase, *Romance of Greeting Cards*, 15; Ettlinger and Holloway, *Compliments of the Season*, 20). Quodlibets originated as a form of advertising in the eighteenth century. They are composed of seemingly randomly arranged trompe-l'oeil illustrations of wares offered for sale by a dealer. Although their use declined in Europe, they were common in America throughout the nineteenth century and, at least on Christmas cards, still survive (Buday *History of the Christmas Card*, 24–25, 80).

39. According to Buday, only a description of the Pease card survives (*History of the*

Christmas Card, 277–78), but Ernest Dudley Chase claims to own one, which he describes as black and white, 4 1/2″ × 6″, designed in the same style as Egley's card, and issued between 1850 and 1852 (Chase, *Romance of Greeting Cards*, 51). A picture of Chase's card is in *Two Thousand Years of Season' Greetings: An Album of Holiday Cards and Their Predecessors, Christmas 1951* (New York: Photogravure and Color, 1951), 13.

40. Buday, *History of the Christmas Card*, 37, 104, 115–16, 119.

41. Ibid., 110; Nathanial Hawthorne, Dec. 26, 1855, quoted in Snyder, *December 25th*, 121. Joel Roberts Poinsett, botanist, South Carolina congressman, and the first United States ambassador to Mexico, introduced the poinsettia into this country (ibid., 129–30).

42. Buday, *History of the Christmas Card*, 78, 114–15. The second side of a card was usually printed in monochrome, and occasionally incorporated longer sentiments or verses (Katharine Morrison McClinton, *The Chromolithographs of Louis Prang* (New York: Clarkson N. Potter, 1973), 76).

43. White, quoted in Chase, *Romance of Greeting Cards*, 31; Buday, *History of the Christmas Card*, 76–77.

44. Tuck (Raphael) & Son, a London company, first originated the idea for design competitions in 1880 (Louis W. McCulloch, *Paper Americana* (San Diego and New York: A. S. Barnes, 1980), 56; Sittig, "L. Prang & Company," 30; McClinton, *Chromolithographs of Louis Prang*, 77. See ibid., 77 ff., for details of winners of these contests. Chase, *Romance of the Greeting Card*, 28; Freeman, *Louis Prang*, 99.

45. Freeman, *Louis Prang*, 102; Buday, *History of the Christmas Card*, 77; Prang, "Autobiography," in Sittig, "L. Prang & Co." Over a thousand entered the contest in 1881, but of the 1500 drawings, only 700 were accepted ("Notes," *Nation*, March 3, 1881, p. 150). Perhaps Prang had attempted to make the Christmas card serve too grand a function. "What the exact test of merit in a Christmas card may be one is naturally at a loss to know," mused the *Nation*. "Possibly these competitions can be regarded as attempts to evolve the ideal type by selection of the fittest."

46. Freeman, *Louis Prang*, 102.

47. McCulloch, *Paper Americana*, 59; Prang, "Autobiography," In Sitting, *L. Prang & Company*, appendix I, p. 154; Chase, *Romance of Greeting Cards*, 26. The public apparently shied from purchasing competitors' inferior greeting cards, but illustrated postcards of all types, which could be sent at the rate of a penny stamp, also cut into the card market. World War I completely closed off the supply of foreign cards. Ultimately, however, these changes opened the market "to quality production." After 1900, Alfred Bartlett, Albert M. Davis, Fred Rust, Paul Volland and "The Gibsons" entered the American field (ibid., 33).

Chapter 9. Gilding Christmas

1. Louisa May Alcott, *Little Women or Meg, Jo, Beth, and Amy* (1868–69; Garden City, N.Y.: Children's Classics, n.d.), 3, 13–14.

2. See, for example, Caldwell, "Christmas in Early Missouri," 129.

3. Milly Richards (Store) Gray, *The Diary of Milly Gray, 1832–1840* (Galveston, Tex.: Rosenberg Library Press, 1967), Dec. 29, 1834, p. 50; William Wood, *Autobiography of William Wood*, 2 vols. (New York: printed for private circulation by J. S. Babcock, 1895), Dec. 26, 1845, 2:136, 138; diary of Sally Knowles, Dec. 25, 1949, Pennsylvania Historical Society, Philadelphia; Robert F. Lucid, ed., *The Journal of Henry Dana, Jr.*, 3 vols. (Cambridge, Mass.: Harvard Univ. Press, 1968), Dec. 25, 1852, 1:526; [Anonymous] diary, Dec. 30, 18 – –, WLCL; Pease and Randall, eds., *Diary of Orville Hickman Browning*, vol. 1, Dec. 25, 1860, p. 444; Ella Benton to Carrie Grant, Jan. 16, 1876, CHS; Nevins and Thomas, eds., *Diary of George Templeton Strong*, Dec. 24, 1855, 2:247;

Juanita Brooks, ed., *On the Mormon Frontier: The Diary of Hosea Stout, 1844–1861*, 2 vols. (Salt Lake City: Univ. of Utah Press, 1964), Dec. 25, 1852, 2:466; Rutherford Hayes to S. Birchard, Dec. 26, 1855, in Williams, ed., *Diary and Letters of Rutherford B. Hayes*, 2: 495.

4. Waits, *Modern Christmas in America*, 50, 51; Luna Frances Lambert, "The Seasonal Trade: Gift Cards and Chromolithography in America, 1874–1910" (Ph.D. diss., George Washington University, 1980), 16–17.

5. Ella Benton to Carrie Grant, Jan. 16, 1876; Williams, ed., *Diary and Letters of Rutherford B. Hayes*, Dec. 26, 1882, 4:99–100; anonymous store manager, quoted in Snyder, *December 25th*, 79.

6. Cheal, *The Gift Economy*, 6, 12, 181; Csikszentmihalyi and Rochberg-Halton, *The Meaning of Things*, 86; Michael Schudson, *Advertising*, 139–40. See also Caplow, "Christmas Gifts and Kin Networks," 383–89, passim, who finds a close relationship between materialism and the concept of family.

7. Ino Churchill, "The Holly Wreath," *Godey's*, Dec. 1875, p. 519. Churchill also observed that "this age of materialization" had made gift-giving more an "onerous tribute" than a "spontaneous offering" (ibid.). "Editor's Easy Chair," *Harper's Monthly*, Jan. 1856, p. 265.

8. For a recent example of the "hype" argument, see Schmidt, "The Commercialization of the Calendar," 887–916.

9. John K. Winkler, *Five and Ten: The Fabulous Life of F.W. Woolworth* (New York: Robert M. McBride, 1940), 69–70.

10. Woolworth letter from Europe, April 17, [1890], quoted in ibid., 94–95.

11. "Merry Christmas," *Godey's*, Dec. 1866, p. 537.

12. Snyder, *December 25th*, 614; Caldwell, "Christmas in Early Missouri," 128–29; "Christmas and Holliday Articles," *Fort Smith* (Arkansas) *Herald*, Dec. 5, 1849. This was the first advertisement for holiday goods to appear in this paper. Except for the "fancy inkstands," the St. Louis firm of Mead and Adriance offered all the items listed above in 1835.

13. *Augusta* (Georgia) *Daily Chronicle & Sentinel*, Dec. 24, 1845; *Wilmington* (North Carolina) *Daily Journal*, Dec. 23, 1859; "Godey's Arm-Chair," *Godey's*, Dec. 1856, pp. 565, 566. In 1878, where always before there had been "Fashions for December," *Godey's* supplied a two-page illustration of "*Godey's* Christmas Gifts" (ibid., Dec. 1878, n.p.).

14. Snyder, *December 25th*, 239; Richards, *How Christmas Came to the Sunday-Schools*, 191; "Holidays," *United States Review*, 65.

15. "Amusing Mechanical Toys," *New York Tribune*, Dec. 22, 1882, p. 7; Child to Sarah Blake (Sturgis) Shaw, Dec. 28, 1879, in Patricia G. Holland and Milton Meltzer, eds., *The Collected Correspondence of Lydia Maria Child, 1817–1880* (Millwood, N.Y.: Kraus Microform, 1980); Ralph M. Hower, *History of Macy's of New York, 1858–1919* (Cambridge, Mass.: Harvard Univ. Press, 1967), 169; *New York Tribune*, Dec. 9, 1894; Winkler, *Five and Ten*, 109. On the importance of window dressing to holidays, see Schmidt, "The Commercialization of the Calendar," 894. Woolworth advised his salesclerks that Christmas was a good time to promote "stickers" or unsalable goods. These, he had found, would sell during the excitement. He counseled his managers to mend all broken toys and dolls every day so that they could be sold at full price. He also warned managers to watch clerks and customers carefully to prevent theft. When the store was crowded, no children should be allowed in the store unless with their parents. Cashiers also needed watching because they had the best chance to steal.

16. Diary of Abiel T. La Forge, Dec. 24, 1867, quoted in Hower, *History of Macy's*, 125n, 201, 281. In 1901, Macy's decided against staying open for evening shopping during

the ten days prior to Christmas, reasoning, in part, that too many employees were on the sick list when they had to work holidays. The results proved favorable enough for it to abandon the practice (ibid., 306–7). Henry Givens Baker, *Rich's of Atlanta: The Story of a Store Since 1867* (Athens: Univ. of Georgia, 1953), 49; advertisement, *New York Tribune*, Dec. 16, 1894, p. 18; advertisement, *New York Times*, Dec. 24, 1898, p. 9.

17. Waits, *Modern Christmas in America*, 20; A. L. Gorman, "Home-Made Christmas Gifts," *Harper's Bazaar*, Dec. 1980, p. 1256, quoted in ibid., 20. In particular, the December issues of *Godey's* carried patterns and instructions for making holiday gifts and decorations. *Peterson's* offered a narrower selection of embroidery patterns and women's wear.

18. Waits, *Modern Christmas in America*, 20.

19. Anna Robeson Burr, ed., *Alice James; Her Brothers – Her Journal* (Cornwall, N.Y.: Dodd, Mead, 1934), 125; Snyder, *December 25th*, 86–87.

20. "Christmas Sport," in "Arm-Chair," *Godey's*, Dec. 1867, p. 547; William Burnell Waits, Jr., "The Many-Faced Custom: Christmas Gift-Giving in America, 1900–1940" (Ph.D. diss., Rutgers University, 1978), 56.

21. Waits, "The Many-Faced Custom," 56; Snyder, *December 25th*, 97; Hower, *History of Macy's*, 333.

22. "Christmas Presents," *Nation*, Dec. 20, 1883, p. 502; Charles Dudley Warner, "Christmas Past," *Harper's Monthly*, Dec. 1884, p. 17; Storekeeper, quoted in Snyder, *December 25th*, 57.

23. Such advice was not uncommon. See, for example, "Holiday Gifts," *New York Tribune*, Dec. 9, 1875, p. 4, and "The Day Before Christmas," ibid., Dec. 24, 1879, p. 4. T. P. W., "Auntie's Merry Christmas," *Godey's*, Dec. 1861, pp. 506–7.

24. Holmes to C. W. Storey, Jan. 4, 1889, in William Roscoe Thayer, ed., *Letters of John Holmes to James Russell Lowell and Others* (Boston: Houghton Mifflin, 1917), 227; "The Seamy Side of Christmas," *New York Tribune*, Dec. 23, 1894, p. 6.

25. Edward E. Hale, *Christ the Giver and Christ the Receiver – Two Sermons Preached at South Congregational Church, Boston, December 25 and December 26, 1880* (Boston: Geo H. Ellis, 1881), 8.

26. Washington Gladden, *Social Facts and Forces* (New York and London: G. P. Putnam's Sons, 1897), 195–96, 198–99, 203–5.

27. "Holiday Gifts," *New York Tribune*, Dec. 9, 1875, p. 4.

28. "Editor's Easy Chair," *Harper's Monthly*, Feb. 1864, p. 417; "Merry Christmas," *Godey's*, Dec. 1866, p. 537.

29. On this point, see Cheal, *Gift Economy*, 181.

30. David J. Rothman, *The Discovery of the Asylum: Social Order and Disorder in the New Republic*, rev. ed. (Boston: Little, Brown, 1990), 172–79, esp. 175.

31. *Raleigh* (North Carolina) *Register*, Dec. 27, 1848, quoted in Guion Griffis Johnson, *Ante-bellum North Carolina, a Social History* (Chapel Hill: Univ. of North Carolina Press, 1937), 700; T. S. Arthur, "Christmas Presents: A Story for the Holidays," *Godey's*, Dec. 1848, p. 371.

32. Strong, Private Journal, Dec. 24, 1841, NYHS.

33. Lydia Maria Child to Anna Loring, Dec. 26, 1843, in Holland and Meltzer, eds., *Collected Correspondence* (emphasis in original).

34. Walter Bagehot, "Charles Dickens," *Works* 2:269–70, quoted in Walter E. Houghton, *Victorian Frame of Mind, 1830–1870* (New Haven: Yale Univ. Press, 1967), 274; "Editor's Easy Chair," *Harper's Monthly*, Jan. 1862, p. 410; "The Christmas Party" (illus.), *Godey's*, Dec. 1867, n.p.

35. "Making Ready for Christmas," *New York Tribune*, Dec. 12, 1877, p. 4; ibid., Dec. 23, 1881, p. 4.

36. Annie Frost, "Christmas for the Rich and Poor," *Godey's*, Dec. 1858, pp. 513–16.

37. Fred Kaplan, *Dickens, a Biography* (New York: William Morrow, 1988), 506–9. The earliest editions of *The Carol* printed in America were "A Christmas Ghost Story," piracy by Henry Hewitt and Richard Egan Lee, in *Peter Parley's Illuminated Library* (n.p., 1844); *A Christmas Carol* (New York: Harper and Brothers, 1844); *A Christmas Carol*, illus. after John Leech (Philadelphia: Carey and Hart), 1844; *Christmas Books*, illus. by F. O. C. Darley and John Gilbert (New York: J. G. Gregory, 1861; and *A Christmas Carol in Prose: Being a Ghost Story of Christmas*, condensed by Dickens for his readings (Boston, Ticknor and Fields, 1867). See "A Chronological List of Some Noteworthy Versions of the Carol" in Paul Davis, *The Lives and Times of Ebenezer Scrooge* (New York: Yale Univ. Press, 1990), 259–70. Dickens gave the first of his public recitations, 127 in all, of *A Christmas Carol* in 1853 (ibid., 53–56). For a description of his American performances, see Kate Field's account in *Pen Photographs of Dickens's Readings* (Boston: J. Osgood, 1871), 23–36.

38. Bayard Tuckerman, ed., *Diary of Philip Hone*, 2 vols. (New York: Dodd, Mead, 1889), Jan. 24, 1842, 2:109–10; "The Dickens Christmas," *New York Tribune*, Dec. 26, 1900, p. 6. The *Tribune* article attributed these assertions to one Stephen Fiske of New York City.

39. Foley, *Christmas in the Good Old Days*, 39–40; Davis, *The Lives and Times of Ebenezer Scrooge*, 7, 9, 49. According to Paul Davis, "Dickens dated the *Carol* from his address to the Manchester Athenaeum on 7 October 1843. He was struck by the goodwill in the faces of the working people in his audience and stirred to write a Christmas story addressed to a similarly broad national audience (ibid., 5).

40. Davis, *The Lives and Times of Ebenezer Scrooge*, 150; *New York Times*, Dec. 19, 1863, quoted in Foley, *Christmas in the Good Old Days*, 27; *North American Review*, quoted in E. Douglas Branch, *The Sentimental Years, 1836–1860* (1934; New York: Hill and Wang, 1965), 104; Whittier to Annie Fields, Dec. 17, 1868, in Picard, ed., *Letters of John Greenleaf Whittier*, 3:186. Walter Bagehot (as do others) credits Dickens with introducing Americans to Christmas and thereby creating the holiday's associations with benevolence and charity (Bagehot, "Charles Dickens," *Works*, 2:269–70). However, this would seem a particularly British viewpoint and in any case overlooks America's own Christmas history.

41. William Gilmore Simms's *Castle Dismal, or The Bachelor's Christmas* (1845), although published in 1845, can be grouped with these earlier expositions of a romantic Christmas. See Chapter 6 for additional discussion of this work. Charles Dickens, *Sketches by Boz* (1833; New York: Walter J. Black, n.d.), 274; Dickens, *The Pickwick Papers* (1837; New York: Dutton, 1977), 374. "A Christmas Carol" was the first and most important of five stories Dickens wrote between 1843 and 1848 that redefined Christmas. The others were "The Chimes," "The Cricket in the Hearth," "The Battle of Life," and "The Haunted Man," collected in Charles Dickens, *Christmas Books* (New York: George Routledge and Sons, n.d.). for a fuller discussion of the meaning of this Christmas set in the context of Dickens's work, see Ruth F. Glancy, "Dickens and Christmas: His Framed-Tale Themes," *Nineteenth-Century Fiction* 35 (June 1980):53–72.

42. Strong, Private Journal, Dec. 25, 1837, p. 162, NYHS.

43. For a thorough and interesting examination of the changing interpretations of Scrooge, see Davis, *The Life and Times of Ebenezer Scrooge*, particularly ch. 3, "*A Christmas Carol* as Secular Scripture," pp. 53–87.

44. Dickens, *A Christmas Carol*, 75–76. On the point of the significance of time, see Glancy, "Dickens and Christmas," 57. Kathleen Tillotson and George H. Ford argue that Dickens's early picaresque novels, ending with *Martin Chuzzlewit* in 1843, treat memory as a past experience. The Christmas stories written between 1843 and 1848 mark a

transition to "time-conscious" novels, the first of which was *Dombey and Son* (1848) ("Dickens and the Voices of Time," *Nineteenth-Century Fiction* 24 (1970):440, quoted in ibid., 54).

45. Tillotson and Ford, "Dickens and the Voices of Time," 44–47. Badly shaken after seeing the emptiness of his own future if he does not reform, Scrooge cries, "Spirit! . . . hear me! I am not the man I was. . . . I will honour Christmas in my heart, and try to keep it all the year. I will live in the Past, the Present, and the Future. . . . I will not shut out the lessons that they teach" (ibid., 70).

46. Houghton, *Victorian Frame of Mind*, 275n; Coffin, *Book of Christmas Folklore*, 157.

47. Warner, "Christmas Past," 17; "A Metropolitan Festival," *New York Tribune*, Dec. 26, 1882, p. 4.

48. Best & Co. advertisement, *New York Tribune*, Dec. 14, 1894, p. 12.

49. Luna, "Seasonal Trade," 85–86; Hower, *History of Macy's*, 201.

50. Woolworth letter, March 17, [1890], quoted in Winkler, *Five and Ten*, 89; Rogers, *Glass Christmas Ornament*, 9–10.

51. Woolworth letter, Dec. 13, 1892, quoted in Winkler, *Five and Ten*, 109–10.

52. Winkler, *Five and Ten*, 123–24.

53. Thomas Nelson Page, *Santa Claus's Partner* (New York: Charles Scribner's Sons, 1899), 101, 110–13.

54. Page teaches a similar lesson in *Tommy Trot's Visit to Santa Claus* (New York: Charles Scribner's Sons, 1908).

Chapter 10. The American Santa Claus

1. I attempt in this chapter to suggest a number of ways in which Americans interpreted and employed the image and legend of Santa Claus. In declining to fulfill what some might regard as an obligation to the reader to draw conclusions about the social, cultural, or religious functions of Santa, I refer to Claude Lévi-Strauss's comment concerning conflicting definitions and usage of myth analysis: " . . . if a given mythology confers prominence to a certain character, let us say an evil grandmother, it will be claimed that in such a society grandmothers are actually evil and that mythology reflects the social structure and the social relations; but should the actual data be conflicting, it would be readily claimed that the purpose of mythology is to provide an outlet for repressed feelings. Whatever the situation may be, a clever dialectic will always find a way to pretend that a meaning has been unravelled" ("The Structural Study of Myth," in *Myth: A Symposium*, Thomas A. Sebeok, ed. (Bloomington: Indiana Univ. Press, 1965), 83.

2. Brian McGinty, "Santa Claus," *Early American Life* 10 (Dec. 1979):103. *The Children's Friend* (1821), a small, paperbound book, is believed to have been the first produced by lithography in the United States as well as the first American book about Saint Nicholas. McGinty also points out that this is the first time that Santa is dressed in red (although red is traditionally associated with bishops' robes). If this was the first lithograph, that is, a color picture, it would be only logical that the printer choose a color that would show the new process to best advantage. Brown, the color of most fur, would not present a great enough contrast with the black of surrounding type. In fact, of all the colors, red would seem to be the most appropriate and arresting choice.

3. Robert W. G. Vail, "Santa Claus Visits the Hudson," *New-York Hist. Soc. Quart.* 35 (Oct. 1951):339–41; Charles W. Jones, "Knickerbocker Santa Claus," ibid. 38 (1954): 383; Snyder, *December 25th*, 224. McGinty suggests that perhaps Weir had seen and been influenced by a copy of *The Children's Friend*. He also thinks Weir added a sword (McGinty, "Santa Claus," 103). Phillip Snyder suggests that "what appears to some to be the

end of a sword scabbard partially hidden behind one leg is just as likely to be the end of a large crucifix" (Snyder, *December 25th*, 224). The 30″ × 24 3/8″ painting was done on wood (Vail, "Santa Claus Visits the Hudson," 338).

4. Philip English Mackey, ed., *A Gentlemen of Much Promise: The Diary of Isaac Mickle, 1837-1845*, 2 vols. (Philadelphia: Univ. of Pennsylvania Press, 1977), Dec. 25, 1841, 2: 247; Mary L. Booth, *History of the City of New York*, 2 vols. (New York: W. R. C. Clark, 1867), 194; Vail, *Knickerbocker Birthday*, 368-70.

5. "Old Father Christmas" (illus.), *Godey's*, Dec. 1867, n.p.; "Old Father Christmas," ibid., Dec. 1868, p. 536; "Welcome, Kriss Kringle, Come In" (illus.), ibid., Dec. 1878, n.p.,; "A Story about a Goose: A Christmas Story," ibid., Dec. 1862, pp. 559-60; Zaidee, "Journeying in the Cradle," ibid., Dec. 1866, p. 507.

6. Sarah to (brother) George Thetford (or Thelford), Jan. 1, 1864, WLCL; Snyder, *December 25th*, 229, 230.

7. Moore, "A Visit from St. Nicholas," 169-75. Darley's Santa was not unlike the one Thomas Nast created in 1863, a coincidence which, according to Charles W. Jones, gives credence to the idea that a standard image of Santa was already evolving (Jones, *Saint Nicholas of Myra*, 353).

8. "Santa Claus and His Works" was composed in ten circles, each with its own title (see St. Hill, *Thomas Nast's Christmas Drawings*, 28). In 1890, in an effort to recover devastating personal financial losses, Nast gathered together the Christmas drawings he had done for *Harper's Weekly* during the previous thirty years and added new ones. The book contained 69 drawings. Santa Claus appeared in 33 of them. Nast used his five children as models and many of the scenes came from his own home. St. Hill, *Thomas Nast's Christmas Drawings for the Human Race* 24. For a brief discussion of Nast's Christmas art before 1866, see Chapter 7. On Nast's illustration of Moore's poem, see Jones, *Saint Nicholas of Myra*, 353. About Santa's red suit, see W. Willis Jones, "From Saint Nicholas to Santa Claus," 8-11, pamphlet presented as a Christmas greeting from Mr. & Mrs. George Arents, 1952, HRC. This pamphlet is an abbreviated version of W. Willis Jones, "The Life Story of Santa Claus," *Amateur Book Collector*, Dec. 1951. Verse author was George P. Webster and book title was *Santa Claus and His Works*.

9. "Merry Old Santa Claus," *Harper's Weekly*, Jan. 1, 1881. Some, including Charles W. Jones, have seen in Nast's portrait of Santa a self-portrait of Nast himself, a comment frequently made on the connection between artist and subject. In the same instance, Jones asserts that Nast's likeness of Santa was his only original addition to the Santa legend (Jones, *Saint Nicholas of Myra*, 353; Albert Bigelow Paine, *Th. Nast, His Period and His Pictures* (New York: Macmillan, 1904)). On the pipe that Santa held in his hand, see Stephen Nissenbaum's discussion on the relationship of pipe lengths to social class, in which he asserts that in giving St. Nicholas "the stump of a pipe," as opposed to a long pipe symbolic of the upper classes, Clement Moore "effectively *declassed*" the saint (Nissenbaum, "Revisiting 'A Visit from St. Nicholas,'" 55-59, quote on 55, emphasis in original). If so, Nast re-elevated Santa Claus in the social hierarchy by giving him a long-stemmed pipe.

10. Julia F. Snow, "Christmas Guests," *Harper's Monthly*, Feb. 1866, p. 345; Paine, *Th. Nast*, 319.

11. Jones, *St. Nicholas of Myra*, 356. That the primary winter sport of the Northeast was sleighing made this sort of travel especially appealing. John Pintard to Eliza Davidson, letter of Dec. 18, 1829, entry for Dec. 24, in Barck, ed., *Letters from John Pintard*, 3:114; Booth, *History of the City of New York*, 194.

12. Isaac Asimov, *Familiar Poems, Annotated* (Garden City, N.Y.: Doubleday, 1977), 181; Bernard Grun, *The Timetables of History: A Horizontal Linkage of People and Events* (New York: Simon and Schuster, 1979), 391; "How to Reach the North Pole," *Nation*,

Jan. 14, 1869, pp. 26–27; "The Search for the Pole," *New York Times*, Dec. 24, 1881, p. 1.

13. Richards, *Diary of Caroline Cowles Richards*, 66. The letter was misdated "North Pole, 10 January, 1869." Jones, "From Saint Nicholas to Santa Claus," 11; St. Hill, *Christmas Drawings for the Human Race*, 29.

14. Snyder, *December 25th*, 235.

15. Charles W. Jones argues that of all the details of Santa's life, only "Santa's Workshop" may be credited to Nast's inventiveness (Jones, *Saint Nicholas of Myra*, 353). Alcott diary, May 7, 1856, Houghton Library, Harvard University, cited in Joel Myerson and Daniel Shealy, *The Selected Letters of Louisa May Alcott* (Boston: Little, Brown, 1987), 31n; "The Workshop of Santa Claus" (illus.), *Godey's*, Dec. 1873, n.p.; Jones, *Saint Nicholas of Myra*, 357.

16. "Arm-Chair," *Godey's*, Dec. 1873, p. 569. From a Marxist standpoint, Hale's comment showed the implicit truth that, as the process of consumption became more sophisticated, an understanding of it as a total process became more difficult. In brief, product and producer became separate, the basis for a classic case of alienated labor.

17. Of course, not everyone imagined Santa in a fur coat, but even the red, ermine-trimmed coat that Nast supplied had a furry look to it. Charles W. Jones writes that the idea for Santa's fur did not come from Old Germany, "with its traditional presumptions that fur covered God's outcast crew of fallen angels and the sons of Cain, the raging beasts of the mummers' world, but originated from the American fur trade, and that those who had become rich, such as the Astors, wore fur during the cold northern winters (ibid., 355). As late as 1913, at least one person expressed outrage that Santa's outfit should be red. In a letter to the editor, one man demanded to know "What Anarchist started the notion that Santa Claus should dress in red?" (*New York Times*, Dec. 11, 1913, quoted in Snyder, *December 25th*, 231).

18. One writer, for example, must have calmed many anxious children who feared Santa might not complete his rounds in time. She sent him out in a "cozy little sleigh" a full twenty-four hours early, on the night before Christmas Eve, to make sure he would not miss delivering toys on time to any deserving children (Snow, "Christmas Guests," 354).

19. Snyder, *December 25th*, 282.

20. Santa Claus to Bessie and Lucy Chase, Dec. 5, 1879, and Santa Claus to Mr. Chase, Xmas Eve 1882, Horace G. Chase Papers, Chicago Public Library, Special Collections, Chicago, Illinois.

21. Wendell H. Oswalt, *Understanding Our Culture: An Anthropological View* (New York: Holt, Rinehart and Winston, 1970), 10; Warren O. Hagstrom, "What Is the Meaning of Santa Claus?," *American Sociologist* 2 (1966):250–51 (emphasis in original).

22. "Germanicus," "The Heathenism of Christmas: A Protest Against Santa Claus," *Lutheran Observer*, Philadelphia, Dec. 21, 1883, quoted in Shoemaker, *Christmas in Pennsylvania*, 16.

23. Philadelphia *Lutheran*, Dec. 22, 1881, quoted in Shoemaker, *Christmas in Pennsylvania*, 45; *The Friend*, Dec. 1906, quoting from the *Evangelical Friend*, quoted in Yoder, "Introduction" to Shoemaker, *Christmas in Pennsylvania*, 10.

24. Josephine Pollard, "A New Christmas" (reprinted from *Demorest's Monthly*), Annual Supplement to *Berkshire Courier*, Great Barrington, Mass., 1891, p. 1.

25. Jacob Riis, *Is There a Santa Claus?* (New York: Macmillan, 1904), 1, 27–29.

26. Editor, "Santa Claus," *Open Court*, Jan. 1899, pp. 45, 47.

27. Francis P. Church, *New York Sun*, Sept. 21, 1897, reprinted in Obituary of Virginia O'Hanlon, *New York Times*, May 14, 1971, pp. 1, 44.

Chapter 11. A Frame of Mind

1. Ruth Russell, "Christmas Spirit and Community Spirit," *World Review* 1 (Dec. 21, 1925):204; Kane, *Southern Christmas Book*, 61. Prototypes of the "new American community celebration," as Ruth Russell called the urban productions, had appeared sporadically throughout the last half of the previous century. The ruling middle class of Philadelphia, for example, had tamed the spontaneous and often unruly mumming demonstrations that immigrant groups held on Christmas Day into a respectable, civic New Year's parade. See Davis, "'Making Night Hideous,'" 185–99.

2. Russell, "Christmas Spirit and Christmas Community," 205.

3. Richards, *How Christmas Came to the Sunday-Schools*, 195. On the transformative effect of Christmas in both public and private places, see Patrick McGreevy, "Place in the American Christmas," *Geographical Review* 80 (Jan. 1990):3, 37–40.

4. Martha J. Lamb, "Christmas Season in Dutch New York," *Magazine of American History* 10 (Dec. 1883):474. Here Lamb refers to an urban population of blacks. Jacob Riis, "Merry Christmas in the Tenements," *Century Magazine*, Dec. 1897, p. 168; Daniel De Leon, "For a Merry Christmas," *Daily People*, Dec. 25, 1900, p. 1.

5. Dorothy W. Nelson, "A Heathen Goes to Mass," in "Contributor's Club," *Atlantic*, Dec. 1930, p. 828; Walter Lippmann, *Preface to Morals*, quoted in ibid.

6. Philadelphia *Times*, Dec. 26, 1877, quoted in Shoemaker, *Christmas in Pennsylvania*, 59.

7. For this paragraph and the next, see "Rabbis' Diverse Views," *New York Tribune*, Dec. 24, 1906, p. 4; "Jews Protest against Celebration of Season in Schools," *New York Tribune*, Dec. 6, 1906, p. 13; Leonard Bloom, "A Successful Jewish Boycott of the New York City Public Schools: Christmas 1906," *American Jewish History* 70 (1980):180–88. The 1906 boycott was just one episode in what has become a lengthy history of protests against and defenses of celebrating Christmas in public schools, not only by Jews, but by other religious and nonreligious groups as well.

8. Louis Witt, "The Jew Celebrates Christmas," *Christian Century*, Dec. 6, 1939, p. 1497.

9. Ibid., 1498, 1499.

10. Editorial, "Jews and Christmas," *Christian Century*, Dec. 20, 1939, pp. 1566, 1567.

11. Rabbi Edward L. Israel, "A Communication: A Jewish Answer to Dr. Witt," *Christian Century*, Dec. 20, 1939, pp. 1580–81.

12. Theodore Caplow, "Christmas Gifts and Kin Networks," *American Sociological Review* 47 (June 1982):390. In this study of Middletown, Caplow found that the entire scale of Christmas had increased greatly since the Lynds had examined it in the 1920s. Of the families studied in 1979, 86 percent had a tree, and 81 percent opened gifts. Toys, money, food, and drink ranked after clothing as the most common gifts. Most of the jewelry went to women, and most of the tools and sports equipment to men (ibid., 383–85, 390). Sue Halpern and Bill McKibben, "Hundred Dollar Holidays," *Crosscurrents* 42 (Fall 1992):365.

13. Schudson, *Advertising*, 138–40, 150–52.

14. Russell Baker, "Less Joy Is More," *New York Times*, Nov. 27, 1976, p. 23; [Margaret Perry], "The Christmas Spirit," *Atlantic*, Dec. 1921, pp. 859–60. On the beginning of advertising's powerful role, see Stuart Ewen, *Captains of Consciousness: Advertising and the Social Roots of the Consumer Culture* (New York: McGraw-Hill, 1976), esp. 157, and T. J. Jackson Lears, "From Salvation to Self-Realization: Advertising and the Therapeutic Roots of the Consumer Culture, 1880–1930," in *The Culture of Consumption: Critical Essays in American History, 1880–1980*, Richard Wightman Fox and T. J. Jackson Lears, eds. (New York: Pantheon, 1983), 3–38.

15. F. E. Manning, "Cosmos and Chaos: Celebration in the Modern World," in *Perspectives on Contemporary Cultural Performance*, F. E. Manning, ed. (Bowling Green, Ohio: Bowling Green State Univ. Popular Press, 1983), 7, quoted and paraphrased in McGreevy, "Place in the American Christmas," 37. This section also draws on McGreevy's use of J. Cohen, *Palace or Poorhouse: The American House as a Cultural Symbol* (East Lansing: Michigan State Univ. Press, 1982), quoted in ibid., 37. Daniel J. Boorstin, *The Image or What Happened to the American Dream* (New York: Athenaeum, 1962), 229–30.

16. Schmidt, "Joy to (Some of) the World," 350–51. On the role of the market in reshaping and echoing American religion, see ibid., 343–56.

17. Lloyd Wendt and Herman Kogan, *Give the Lady What She Wants: The Story of Marshall Field & Co.* (Chicago, New York, and San Francisco: Rand McNally, 1952), 365–69.

18. "Greet Santa Claus as 'King of Kiddies,'" *New York Times*, Nov. 28, 1924, p. 15; Henning Cohen and Tristram Coffin, eds., *Folklore of American Holidays* (Detroit, Mich.: Gale Research, 1987), 348–49.

19. Wallace G. Chessman, "Thanksgiving: Another Experiment," *Prologue* 22 (1990): 273–85; Tom Mahoney, *The Great Merchants: The Stories of Twenty Famous Retail Operations and the People Who Made Them Great* (New York: Harper & Brothers, 1947), 102n3. Two years elapsed between FDR's declaration and Congress's resolution because of the changes necessary in football game schedules, school holidays, railroad timetables, and other calendars that had been planned well in advance.

20. Wendt and Kogan, *Give the Lady What She Wants*, 368–69; quotes on 368, 369; a fuller description of Christmas at Field's can be found on 365–69. Uncle Mistletoe remained popular for a number of years. Hundreds of children thronged to visit, telephone, and send letters to him. They watched him on television, sang songs published about him, and joined his "Happiness Clubs."

21. "Santa Claus Association, N.Y.," *New York Times*, Dec. 6, 1913, p. 11:7; editorial, Dec. 19, 1913, p. 10:4; Dec. 25, 1913, p. 4:3. According to Waits, the Salvation Army, as part of a general decline in the use of Santa, stopped employing him as a bell-ringer in the late 1930s, thinking that his burgeoning numbers had begun to arouse the suspicions of children. Waits, *Modern Christmas*, 131.

22. Waits, *Modern Christmas*, 25; David Brown and Ernest Lehman, "The Santa Claus Industry," *American Mercury*, Jan. 1940, p. 26. In previous decades, Santa Claus had appeared in 3 to 5 percent of the advertisements in these magazines. Waits, *Modern Christmas*, 212 n18. Waits theorizes that Santa's major role in commerce (at least until 1940) was to "decontaminate" manufactured goods, making them a product of his bounteous bag of gifts (ibid., 25). For another interpretation of Santa's appearance in advertising, see Russell W. Belk, "A Child's Christmas in America: Santa Claus as Deity, Consumption as Religion," *Journal of American Culture* 10 (1987):87.

23. Brown and Lehman, "The Santa Claus Industry," 26–29. Waits briefly discusses the rising number of Santas and subsequent concern by sponsors that his nearly ubiquitous appearance might affect children's belief in him, in *The Modern Christmas*, 130–31. For a similar point, see Daniel J. Boorstin, *The Americans: The Democratic Experience* (New York: Vintage Books, 1974), 160–61. However, neither offers evidence that this worry had much, if any, long-term effect on the proliferation of Santa Clauses.

24. All quotations in this and the following paragraph are from Robert L. May, *Rudolph the Red-Nosed Reindeer* (Chester, Conn.: Applewood Books, 1967), n.p. (ellipses and emphases in the original). I am indebted to James H. Barnett for his clever and convincing interpretation of *Rudolph* in *American Christmas*, one that I draw on here (Barnett, *American Christmas*, 108–14). Barnett supplies additional information: May based *Rudolph* on

the "Ugly Duckling" story, selected the name Rudolph through a combination of chance and alliteration, chose a large nose because it was shunned by "Western culture," and made Rudolph's nose red to draw attention to it (ibid., 110–11).

25. May, *Rudolph the Red-Nosed Reindeer*, bookjacket, n.p. See also Barnett, *American Christmas*, 109.

26. Crosby sang "White Christmas" again in the 1954 film *White Christmas*, a partial remake of *Holiday Inn*.

27. John Springer, "Master James Is Home for Christmas!," *American Heritage*, Dec. 1983, pp. 47–48.

28. See Valentine Davies, *Miracle on 34th Street* (New York: Harcourt, Brace, 1947), Kris Kringle, quoted on 30. For an interesting and slightly different analysis of the movie, see Barnett, *American Christmas*, 114–18. William Gilmore Simms's "Maize in Milk" is discussed in Chapter 6.

29. Davies, *Miracle on 34th Street*, 3–13, 18.

30. Ibid., 19–22, 27–28, Kris Kringle, quoted on 4.

31. Ibid., 15, 16, 23–25, 29, 32–34, 62–72. In contrast to Frank Church's response to Virginia O'Hanlon, which used the language of mystery and religion, here opponents of Santa, led by store psychologist Albert Sawyer, turn to the twentieth-century language of psychology. See ibid., 63.

32. Ibid., 79–113. In at least two instances, judges, tongue-in-cheek, had already confirmed Santa's reality. See opinions of Judges Michael A. Musmanno and John Hatcher, quoted in Coffin, *Book of Christmas Folklore*, 75n.

33. Santa Claus faced another, serious demotion in 1970 when the Vatican permanently removed St. Nicholas's Day (Dec. 6) from the universal calendar of the Roman Catholic Church.

34. Francis P. Church, *New York Sun*, Sept. 21, 1897, reprinted in Obituary of Virginia O'Hanlon, *New York Times*, May 14, 1971, pp. 1, 44. A discussion of Virginia's letter to the editor is in Chapter 10.

35. Moore, "A Visit from St. Nicholas," in *Yankee Doodle's Literary Sampler*; Charles Dickens, "A Christmas Carol," in Charles Dickens, *Christmas Books* (New York: George Routledge and Sons, n.d.), 1–77; Willa Cather, "The Burglar's Christmas," *Home Monthly*, Dec. 1896, in Susan Koppelman, ed., *"May Your Days Be Merry and Bright" and Other Christmas Stories by Women* (Detroit: Wayne State University, 1988), 95–105. An early example of a woman, but in this instance, a young, unmarried one, tempering conflict between father and lover can be found in Lizzie McIntyre, "The Christmas Tree," *Godey's*, Dec. 1860, pp. 505–6.

36. Davies, *Miracle on 34th Street*; May, *Rudolph the Red-Nosed Reindeer*; Gian Carlo Menotti, *Amahl and the Night Visitors*, RCA recording. See Alan Dundes's insightful discussion of this opera in *Christmas as a Reflection of American Culture*, 20–22.

37. Dr. Seuss, *How the Grinch Stole Christmas* (New York: Random House, 1957). For a thorough explication of the Grinch's story, see Thomas A. Burns, "Dr. Seuss' How the Grinch Stole Christmas: Its Recent Acceptance into American Popular Tradition," *New York Folklore* 2 (1976):191–204; on the point of Christian symbology in the story, see pp. 195–97.

38. Seuss, *How the Grinch Stole Christmas*, n.p. Emphases and ellipses in original.

39. Thomas Burns writes that Cindy-Lou Who represents "a victory for the young, the small, the weak, and the child" (ibid., 203). To this may be added "the female."

40. As John Springer has noted, Christmas "has a way of turning up in movies that ostensibly have nothing to do with the holiday." See, for example, *Meet Me in St. Louis* (1944), *Going My Way* (1944), *The Bells of St. Mary's* (1945), *Say One for Me* (1959),

High Time (1960), and H. G. Well's *Things to Come* (1936). Springer, "Master James Is Home for Christmas!," 46.

41. About *Batman Returns*, Laurence A. Hoffman writes, "Christmas stands symbolically for a secular version of redemption: Jesus doesn't save; Batman does. If evil has been eradicated it must be at Christmas . . ." (Hoffman, "Being a Jew at Christmas Time," *Cross Currents* 42 (Fall 1992):361).

Index

Pluralism, 16, 33
Plymouth Colony, 172. *See also* William
  Bradford
Poe, Edgar Allan, 73
Poinsett, Joel Roberts, 199 n. 4
Poinsettia, 120
Potlatch, 70
Prang, Louis, 118–19, 120–22, 124, 140.
  See also Cards
Presbyterian Church, 22, 31, 68, 96;
  Scots-Irish, 175 n. 21
Presents. *See* Gifts and gift-giving
Price, Patience, 111
Prince, Hezekiah, Jr., 25
Progressives, 156, 196 n. 3
Protestants, 43, 58, 73, 106, 108, 110,
  131, 132, 144, 152, 157; and commer-
  cialism, 54, 56. *See also* Home religion;
  specific denominations
Prynne, William, 7
Puritans, 7–8, 14–15, 26, 34, 35, 48, 55,
  61, 65, 93, 94, 95, 96, 107, 108, 109,
  122, 152, 154, 175 n. 21, 179 n. 34,
  196–97 n. 5, 197 n. 7; English, 7–8. *See*
  also Cromwell, Oliver

Quakers, 9, 11, 31, 34, 39, 41, 65, 68,
  175 n. 21
Quattelbaum, Junius, 89
Quodlibet, 198 n. 38

Ranger, Terence, viii
Redner, Lewis, 109
Reformation, 18, 44, 45, 58
Reid, Ira, 87
Reindeer, 48, 119, 145, 147, 150, 151,
  164–65. *See also* Rudolph
Renaissance, 45
Restoration, 109
Revelry, 7, 9–11, 35–41, 109; in America,
  10–11, 15; and class consciousness, 40–
  41; efforts to quell, 38–39; in Europe,
  10, 11, 35, 38; and fireworks, 35; as frolicking, 8, 9; on frontier, 36–38; and general rowdy behavior, 19–20; and
  masque, 7; amongst slaves, 84–86, 87,
  89. *See also* Koonering; Shooting; Fireworks
Revolution. *See* American Revolution

Richards, Caroline, 62
Riis, Jacob, 153, 157
Ripley, Eliza, 80
Risk, Robert Blair, 61, 68
Robbins, Thomas, 31, 32–33, 68
Rochberg-Halton, Eugene, 125
Rodman, Samuel, 25, 31, 68
Roman Catholics, 18, 26, 31, 32, 41, 43,
  56, 58, 108, 175 n. 21; holidays of, 18
Roman customs, 57, 65, 157
Roosevelt, Franklin, 162, 164
Rudolph the Red-Nosed Reindeer, 164–65,
  166, 169
Ruffin, Edmund, 90
Russell, Ruth, 156

St. Francis, 58
St. George, 46
St. Nicholas, 19, 46–47, 50, 143, 144,
  145, 146, 163, 182 n. 7, 203 n. 2; in
  American Revolution, 45; birth legend
  of, 45, 47; as Dutch saint, 45–46; as
  folk hero, 56–57; and Washington Ir-
  ving, 48. *See also* Santa Claus
St. Nicholas Day or Eve, 46, 50, 67, 151,
  208 n. 33
St. Nicholas Society, 145
Saint societies, 45–46
St. Tammany, 46
St. Winfred, 57
Salmagundi, 47
Salvation Army, 207 n. 21
Sandys, William, 109
Santa Claus, vii, 45–56, 57, 68, 72, 73,
  89, 90, 107, 119, 121, 128, 142, 143–
  54, 155, 161, 163, 166, 171; alternative
  spellings of, 51, 162, 203 n. 1; and charity, 162–63; and commerce, 149–50,
  151; correspondence with, 54–55, 151;
  decline of, 168, 207 n. 21, 208 n. 33;
  early American images of, 144–45; family of, 147, 148–49; as folk character,
  143, 150; fur coat of, 205 n. 17; history
  in America of, 143; late 19th-century images of, 145–46; legal stature of, 208 n.
  32; Marxist interpretation of, 151,
  205 n. 16; and the north, 145, 148; and
  parents, 54–56, 143, 150–54 passim,
  185 n. 34; physical description